OCEANSIDE PUBLIC LIBRARY
615 FOURTH STREET
OCEANSIDE, CALIF. 92054

D0054103

OCEANSIDE PUBLIC LIBRARY

3 1232 00253 1830

A SAILOR'S TALES

Books by *Bill Robinson*

The Science of Sailing (1960)
New Boat (1961)
A Berth to Bermuda (1961)
Where the Trade Winds Blow (1963)
Expert Sailing (1965)
Over the Horizon (1966)
The World of Yachting (1966)
The Best from Yachting (editor) (1967)
Better Sailing for Boys and Girls (1968)
The America's Cup Races (co-author) (1970)
Legendary Yachts (1971)
The Sailing Life (1974)
The Right Boat for You (1974)
Great American Yacht Designers (1974)
America's Sailing Book (1976)

791.124
ROB

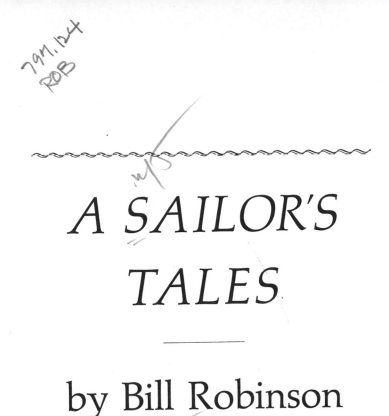

A SAILOR'S TALES

by Bill Robinson

W·W·NORTON & COMPANY·INC·

NEW YORK

OCEANSIDE PUBLIC LIBRARY
615 FOURTH STREET
OCEANSIDE, CALIF. 92054

Copyright © 1978 by W. W. Norton & Company, Inc. All rights
reserved. Published simultaneously in Canada by George J. McLeod
Limited, Toronto. Printed in the United States of America.

FIRST EDITION

Library of Congress Cataloging in Publication Data
Main entry under title:
A sailor's tales.
   1. Sailing—Anecdotes, facetiae, satire, etc. 2. Sailing
I. Robinson, William Wheeler, 1918–
GV811.S25 1978   797.1'24'0207   77–11199
ISBN 0–393–03211–6

1 2 3 4 5 6 7 8 9 0

4495

APR 3 1979

This book is dedicated to my grandchildren,
Elizabeth, Willie, Julie, Sam, and Katherine, and any more
who may eventually join them,
to save them the hours of having to listen to
their grandfather in his old age

Contents

VI Back Home—and a Family

VII With the Big Boats

Preface

This is a book of what I have always called "sea stories"—"sea stories" in quotes as opposed to formal sea stories like *Two Years before the Mast, Sailing Alone around the World,* or *The Sea Wolf.*

"Sea stories" of the kind in quotes are to sailors what big whopper tales are to fishermen or nineteenth-hole postmortems to golfers. These are the funny incidents, the odd happenings, the adventures, misadventures, personalities, and the boats themselves that end up being talked about in gatherings of nautical types, on the club pier after the race with appropriate angling of hands and graphic arm gestures, in the cockpit over an anchor cup after a day of cruising, or at winter get-togethers when nostalgia stirs memories.

They are also the stories that seldom find their way into the formal coverage of a race or cruise, the sidelights that give flavor and color. Most of them have never been in print, and in some of them, names have been changed when fictionalization would seem to be kinder.

I first became aware of the "sea story" genre in the subchaser Navy in World War II. When an SC sailor joined a group of shipmates or friends from other ships who were already chatting, the greeting would usually go something like this.

"Telling 'sea stories,' eh?"

"Of course. What else. Heard anything new lately?"

They would range from gossip of oddballs in the fleet, complaints about superior officers and problems of food, fuel, maintenance, and mail, to accounts of storms, strandings, and enemy action, and they could go on for hours, with one story begetting another in an associative process.

The practice lives on—in the Navy, I'm sure, and in similar sessions of sailors after one-design competition, ocean racing, and short and long cruises. Join a gathering at such spots as the bar of the San Diego Yacht Club, the lawn of The Royal Bermuda Yacht Club, the pier at

Coinjock, North Carolina, or the quay at Papeete, and "sea stories" automatically begin to flow.

These, then, are tales gathered over the years from sailing and the Navy, and from the seafaring past of my family. I have spun them out in a rough structure of categories, but mainly they have come from that process of association in which one story is a reminder of another one, and so they continue. I hope they remind you of similar tales in your own experience, and perhaps you know or recognize some of the people, and I hope you enjoy them half as much as I did (well, most of them) in living them.

Rumson, New Jersey
February 1977

PART I

~~~~~~~~~~

The Gulf Stream

Perhaps because it is so unpredictable, the Gulf Stream seems to have figured in a great many of the memorable things that have happened to me afloat. Although I have been in it on the way to Bermuda and off the mid-Atlantic Coast, I'm thinking mainly of the Florida Straits, where its influence and very presence are so overwhelming and where its peculiar characteristics have such a direct effect on all operations. Even when I was on it every day for weeks at a time, there was seldom one that could be called "routine." Routine usually meant excitement, and I have had enough of that on the surface of the great deep blue ocean river for it to merit a special chapter of these sea stories.

The Mary E *Story*

When we went to bed the night of February 22, 1976, in our hotel overlooking Biscayne Bay, thunder and lightning filled the air outside and rain squalls clattered against the northern windows. In the morning, awakening to the rustle and slash of palm fronds and the glimpse of a flag at the marina across the way giving off little machine-gun–like *whaps* as it vibrated stiffly in a norther, I was stirred by a sense of foreboding and an unhappy, long-remembered feeling in the pit of my stomach.

I knew what it would be like in the Gulf Stream that afternoon when the Miami-Nassau Race started, and deep down inside I knew I didn't want to be there. Too many times, on subchaser duty in World War II and on eleven previous Miami-Nassau races, had I seen these big mountains of blue water building against the northward thrust of the Stream, looming at eyeball height on the flying bridge of a subchaser or spreader height on an ocean racer, before hurling cascades of white water against the topsides to burst over us with the always surprising reminder of Gulf Stream warmth that only makes the wind seem colder afterward. I knew what it would be like clinging to the windward rail of *J & B*, alternately prey to stinging but warm hosings and cold wind blasts, muttering, "What in hell am I doing here?"

Even when I'm not reluctant because of conditions of the day, I'm never particularly happy to leave Jane for sea, a feeling that goes back, I guess, to the many subchaser sailings of the war. This time, as I listened to the nervous rattle of the palms, there was a heavier than usual reluctance to forsake the comfortable companionship of the double bed and the luxury trappings, no matter how impersonal, of the room. This was our first travel since she had recovered from a serious illness, and even though she was fine and would be with the other *J & B* wives, old and good friends all, I would have liked to be with her on the plane to Nassau. And, purely selfishly, that inclination grew ever stronger as we drove up Bayshore Boulevard to Miamarina under the lash of palm fronds against a sky that had that hard, blue look of air straight from Canada.

Too late to chicken out, though. I had sailed with Jack Sutphen and Mort Engel, veteran co-skippers of *J & B*, for several years now, and despite that stab of reluctance deep in my gut, I knew there was no way to back out gracefully. A few years ago, such thoughts would hardly have crossed my mind, but the fifty-seven-year-old body remembers those Gulf Stream thumpings in a different way.

Miamarina was aquiver with last-minute preparations. *J & B* lay alongside the seawall in front of the marina office, where long lines of race sailors queued up for the two pay telephones. She surged uneasily, with ensign and burgee flapping and slapping noisily and the breeze humming in her shrouds as I kissed Jane goodbye and clumped aboard with my gear. The name *J & B* has nothing to do with Scotch whisky, by the way, although the distiller did wake up to the promotional possibilities and send her some of the product when she did some winning. Jack and Mort's wives are Jean and Barbara, and the boat was originally to be called *B & J*, until someone remembered that there was a female whose nickname sounded like that who had been rather well known around the SORC fleet for quite a few years. To avoid any confusion, the initials were reversed, and the Carter 39 sloop could identify with well-aged Scotch, not an ocean-racing groupie of somewhat the same description.

Gradually, around the marina, crew members working high up on masts were lowered in their bosun's chairs, wives gave last kisses and waves (and some came along), and, amid noisy banter, the mutter and rumble of engine exhausts, and the skitter of dark wind gusts across the protected water of the marina, the fleet unscrambled from slips and berths and headed for Government Cut in a long, irregular procession.

I munched a sandwich and drank some iced tea, reflecting mournfully (and so correctly) that it would be the last real sustenance for some time, as we struggled into foul-weather gear and sniffed the fresh, uneven puffs sweeping across MacArthur Causeway from the north. We headed into them at the Miami Beach Channel to hoist a reefed main, and Peter Wilcox, the "do-everything" man in the crew, jumped overboard to put a rubber band on the folding propeller at the correct alignment. With droplets blowing off his matted hair and beard, he was shivering with duck bumps as he climbed back on deck and quickly got into his foul-weather suit.

"Hey, the water's great!" he said, laughing, "—but, oh, that wind!"

J & B bore off and surged toward the entrance of the Cut, where pale green breakers frothed across the darkly jagged rocks of the breakwater. The boats ahead of us could be seen rearing their bows high and crashing down through wings of spray as they met the first seas outside the tide-roiled Cut. Soon we were bouncing along with them out of the lee of Miami Beach in the unhindered sweep of the wind, close-hauled and jogging toward the starting area. With somewhat misplaced optimism, we decided on the No. 2 reefable jib, and the deck apes scurried around surefootedly setting it up.

Class by class, the fleet got away, big boats first, close-reaching through the powdery green of the short, steep inshore seas toward the line of blue lumps that marked the edge of the Gulf Stream about a mile to the eastward. Jack makes as good starts as anyone I've ever sailed with, and we settled down to the business of it as our time came. We were in a class for stock boats, a new division in this series designed to bring back this type of boat to Southern Ocean Racing Conference competition. Ten years ago, stock boats had been dominant, but the change to the IOR Rule and the development of super-fancy, custom-built racing machines had driven stock boats from the circuit in the past few years. There were only six boats in our division, but they had been engaged in intense, closely fought competition over the previous four races, with at least four of the boats still holding a shot at the class SORC title, and everyone was very intent on the starting process. This race would probably be the clincher.

Jack is such a competitor that tension always hums across the deck while the time ticks away, called by Mort in fifteen-second intervals. Jack, his voice rising and edgy as the minutes narrowed down, fired questions about the other boats and the location of the buoy at the far end of the line. We were a little early, and we had to slack sheets while Jack sashayed *J & B* on a zigzag course to slow her down. With only six boats, we could get away with a tactic that would never have worked in a crowd, and we hit the line a second or two behind the gun, with *Mary E*, a Standfast 40 and our closest competitor, right on our stern, and the Tartan 41 *Vagary* and our near sister, *Phoenix*, the other two boats in the running, right alongside us to leeward.

As we charged and leapt eastward within a few boat lengths of each other, bows soaring high and crashing down in great clouds of spray, with crews huddled to windward and lee rails awash, the sun, in its low winter path over the receding silhouette of Miami Beach hotels, was blotted out more and more by clouds marching in from the horizon in close-order formation. Watery shafts of light slanted through breaks in the pattern, picking up the tiny, heeling splinters of black that were the class behind us.

On the rail, with the cockpit coaming jammed into the small of my back, I spent the first hour trying to keep dry under the repeated onslaught of wave tops, but finally gave up as the Gulf Stream

J & B heads into the Gulf Stream after the start of the race. Even at this distance, it can be seen that I (white hat) am not too happy. Reefed jib is scooping seas

gradually worked its way down my neck and into the legs of my foulweather gear. My dry areas slowly contracted into a small panel below each arm, but those didn't last long. From then on, immersion was as total as that of the most devout Baptist wading into a river. All the while, I couldn't help remembering the various dismastings and rigging failures I had witnessed in this area on previous races, plus the dismasting of a previous Engel-Sutphen boat, *Bones*, in the Nassau Cup, and visions of disaster dodged through my mind as I sat on the cramped, damp panel of deck space—just too narrow for one sideways buttock to find a perch that could be lived with—and automatically dodged the showers of spray, even though it no longer did any good.

It was no surprise when the reefed jib, rolled and tied so that the reefed section faced inboard and therefore filled with water whenever the jib scooped, which it did quite often, began to rip at the reef points and had to be replaced with a No. 3—plenty of sail anyway for the way the wind and seas were building. Clouds had completely taken over the sky before sunset, and twilight was gray and unfriendly, making the seas look bigger, blacker, and more menacing. By now the wind was well over 30, and an occasional gust had more authority. It began to feel lonely out there as the other boats washed out of sight in the dusk.

There was no thought of a real meal at suppertime, and, after some extra exertion on a winch on a sail adjustment, I had my first experience with seasickness in fifty years of sailing. On powerboats and subchasers, yes, and often, but never before on a boat under sail, and, perhaps because of this lack of experience, I didn't handle the usual position of ignominy at the leeward rail very well. In fact, I lurched out of sync with the boat, and the genny track jumped up out of its smother of foam and gave me a good whack on the mouth. From then on I had a fat and tender lower lip that didn't really cure itself for a couple of weeks, but it was also the end of mal de mer. There was too much else to think about.

In darkness, the only relief from total inkiness was the bob and blink of running lights of the other boats, the luminous rush of white-caps out of the wall of night, and the pale, wavery ghostliness of our starboard running light reflecting back off our bow wave in uneven, occulting flashes.

I had no intention of going below no matter what the watch schedule, and I happened to be looking off to starboard when a blob of red arced up briefly from the nonexistent horizon, followed by a couple more.

"Flares off the starboard bow!" I called, and almost simultaneously the VHF radio crackled with a clearly heard "Mayday" from *Mary E.* Then there was another flare. The time was 2040.

Twice before, Jack and Mort had had SORC races interrupted by rescue operations, once to stand by a sinking tug off Key West, and once to help a competitor in trouble, and from Jack at the wheel and Mort below at the radio came the absolutely simultaneous cry: "Oh shit! Here we go again!"

Aside from my natural reaction of excitement and concern, the thought popped up that here, after thirty years as a sportswriter and boating editor covering predictable, scheduled events, was the "real thing." The old phrase "This is it!" also jumped into my head. I remembered having the same reaction, with the same phrase, the first time I saw Zeros coming directly at us in the Southwest Pacific. It wasn't something from a movie or novel any more, and I felt like a cub reporter chasing his first fire engine.

Mort immediately started to talk to *Mary E*, and I gave the approximate bearing of the flares I'd seen. We eased sheets and headed over that way without any definite point to aim for, and Channel 16 came alive with other yachts in the race responding to the message. *Mary E* reported that she was leaking badly and that the water was gaining faster than they could pump. She had eleven in crew, including two females, a large complement for a forty-footer. As we drew closer to her supposed location, a swarm of running lights began to flock together like lightning bugs gathering in a garden—some windy, dark garden—and we had no idea which one was *Mary E*. At least five boats were in the area, all but one of our class, but, gradually, it was sorted out that *Phoenix* and *J & B* were probably closest and would take over the duty of standing by.

Someone had the bright idea of telling *Mary E* to upend a man-overboard strobe light so that we could pick it out from the welter of running lights and aim for the right place, and its quick, distinctive flash solved the problem immediately.

Searchlight beams stabbed across the water, picking up the cresting, breaking wave tops and then the mothlike apparition of a white boat lying ahull and wallowing in the seas. Her sails were down and lay messily across her decks, and her jib trailed over the bow and into the water. At first we thought this was just an evidence of hasty action, but we later learned that it had been rigged this way as a drogue to keep her bow on one heading, and it proved remarkably effective in holding her steady, without yaw, and with minimum leeway.

Mort, ever cool and matter-of-fact, had been on the microphone gathering all the information he could and then began an attempt to raise the U.S. Coast Guard in Florida, now about forty miles away, to tell them of the situation. Line-of-sight VHF did not have enough range to make it, but the cruise ship *Emerald Seas*, on her way from Miami to Nassau and just over the horizon to the eastward in the vicinity of Great Isaac Light, picked up the transmissions and reported in that she would notify the Coast Guard.

Meanwhile, Chuck Coyer, Jr., and Denny Sanford in *Phoenix* had reported that they were alongside *Mary E* and would begin taking crew off, ladies first. Both *Phoenix* and *J & B* had taken sails off and were under power, heaving and pitching over the steep seas, and we watched in some awe and trepidation as *Phoenix* slowly approached *Mary E* from leeward. *Mary E* had running and spreader lights on, and flashlights playing over the scene made eerie silhouettes and sudden splotches of brightness as they hit on a white hull. Both boats were gyrating wildly in the seas, *Phoenix* more so than the stabilized *Mary*

E, as the bow of *Phoenix* slowly approached the stern of the disabled boat. In the wavering light, we could see moving figures as the two boats came together, bow and stern rapidly rising and falling past each other, and there was a tense moment of hesitation before *Phoenix* backed away. On the radio they reported that both girls had made the transfer safely but that it was much too dangerous to try the maneuver again. By radio conference it was agreed that *Mary E* would drop one man at a time down to leeward in an Avon inflatable dinghy on a long line as a much safer method of transfer, and this was done three times while we watched. *Mary E* had about half her normal freeboard and was wallowing sluggishly, but she did not appear to be sinking rapidly. The word was that the water below was over the table in the cabin and that the pumps were clogged.

Phoenix took on three men, and it was then agreed that *J & B* would take off the remaining six, splitting the load as evenly as possible between the two rescuers. *Phoenix* moved out of the way, and Jack Sutphen maneuvered *J & B* up from the leeward side of *Mary E* as the rubber dinghy dropped down to us with one man at a time. It was tricky boat handling, and he did it flawlessly despite the heave and bobble of the seas and the lash of spray flinging across us in the wind, which *Emerald Seas* reported was now up to 40 knots.

Six times the black blob of rubber bounced downwind to us, and each time Jack put *J & B* close enough for our crew, under Peter's leadership, to throw a line across to the man in the Avon and then haul him alongside. It was like landing a slippery tuna to wrestle some-one in foul-weather gear out of the inflatable and over the rail of *J & B*, and it was not exactly a graceful operation, but one by one they made it, landing heavily on deck with a sodden thump. There was re-markably little talk and no aimless shouting or evidence of panic. Jack's orders and the communications between our crew and each man in the Avon were calm and only loud enough to be heard over the whistle of the wind. *Mary E*'s gradually fading spreader lights and the erratic stabbing of flashlight beams from *J & B* cast a flickering half-light over the action, with the bulky, glistening figures of rescuers and rescued, faceless and impersonal in their foul-weather gear in the uneven light, forming a growing blob of congestion in *J & B*'s cockpit.

At a moment when I had no hold on anything and was moving across the cockpit to lend a hand to someone, a *Mary E* crew member, tired and groggy and not sure of himself, lost his balance from a perch on the windward rail and came flying down across the cockpit, hitting me at the waist with the kind of block good enough to be shown on instant replay. With a great "ooof" of escaping air, I was upended and knocked over the leeward coaming. Because of the crowded conditions that made moving around so difficult, none of us had harnesses on, and my instant thought was that I was headed for a swim, but I didn't fly quite that far. Instead, I crashed onto the leeward deck on the point of my left shoulder.

The pain was immediate and sharp as I landed heavily, and I remember bellowing an enraged "God dammit!"

I was sure that the shoulder was broken, but this proved overly dramatic. From then on (and forever afterward, as a matter of fact) it hurt. Motion was possible but painful, and between it and my fat lip I was far from happy. At least I wasn't seasick any more.

The last one off *Mary E* was her skipper, Chuck Benson, glum and subdued but matter-of-fact as he checked to make sure everyone in his crew was safe. Most of them had brought a duffel with them in the Avon, and these were hurled down to the cabin sole, where they made a great wet mountain of lumpy canvas for the rest of the trip. *Mary E* was equipped with an inflatable eight-man raft, and they had broken this out soon after the "Mayday." When it popped open, it also had a canopy, a fine idea for protecting survivors if they have to remain afloat for several days in foul weather or tropical sunshine, but a severe hindrance in abandoning ship. Getting into it through a slit in one end of the canopy proved just about impossible as the raft and *Mary E*'s hull roller-coastered by each other on the Gulf Stream seas.

They had ended up loading it with bags and savable equipment and sent it to *Phoenix* on a long line. They did manage to get the gear out and then cut the clumsy raft adrift, as it proved much easier for one person at a time to jump into the open Avon dinghy. Undoubtedly the canopy could have been folded down, but no one realized it.

Now, with the little knot of boats clustered in the wild night, the question was: What to do next? By this time, Mort had word that the Coast Guard had received the message from *Emerald Seas* and was on its way. First would be a fixed-wing patrol plane to establish position, then a helicopter to drop high-capacity pumps, and finally the ninety-five-foot cutter *Cape Shoalwater* to attempt salvage. *Phoenix* was relieved, and we were asked to stand by. With her extra complement of five, *Phoenix* made sail again, wished us good luck on VHF, and disappeared into the heaving darkness in the direction of Great Isaac, whose loom could occasionally be picked up to the eastward, perhaps sixteen miles away. It was the first mark of the course, a third of the way to Nassau, and, oh yeah, there was still a race on. In the back of our minds was the realization that the boat that had rescued survivors of *Wimoweh* after she hit rocks off Isaac and sank in the 1974 race had been awarded such a big time allowance for the rescue that she ended up winning the race, but we had no idea what would happen this time. We weren't through here by any means.

Mary E was a bit lower in the water, but not sinking fast, and we learned the crew's story now as we waited for the Coast Guard while staring across the mess of sea at her half-awash form. They had been doing well in the race, gradually moving out on us, which they had to do, since they gave us some time, when the skipper's wife went below to do something about supper at about 1830. She noticed that there was water sloshing around on the cabin sole and commented on it, but this didn't make much impression. Lots of water had been coming aboard, and it was no surprise to find some below. The men on deck told her not to worry and to go ahead with supper, but they did turn the pump on.

After a while, in a sharper tone of voice, she called up, "Hey! There's a LOT of water down here!"

At first the reaction on deck was chauvinistically male—"how silly women are to worry about a little water" sort of thing—but Benson felt there was real conviction in his wife's voice and thought it best to check.

"God. You're right," was his reaction as he stepped into a slosh of water over the cabin sole. It was obvious this was more than anything that flying spray had put aboard, and they got auxiliary pumps going and began a check of all through-hull fittings and other areas of possible trouble. They could find nothing, as the water continued to rise far faster than they could pump with every regular and auxiliary piece of equipment they had. They stopped driving her hard and eased sheets, falling off to leeward to see whether that would ease some strain on the hull that was causing the leakage, but it hardly changed the rate of increase.

Someone on deck, happening to grab a shroud in passing, noticed that the whole rig had gone slack, and this created the suspicion that something had happened in way of the mast step. Her fiberglass construction consisted of two half-hull sections joined at the centerline, and there had been a previous history in this model of leakage on this seam just forward of the keel. *Mary E* had actually been beefed up with extra fiberglass there while under construction in an attempt to correct the propensity.

This might have been the trouble, and in fact was the best bet, but there was no way of checking it while she heaved and lurched over Gulf Stream seas. Gradually, the pumps began to clog, as clothing, can labels, and other paper fouled the intakes, and the water came inexorably higher. There had been a thought to cut the water intake hose of the auxiliary engine and let it act as a pump, but the engine was already under water when this idea came up, and it was too late.

Finally, there seemed nothing else to do but send the "Mayday," and now it became a question of the best way to keep *Mary E* from sinking. Perhaps the Coast Guard pumps, if they arrived in time, would take care of the situation. There was not much more to hope for.

The rescue effort had taken almost two hours, so there wasn't long to wait before the lights of a plane could be seen dodging through the clouds, and Mort got the message that it was the Coast Guard patrol plane homing in on our transmissions. She began to circle over us and sent word that a helicopter was on its way.

There was an inevitable feeling of "Here come the Marines!" when the brilliant, searching light of the helicopter appeared low in the sky to the west, and the peculiar whickering rackety-rack of its engine and rotors broke through the constant smash of waves and whine of wind. Closer and closer it came in an advancing avalanche of sound and light until it hovered right over *Mary E* just above mast height, flooding the scene with an intense electric-blue bath of light that turned the black water to a frothy, tossing expanse of whipped cream and glinted and reflected in smaller flashes off *Mary E*'s gyrating spar and wet hull. I've never seen St. Elmo's fire, but there was an eerie glow around the edges of the panorama that brought descriptions of it to mind.

Mary E's Avon dingy had been left attached to her by a long painter, and it was worked out by Mort and the helicopter crew via VHF to put two of *Mary E*'s men back aboard to receive the drop of a high-capacity pump. When she was abandoned, *Mary E*'s radio transmitter key had been left open, and the slurp and slosh of the water in her cabin was a weird background to all the transmissions. Her batteries remained operative all night, though the running lights gradually dimmed and her spreader lights were no longer working.

It was again a tricky bit of boat handling to put *J & B* up against the Avon to transfer the men one at a time, but Jack moved her in unerringly, and they made their way aboard. Over the still-functional radio, they said that the water was higher than ever, completely covering the table, but that its rate of gain seemed slower.

When all was ready, the copter moved in directly over the wallowing sloop, enveloping us in sound, and its downdraft added even wilder swirls to the whirlwind of broken water around her, setting up a dense mist of spray in the harshly glaring light. With breath held, we watched the bulky pump pop out of the copter's belly hatch on an umbilical and start downward in jerks and halts until it landed with amazing accuracy right in *Mary E*'s cockpit. When it was detached, the copter turned off its light and soared upward to circle around us, which uses less fuel than hovering, and its clattering roar continued to engulf us.

After all this excitement, it was a long-drawn-out anticlimax to have the pump not work. Anyone who has played with a gasoline handy-billy knows they are recalcitrant on a warm summer day on dry land,

and the heaving, slanting, spray-strewn cockpit of a disabled boat made an impossible working platform. The pump was covered with heavy grease, and the men struggled with it, hauling frantically on the pull cord and priming it time and again, but it never did more than sputter a few times. There were instructions with it, but they were on ordinary paper, which soon disintegrated into pulp, and it seemed that there was also water in the fuel supply that was dropped with it. Whatever the reason, after what seemed an eternity of suspense that probably lasted less than a half hour, there was an admission of defeat from the two on *Mary E.* I hope no FCC official was monitoring what they had to say on the radio about the antecedents and functional ability of the pump.

The helicopter then advised that it had another pump and that this would be dropped on *J & B* for transfer to *Mary E.* Mort knew this down below at the radio, but we had not had the word on deck when the whirlybird suddenly swooped in over us just above the mast. The floodlight came on again, so bright it was like a physical force, the downdraft splattered around us amid a hurricane of sound, and I looked up in fascination to see whether the truck of our mast was safe, so low was the copter above us. There was something hypnotic in the excess of noise, light, and blasts of air, and I had no idea what was going on or why we had this roaring monster hovering overhead, when I felt a moderate thump on the side of my head and found a line draping over my shoulder and down my front. A small sandbag was in my lap, and the line stretched up like the coil of an Indian ropedancer, lost when it disappeared into the blinding brilliance overhead. Although the sandbag hadn't really hurt, I was stunned for a moment before waking up to the fact that it had been dropped from the copter.

Just as I began to make sense, the line went slack and draped over the stern, and there was a big splash in the water at the limit of the circle of light.

"Hey!" I cried. "They're dropping something!" and I began hauling in on the line. Mort then called up that they had dropped us a pump, and a couple of us began heaving on the line as rapidly as we could. It offered suspiciously little resistance the more we pulled it in, and finally we came to a frayed, unattached rope end. Whatever had been attached to it no longer was, and thus ended the episode of the helicopter and the pumps. It had been exciting but unproductive, as their supply consisted of the two that had been dropped.

The helicopter had nothing more to offer, and it and the patrol plane checked out, heading back to Florida and saying that *Cape Shoalwater* was on her way. It was then about a half hour after midnight, and her ETA was some four hours off. We had nothing to do in the interim but stand by *Mary E*, slowly decreasing in freeboard and with more and more waves breaking across her. Would she last until the cutter got there? Her red and green lights still glowed fuzzily, her open radio transmitter still sent us the slosh of water in her cabin, and the jib over her bow held her on a steady heading, but the prospect was not too good.

Mary E's emotion-spent survivors had gradually drifted below to spread out over the great wet mass of duffels in the cabin, and Jack, Mort, and the members of the crew who had done the toughest physical work of staging the rescue and wrestling the survivors aboard were all dead on their feet. I had no desire to descend into the incredible mass of bodies, wet duffels, and seasick buckets in the main cabin despite the lash of spray and cutting howl of the wind. Knowing that I would be next to useless in normal operations with my damaged shoulder, but feeling able to steer with one hand while we stood by under reduced sail, I offered to take the wheel for a while, and Charlie Booz, who evidently shared my feelings about conditions belowdecks, said he would stand watch with me.

For the next several hours we reached back and forth across Mary E's position, keeping the dim glow of her lights in sight and watching her wallow lower and lower, more and more down by the bow. Now and then one of her crew would slip into the cockpit and silently watch her for a while before ducking below again, and Mort kept radio watch below, talking to Cape Shoalwater as she pounded her way toward us from Fort Lauderdale through the smashing seas. It was like waiting for the other shoe to drop as we watched Mary E settling down. Here was $100,000-plus on the ragged edge of extinction, and it was a morbidly fascinating sight. Sometimes, as we reached the end of an orbit and jibed around, we would lose sight of her for a few moments, and you wondered then "Has she gone?" "Did we miss it when she went under?" Each time, though, the blurred glow of one of her running lights would wink across a wave, and from time to time a late moon would break through a small parting in the clouds to send a beam down to glint off her hull and spars. Our motion was relatively easy as we jogged back and forth on a reach. The wind had never let up in the slightest, and the waves were still steep and nasty, but, whether it was due to the easy reaching course or the long exposure, they didn't seem quite as awesome any more, and our thoughts were constantly on the race for time between Mary E's impending disappearance and Cape Shoalwater. As the cutter came closer, she asked us to put a strobe light at our masthead to help her find us, so we put it on a halyard and sent it up, and its nervous blink skittered down on us. Just as the first dim change from inky blackness to a hint of gray began to appear in the east, Cape Shoalwater's lights came over the western horizon and gradually grew sharper. By the time she was alongside, morning twilight had evened everything to gray pallor under a solid overcast, and

Mary E was still there, her bow barely showing as waves smashed across it. *Cape Shoalwater*, rolling and pitching her underbody halfway out of the waves, checked details out with us, thanked us for our assistance, and relieved us to go on our way. As we left, the cutter was trying to come close aboard *Mary E*, and this was our last sight of them.

The crew struggled back on deck, the No. 3 jib went up again, and Jack took over, squaring us away on a hard beat for Great Isaac. As soon as we started moving into the seas at best speed, the easy jogging motion of the reaching we had been doing changed to leaping, smashing plunges, and the longest, nastiest twenty-four hours I have ever spent in a boat—or anywhere else—followed. We were a glum, physically beat crew who had lost any enthusiasm for competition, companionship, or anything else but survival and the passage of time, and never have the hours dragged slower as we tacked around Isaac and set off on a long port tack toward Stirrup Cay, sixty miles to the eastward and the next turning point on the three-legged course.

Life settled down to considerations such as whether to eat a hardboiled egg or an apple and how the hell to take a leak, finally a necessity despite almost complete lack of consumption. It became a clumsy balancing act on your knees on the leeward corner of the stern, with more than usual difficulties with layers of soggy clothes and the openings in them, and, with cascades of water streaming over you through the whole process, it was a very good question whether you had been able to clear your own fly, much less the rail of the boat, with whatever you could produce.

The longest day wore on to the accompaniment of constant pounding and clouds of spray, colder now that we were out of the Gulf Stream and into Northwest Providence Channel, a body of water I've never had much affection for and now grew to hate with an active passion. The day remained gray, the wind remained at about 40, and the seas remained unrelenting, much shorter and steeper than Gulf Stream monsters, but, if possible, even nastier. There was not another boat, not a plane, not even a fish or a bird in sight, and the radio told us nothing of the fate of *Mary E*.

Our boat had been built in Greece, *Mary E* in Holland, and, as we slugged through the seas, lower and heavier because of our extra burden and resounding with nasty cracks and crashes as each wave hit, I began to think of *Mary E*'s fate more and more and couldn't help wondering about the comparative boatbuilding skills of Greeks and Dutchmen. If something happened to us out here, we were out of VHF radio range of anyone, we did not have enough life jackets or rafts for the fourteen souls now jammed on board, and we were very far from land. Just a few pleasant thoughts to pass the time as the spray lashed across you, and I couldn't help but be amused at my concern the afternoon before, which now seemed as though it had been in another century, about staying dry under my foul-weather gear. Ha!

I tried it below once or twice, but conditions were beyond belief and description. Almost everyone was being unrestrainedly seasick at frequent intervals, and I won't go into the atmosphere created by this activity plus a dozen or so bodies in wet clothing, the great wet pile of duffels, and the slosh of bilge water. Perhaps a slave ship in bad weather might have had somewhat the same ambience.

We thrashed around Stirrup on two long tacks that took most of the evening, thinking that once we had cleared it and could head off southeastward for Nassau, reaching would be more comfortable. Another "Ha!" Boat speed picked up, but so did the velocity of the spray, which now smashed across the cockpit with the intensity of a fire hose, and I finally decided that the Black Hole of Calcutta below was the better choice. Also, it had started to rain.

Nursing my shoulder, fat lip, and an incipient case of diaper rash under the salt-sodden clothes, I wedged into a corner of the cabin on a couple of lumps of duffel and listened to the sounds of regurgitation as *J & B* lurched on her way. The sensation, and the roar of rushing water echoing through the hull and clattering across the deck, were akin to being trapped in a runaway subway train in imminent danger of derailment. Jack and Peter kept her driving through the mess, stalwart in the avalanche of spray and showing incredible stamina.

Somehow Nassau finally appeared in the next dim dawn, twenty-four tortuous hours after the one in which we had left *Mary E* and *Cape Shoalwater*, and we still didn't know what had happened. *Mary E's* crew had kept a very low profile during the ordeal of the sail to Nassau, and we could imagine how they felt. We had all been equally uncomfortable, but we at least had our vessel under us.

Our wives, who had heard about *Mary E's* being in trouble and knew we had been standing by, but had had no further word for twenty-four hours, even though Mort had asked the Coast Guard plane to relay a message about us, were waiting at Yacht Haven when we straggled in. They had been up all night hoping for some information, and the reunion was subdued but emotional.

Jane had a rental car, and we staggered to it in driving rain, anxious to get to the hotel and a hot shower, as my diaper rash was now in full flower, stinging painfully under the salt-soaked clothes. When we got in the car, there was a sudden strong smell of alcohol and sweat, and I was just beginning to react to it when a form lurched up out of the back seat behind us. For a moment, I thought it was a mugging—just what we needed at the moment—but all that happened was a mumbled "Huh—wha—?" We had awakened a drunk who had taken refuge from the rain in our car, and he quickly opened the door and stumbled out into it before we had time to do anything ourselves.

After all this, it was somehow no surprise that the water in the hotel was off and did not come on until 10 A.M.

And what happened to *Mary E* and in the race? From sketchy reports, we gathered that *Cape Shoalwater* did put pumps aboard, but they were hampered by debris in *Mary E*'s cabin and wouldn't keep working. The cutter tried to take her in tow, but she was too far gone for this and finally dipped below the last blue Gulf Stream mountain to wash over her and sank in several hundred fathoms of water about two hours after we left her. No one will ever know for sure what her trouble was, as the proof lies hidden deep on the floor of the Florida Straits.

As for the race, since five of the six boats in the class were involved to some extent in "Operation *Mary E*," it had not been a real race for anyone in the class. Because the wind kept swinging into the northeast while we were standing by *Mary E*, *Phoenix* and *J & B* had different conditions from the rest of the fleet, and *J & B*, leaving the scene four hours after *Phoenix*, took five hours longer to get to Nassau because of added windward work. The committee decision, which was generally accepted as a fair solution, was to arbitrarily award *Phoenix* and *J & B* a tie for first-in-class. *J & B*, incidentally, then went on to win the class SORC title by taking first-in-class in the finale, the Nassau Cup.

As for me, I knew I "shoulda stood in bed" the morning we awoke to the uneasy thrash of palm fronds. If I had obeyed the feeling in the pit of my stomach, I just might have continued ocean racing a little bit longer instead of retiring to the press box as of February 24, 1976. But then, if my twelfth Miami-Nassau Race had been like this, what would my thirteenth bring? I'll never know.

George Hinman and the Strange Coffin

There was another Miami-Nassau Race when, for a few moments, it really looked as though I "shoulda stood in bed."

In the mid-1960s I sailed for several years in the SORC with Jack Brown in his forty-three-foot Sparkman & Stephens yawl *Callooh* as one of the few "Indians" in the crew. Jack, a fine skipper and always great to sail with, was one of the champions at following the SORC custom of collecting an all-star group of top racing skippers who were happy to come south and crew in someone else's boat. This made for a

Bus Mosbacher and Ed Raymond, part of the "all-
star" cast usually sailing *Callooh*

lot of "chiefs" and very few "Indians," but as one of the latter I had
a chance to be shipmates with such luminaries as Bus Mosbacher,
George Hinman, Ed Raymond, Vinnie Monte-Sano, Art Wullschleger,
Bill Heine, and several others, all well-known racing skippers in their
own right.

In 1965, the Miami-Nassau Race produced somewhat similar conditions to those of 1976, though the wind was more in the west and not
as cold or strong. We had a fast spinnaker run across to Isaac, as the
wind continued to build. *Callooh* was at hull speed–plus, with every
sheet and guy humming tautly as she surfed eastward, and steering was
a tough exercise in keeping her under the chute and avoiding a broach.

It was dark and cold as we roared by Great Isaac Light, and, our
watch over, I headed below for some sack time. My assigned bunk
was a quarter berth on the starboard side, which had a rather peculiar
feature. The navigator's table was located over it at a 45-degree angle
and had to be raised so that someone could get in the bunk. Then it
would be lowered back in place and hooked. Air spaces on either side
of it kept the bunk ventilated, but the table had to be unhooked and
raised to let the occupant out.

Wullschleger was the navigator, and, ever-present cigar clenched
in his teeth, was working out a fix when I made noises about using the
bunk. *Callooh* was in that crucial area where the turn at Isaac must be
figured exactly to avoid the unmarked Northeast Rocks, which had to
be left to starboard before course could be set for Stirrup Cay. Art

allooh, on an even keel at the moment, running for Nassau. I am sitting right
ver the location of the navigator's bunk

who normally puts on a gruff, abrupt manner as part of his nautic character anyway, was concentrating hard and annoyed at bein interrupted, and he muttered and grumbled as he lifted the table so could crawl in.

"How do I get out of here?" I asked as he lowered the table an secured the hooks. I'd never used this bunk before.

"Shut up and go to sleep," he growled. "I'm working a fix here. Don worry, we'll wake you up when it's time for your watch."

It was a disorienting experience to be encased in the quarter bert by the angled table, but, as the boat yawed and surfed her way throug the night, I managed to wedge myself into a comfortable position an fell asleep with the water roaring by outside the hull a few inch from my ear.

The next thing I knew, I was being bounced around in the bur like dice in a croupier's cage. With the slanting table over me, it w hard to tell just what angle the boat was at, but I began to feel th she must be completely over on her ear, knocked down on her bear ends. From the deck I could hear shouts and thumpings, and, mo ominous of all, there was the loud splash of a cascade of water comir into the cabin. As far as I knew, the only opening was the main hatc which was on the starboard side of the cabin trunk. If water w coming in that, we were in real trouble, maybe a rollover.

Thrashing around like a third-rate Houdini trying to escape fro a coffin, I had no idea where the hooks on the navigation table wer and I was yelling, "Hey! Get me out of here! Someone unhook t table," as I groped around it trying to locate them. The cabin w empty, and the sound of water pouring in continued, and I had a stror mental image of the quarter berth becoming my permanent coffi What a way to go!

Finally, my fingers found the hooks and I managed to undo the lift the table, and scramble out. By now, freed from the crazy pe spective of the navigation table, I could get a better idea of the ang of the boat, and I realized that she was well over to port, but gradual straightening up. Dashing up the companionway to the cockpit, I cou see George Hinman fighting the wheel and bringing *Callooh* und control, and figures in foul-weather gear were busy around the winch

"What the hell happened?" I asked George.

"Where were you, Bill?" he said. "We called all hands on deck. W had a little broach, but it's under control now."

"Where was I? I was trying to get out from under that godda navigator's table. That's where I was. And what was all the wat pouring in the cabin?"

"Water?" Jack Brown overheard me and jumped below to chec muttering and cursing. After investigation, the anticlimactic answer w that the paid hand had opened the port in the trunk above the galley while cleaning up after supper and had forgotten to close it. That's where the water was coming in, not the main hatch, and we had not been in the rollover I had imagined—just a "routine" broach.

From then on, whenever I run into George Hinman, a dignified "elder statesman" of yachting and former Commodore of the New York Yacht Club, he always breaks into a broad grin.

"I can't help it, Bill," he says. "Whenever I see you, all I can think of is you thrashing around in that quarter berth trying to fight your way past the navigator's table."

An Early Humiliation

Despite these experiences, the Gulf Stream, as I've already mentioned, could hold very few surprises after subchaser duty, wicked as it was on *J & B*. Going back to my introduction to it in the weeks of training and then shakedown on new ships at Miami's Subchaser Training Center (SCTC) back in 1942–43, we saw it smiling under placid skies on occasion, but more often it was kicking up those blue monsters against the flow of the current or was chopped by the short, quick seas of the "southeast trade" blowing with it, and I've never thought of it as anything but rough and unreliable. SCs, 110-foot wooden splinters of eighteen-foot beam, were wet and rolly, and they seemed to be designed perfectly for hitting whatever period the seas had—short and quick or long and rolling—just wrong. Forty-five-degree rolls (in a six-second period) and showers of spray inundating the flying bridge were standard operating procedure—as they used to say in the Regular Navy.

During training at SCTC we had to go out in it in every kind of weather short of a hurricane while undergoing the endless drills that were the major part of the course there. Then, when you came back in a newly commissioned ship for shakedown, you had to go through the whole routine again to see how the ship was set up to handle such things as man overboard, fire in the paint locker, abandon ship, collision forward, collision aft, emergency steering, and just about everything short of earthquake.

My introduction to the drills was not such a good one. Students at

SCTC went out by the day on ships assigned to the school and were put through the drills to see how they handled the conn of an SC under various circumstances. My first turn came in a man-overboard session, where an object—crate, box, life jacket, or life ring—was thrown overboard without warning and you were suddenly told you had the conn and had to pick the "man" up as quickly as possible. It was rough and bouncy, and I had no feeling of being in control of the bucking little ship as I took over.

Sweating as nervously as a novice actor in his first moment onstage, with my classmates standing around hoping devoutly that I would do worse than they did, while the instructor sat by impassively, I gave orders to the helm and engine controls and soon had the ship bouncing in ever-decreasing but concentric circles around the box bobbing so innocently on the deep, heaving blue of the Stream. Somehow I could never seem to make a part of the circle coincide with the position of the box. The instructor kept checking a stopwatch as we whirled tightly around the damn thing, and finally, suppressing a yawn and without even looking at me, he stopped the watch with a click, made a short notation on his pad, and said, "You're relieved, Mr. Robinson. Your man overboard just drowned."

The Roughest Ever—with Cockroaches

That humiliation had been on a day of no worse than moderate conditions, but before the four-week course was over, we'd seen most of the variations the Stream could throw at you, and it always seemed especially ironic to be subjected to these indignities within sight of the fairyland profile of the Miami Beach skyline. That silhouette wasn't as outlandish as it has become in the post-Fontainebleau period, but the whites and pastels of the hotels gleaming in the sunlight always seemed to mock us as we rolled and pounded our way, enveloped in spray, not far off their pools and cabanas.

In two years of sea duty in SCs between the unlikely geographic limits of Nyack, New York, and New Guinea, I saw a lot of rough water and did my full share of rolling, pitching, yawing, and pounding. The biggest waves I saw were in a clear norther in the Windward Passage, and the worst storm we met was in the Bismarck Sea north of New Guinea, but for sheer messy, uncomfortable—in fact, down-right nasty—conditions, the Gulf Stream right off Miami was the champ. It all took place with the orangy bulk and distinctive central tower of the Roney Plaza Hotel (Walter Winchell's favorite winter hangout) right there on the horizon.

This was doubly disheartening because it came so unexpectedly, minutes before I was expecting to take off for a pleasant Saturday-night party with Jane and some good friends. My performances gradually improved until I qualified for command, and my first, SC 743, which I had taken over from the builder, Julius Petersen of Nyack, New York, was undergoing shakedown at SCTC in April 1943. This involved a couple of weeks of putting us through all those drills, checking out my and the ship's efficiency prior to sending us on to the realities of life in some (as yet unknown) combat zone.

On a blustery Saturday, with our shakedown complete, we were loading stores and preparing for a Monday departure for Key West and a final run-through of the latest ASW doctrines (which seemed to change more rapidly than you could flick pages off a calendar), and the job was about half finished by midafternoon. When it was completed, liberty would begin, split between the two watches of the crew between Saturday and Sunday, with one of the three officers remaining aboard at a given time, and Jane and I had an average drink-'em-up Naval Reserve Saturday night in prospect.

It was our routine when taking on stores to break open all crates and cartons on the pier, removing cans and produce for individual stowage, in an attempt, which had been successful this far in the ship's young life of three months, at keeping cockroaches off the ship. There was a great pile of open, half-open, and unopened stuff on the pier when a messenger arrived in a rush and invited me to make a quick visit to the Operations Office.

"Are you ready for sea?" was barked at me as I walked in there, and I hesitated for just a moment, thinking of the jumble on the pier.

"Almost, sir. We're just loading stores."

"The hell with stores. Leave 'em or throw 'em on deck. You've got to get under way immediately. How's your fuel?"

"We're topped off."

"Good. Come on in here and I'll show you what's up." He motioned me into an inner room, where several SC skippers were standing in nervous anticipation.

On a large chart of the Florida Straits, he pointed out several X's starting down near the Cay Sal Bank off Cuba and progressing up the Florida Keys halfway from Key West to Miami.

"These are sinkings." He paused for effect. "An enemy submarine has been hitting ships in the Straits and seems to be working slowly northward. We are going to put you out in a picket line between Fowey Rocks and Gun Cay in the Bahamas on the other side of the Gulf Stream, and I hope somebody will pick him up as he tries to come north. Every ship in the base is going to be out there, spaced at 2,000 yards, which should keep you in visual touch in daylight, and you are to hold the station assigned until relieved."

There was a hedge of arched eyebrows around the room as he went on with details of communications, station assignments, and operational instructions. Most of the SCs there were on shakedown, except for few school ships, and we were none too confident of our ability to detect and attack a German submarine. Soon we were shooed out to man our ships and get under way as quickly as possible, and we shrugged helplessly at each other as we dashed back to the pier.

The groans from the crew were predictably loud when I passed the word, and the cook made the loudest noise of all about what would happen to his stores. Without ceremony, we tossed all the freight onto the deck whether opened or not, and soon we were backing away from our berth along with the rest of the ships, leaving the usually crowded pier deserted in a haze of diesel smoke. There had been no chance to call Jane even if security had permitted, and I thought glumly of the lonely night ahead for both of us and of how worried she must be over my not showing up, although she was thoroughly used to the vagaries of life as the wife of an SC skipper.

The crew tossed boxes into the lazaret and hurried to clear the deck before we hit Government Cut, because it was obvious things would be wet outside. The wind was northeast, gusting well over 20 knots, and we all knew what it would be like. We had drawn the second station east from Fowey Rock Light, which is a few miles southeast of the Cut, fairly near the axis of the Stream, where the current would be strongest and the waves the lumpiest.

It was a nasty gray day, cold for the time of year, as we rolled our way through the green inshore seas. When we reached it under the colorless sky, the Gulf Stream was a menacing black, with its deep, inky blue apparent only when you looked directly down into it, and the whitecaps hissed and curled, blowing off the breaking tops in sheets of spray. The other SCs, PCs, YPs, and assorted patrol craft that had been hastily organized set out on their slowly divergent courses to the eastward, rolling, heaving, throwing spray, and generally making heavy weather of it as we moved down to our station, taking bearings on Fowey Rocks visually and by radar. When we arrived at it, we could see one SC inshore of us and another was a dot on the heave of the eastward horizon, while the rest of the fleet moved out of sight toward the Bahamas.

I had often wondered which way to face a storm or hurricane sea

SC 743 at sea

in an SC—bow on or stern to, and I didn't have much confidence in
either method. We had a bow that seemed perfectly designed for
scooping green seas and throwing heavy spray, and the two small
rudders behind each of our propellers were intended to give good
control for tight turns and quick maneuvers during a depth-charge
attack but were not much good in a steep following sea. Fortunately,
I never had to face the ultimate decision in severe conditions, a might-
have-been I don't regret at all, but this time there was no choice. We
were there on anti-submarine picket duty, the sub was presumably
coming from the south, and our sonar was much better in an ahead
search than in working astern through the sound of the propellers.
The propellers would have to be turning at intervals to keep station
against the 2.5-knot current of the Stream.

And so we sat there as the northeaster built up and blew well over
30, with higher gusts, and the waves built with it. The ship rolled and
corkscrewed and was extremely difficult to keep on a heading. Each
wave looming over the low, flat stern seemed sure to break aboard
and engulf the deck, but somehow the boxy stern rose to most of
them. A few did smash aboard, and the after crew's quarters and
galley became a sodden mess. The galley was drowned out and it was
"horsecock" (the Navy name for cold cuts of any description) or
nothing from then on. Almost everyone became seasick to some extent,
as this was our first exposure to really rough weather, and the men
in the sonar compartment and radio shack sat with wastebaskets between their knees as the only way to stay on duty. We had a few
stalwart souls able to stand a wheel watch, and even the officers had
to pitch in, as this was the toughest duty of all.

Night came, black and menacing, seeming to add to the height of the waves as they threw crazy white horses at us out of the darkness, glowing with a fierce phosphorescence, and rain added its sting to the general mess. Through it all, with the sonar giving out its monotonous, metallic ping, I had a truly physical fear that the next thing to hurl at us out of the black would be the sharp steel bow of the submarine, splintering our wooden hull before we had a chance to do anything. I certainly had no confidence whatever that our sonar could pick up a contact out of the mess around us. Being out in that sea was enough of a trauma in itself, but the submarine dominated our awareness like a monster in a nightmare. None of us slept more than a few dozing nods propped in a corner of the bridge.

Somehow the dawn always does come after a night like this, but now it almost seemed worse to have to look at the waves in the daylight, as they certainly weren't any smaller.

Songer, our toughest engineer, managed to get a fire going in the galley and cooked up the worst-looking mess of scrambled eggs and horsecock ever imagined. There were a few who could eat it, but to most it was just an added impetus to seasickness.

Finally, late Sunday afternoon, the radio brought the welcome news that we were relieved of duty and could proceed to base. It seems there had been a sinking off Daytona, and the sub was presumed to have gone through. Even the crash and smash of the seas on the bow as we pounded our way to Government Cut was a welcome change from the wallowing motion of station keeping, and it was a bedraggled mess of a fleet that gradually staggered in to SCTC's piers and made fast.

When I reported to the Operations Officer, who was freshly shaved and wearing clean, pressed khakis, he laughed and said, "Little bouncy out there?"

"Yes, sir. It sure was."

"I gather you didn't see anything."

"No, sir."

"Well"—he laughed again—"it was still a good idea. I didn't expect any sonar to pick him up, but I figured if we put enough of you guys out there in that mass of sea, he just might bump into one of you"—my nightmares of that very vision came sharply back—"and it almost worked. A banana boat coming in from Cuba did have a collision with a YP boat we had out there, so I guess the theory wasn't too bad."

P.S. And from then on we were never without our complement of cockroaches.

Crate Overboard

Those shakedown drills had been quite an ordeal for the crew, and they were thoroughly sick of them long before they were finished. Most of them were fairly new boots who had never been to sea, and they needed the training, but Songer, our oldest engineer, stocky and potbellied, with a bulldog face, was a Regular Navy veteran who had been on cruisers and battleships and was tolerantly amused at the antics of boots and reserve officers running little spitkits.

One day on shakedown off Miami he was lounging in the engine-room hatchway sucking on a toothpick and catching a breath of air when a young shakedown officer standing near him picked up an orange crate and dropped it over the side.

"Man overboard," he said, looking meaningfully at Songer.

Songer looked back at him blankly without reacting.

"I said 'man overboard,' " the officer said, pointing to the orange crate bobbing in the wake.

Fixing him with an unblinking stare, Songer removed his toothpick and said, "Mister. That ain't a man. That's an orange crate," and turned without another word and went back down the ladder to the engine room.

Havana with Tears

After our experience of Fowey Rocks, things seemed to be looking up when, instead of heading immediately for Key West, we were ordered to take a convoy to Havana. The Operations Officer was as fatuous as Santa Claus when he told me the orders, and the prospect of liberty in Havana did seem almost as exciting as Christmas. When I got my typed papers, they included a little mimeoed notice over the name of the commanding officer reminding us that it was against Navy Regs to transport liquor in a Navy vessel, and, with his other hand, the Operations Officer handed me a handwritten memo.

"Oh yeah," he said. "Here's the old man's order for what he'd like you to bring back," and he gave me the list of so many rums, Scotches, and gins and the name of the best liquor store on the Havana waterfront.

The convoy down was uneventful except for the fact that one of the ships in it, a Seatrain, was much bigger and faster than the other old tubs wallowing along at about 8 knots. Evidently her skipper felt he was safer going ahead on his own at full speed rather than looming up like a warehouse as a sitting duck among the smaller ships under the not so awesome protection of an SC, and he began to move up through the convoy until he was the lead ship and rapidly growing closer directly on our stern. The bow loomed over us like a great cliff, and I wasn't too sure just how to make my fractious charge behave. Radio silence was only to be broken in an extreme emergency, so we started blinking an Aldis lamp at him, a directional lamp shaped like a gun for maximum security in signaling, telling him to slow down and resume station. We blinked and blinked, and on he came, the bow waves shining like great white jaws in the night, and their hiss could be heard over the rumble of our engines. All on deck had their heads turned to me and I could imagine the questions in their eyes. Several edged nervously toward the rail.

Finally, just when I was going to have to give the order to turn out of his way, and the feeble glow of the Aldis was actually reflecting off his hull as it towered above us, the size of the bow wave lessened noticeably and the great ship slowly dropped back to position.

As we approached Havana the next day, its buildings gleaming whitely in the sun above the bright blue of the Stream, the crew was as busy as I've ever seen it, shaving, washing, combing hair, and using up great quantities of Mum, all in a gale of goosey giggles. Tall tales of what was going to happen to the girls of Havana were shouted around as the Mum was slapped on by the fistful, and the ship hummed with excitement.

The consternation was complete, then, when we were greeted by a patrol boat off Morro Castle with the word that we had half an hour to tie up while I reported for orders to take a convoy to Tampa, and we had the best-smelling, most evil-tempered crew in the Caribbean as we came alongside a wharf. I went ashore to the convoy office, and Worthy, our Exec, made a dash for the liquor store to load up with contraband and some Havana cigars for my father-in-law.

As soon as we came back aboard, it was time to leave, and I gave the order to set the special sea detail. Since this was at the end of the shakedown period, and we had been put through endless drills by the shakedown officers, everyone knew his station, and the crew, numb from the disappointment over no liberty in Havana, went about the duties mechanically, as though it were still part of shakedown.

Part of the special sea detail was to lower the jackstaff on the bow, which was hinged so that it could lie flat on deck out of the way of the 40-mm. gun on the foredeck. Our youngest seaman, Loomis, a bashful country-bumpkin type who spoke with a lisp, had the job of lowering it, but something was stuck, and the chief boatswain, a soft-talking but very experienced North Carolina fisherman, took over from him brusquely, eager to get the job done. He gave the sticky staff a mighty wiggle, and it collapsed forward instead of aft, catapulting him over the bow into the oily waters of the harbor. Boats broke the surface with a thoroughly abashed grin on his face, and Loomis, standing there openmouthed for a moment, finally came to with a start and turned around and shouted up to the bridge:

"Man overboard! No thit thith time!"

A Nice Girl

On a rather rough day in the Gulf Stream, we had had another real "man overboard" when O'Hegan, one of our engineers, lost his balance as he came on deck in the middle of a heavy roll and went over the side. The crew went into its drill like the Marx Brothers gone crazy, coming up with ladders, nets, grapnel hooks (that would have killed anyone they hit), antishark rifles, and all the other required items, and he was picked up safely, wet, embarrassed, and o.k. except for a strained arm muscle.

Later that day, back in port, Jane came aboard to meet me, and was standing just around the corner of the deckhouse from O'Hegan when he happened to be telling one of the other men what had happened. He didn't know Jane was in earshot, and he said, in the perfectly normal Navy language that applied the word to everything from guns to butter, "Boy, I really fucked up my arm today."

Stonily ladylike, Jane turned away pretending she hadn't heard him, as he gulped in embarrassment. Later on, after we'd left the ship, my wife endeared herself to me forever, proving what a nice girl I'd married. A supposedly sophisticated graduate of Smith College, who was known to bandy naughty words about a bit herself, not the usual thing in 1943, she said to me, "What was O'Hegan talking about? I thought I knew what that meant, but how could it happen to an arm?"

Bumbling into Bimini

My last subchaser brush with the Gulf Stream was the 743's eventual departure from Key West after about our seventy-fifth reindoctrination in ASW techniques, each one different, for parts unknown via Guantánamo and Panama.

We had been partying well in Key West, knowing that the next goodbye would be a long one, and I was not in shape for the dusting we got as we headed toward the Old Bahama Channel along the north coast of Cuba into the usual heavy easterly. Leaving Jane for who knew how long was bad enough for morale, and first-day stomach, a phenomenon that had only begun to hit me after I became skipper, helped not at all and was made doubly unpleasant by the receipt of an urgent radio message.

This was the kind that had to be decoded by pushing little yellow strips of letters across a metal tray, a great exercise for seasick eyes, and I resorted to the wastebasket-between-the-knees solution to get me through it. It was about some sinking on our route, and again the vision of a big black submarine looming up in the night added to the tension of pounding and crashing into head seas, but no contact was made, and I was through with the Gulf Stream for quite a while.

We did have a little seventeen-foot cabin sloop my last year of duty when I came back to Miami to teach at SCTC, now dignified by the designation of Naval Training Center. Just before the war was completely wrapped up, we were finally allowed to take her out of Biscayne Bay, and we slid through Government Cut in fair weather for some delightful day sailing. What a contrast!

Then it was more than a dozen years of northern living and sailing before I cruised from Fort Lauderdale to the Bahamas in the motor sailer *Rolling Stone*, crossing to Bimini in an oily calm that almost made me forget subchaser days.

Mar Claro offshore

The next real brush with the Stream was in our own twenty-four-foot Amphibi-Ette class sloop *Mar Claro,* which we had trailed to Florida for the winter of 1958–59. Jane and I were messing around in the Keys in her in April when we took a notion, on a day of bright sun and a fresh southerly breeze, to head across the Stream from Ocean Reef to Bimini. We hailed a charter fishing boat out of the Ocean Reef Club working the edge of the Stream, told him we were heading across and would check back with Ocean Reef on arrival, and sailed away from his openmouthed amazement.

It was a glorious sail until the wind quit, and we had the silly experience of putt-putting across sizable swells on the Stream's axis with a six-horse outboard. At nightfall, the breeze came back, and I decided to change from genoa to working jib for after-dark safety in case it breezed on heavily. Jane, who has never had much confidence as a helmsman, took the tiller, and I went forward to make the switch. As I was tacking down the working jib and had hands full of shackle parts and a cotter pin in my mouth, I called back something about "be careful not to come about," as I thought she was a little high, and only the last phrase, the "come about" part, got through to her. Suddenly I was whapped against the pulpit by the genny and found myself in a pretty precarious position for a few minutes, with no hands to hold on with and a cotter pin clenched in my teeth.

The pulpit kept me aboard, and I gradually collected myself and the rigging parts and finished the job, all the while hurling rather caustic remarks back to the helm.

There was little rapport between skipper and crew for the rest of the crossing, but we finally eased across the Bimini bar about 0300, and, feeling smug at negotiating it, I relaxed a bit as we turned to port and headed up the harbor toward the marina lights. Suddenly I was aware of some change in the water color ahead, a darker darkness in the dark, and started to say "What's that thing in the waaa—ter," which is as far as I got before we ran aground.

Mar Claro had a two-foot-four draft, so it was a simple matter to hop out and push her off, but I had strayed from the channel at a bend and ran aground again right away. There was a stringpiece just inshore of us, so I decided to ease the few feet over to it and tie up for the little bit of night remaining. It was narrow, with no railing, and I teetered along it making the lines fast before tumbling back aboard and into the sack. (We straightened out the "come about" business the next day.)

In daylight, I poked my head into the cockpit to see just what kind of place we'd ended up in, and it was something of a shock to gaze through a heavy wire netting that was underneath the catwalk we were tied to. We were at the Lerner Marine Labs, and the catwalk I had teetered on at 0300 was the outer edge of the shark pen at the Lab. Great gray monsters, at least a dozen of them, were lazily nosing around the sandy bottom behind the wire, which was only a couple of feet from the hull.

We didn't stay there very long.

*

Tornado Warning

We had excitement of a different sort on the return trip. After messing around Bimini and Cat Cay for a few days and enjoying the first-time thrill of sending in our own boat over the pale, incredibly clear waters of the Great Bahama Bank we picked a day with a strong southerly for the return to Miami.

A pre-dawn departure was set to give us an early afternoon landfall, and we weren't worried by the forecast of a cold front due to cross

Florida "sometime around midnight." We would be in long before that. There was a little excitement as we were negotiating the tricky turns in tide-roiled Gun Cay Passage from the Bank out to the Stream, when the outhaul of the club-footed working jib parted. It would have been impossible for me to give helm orders from the foredeck in those restricted waters, so Jane was elected to inch her way forward and get the wildly flogging jib down and lashed until we could get into open waters and put on a new outhaul.

Maybe I was thinking of our experience on the way over when I decided to stay at the helm!

For nine hours *Mar Claro* charged across the uneven seas, short and quick, close-reaching toward Miami, and a fast passage was in prospect when we began to see the towers of the beach hotels popping over the horizon. The wind was gradually heading us and swinging southwest, however, a big ring was building around the slowly dimming sun, and the western horizon had a dirty orange-brown look. The front had evidently stepped up its timetable, but the Miami radio stations were not changing their prediction of a daylong southerly.

Evidently no one was looking out the window, as the wind was now well around in the west, and we could not lay Government Cut close-hauled any more. I kicked myself for not holding higher on the crossing, but I had originally aimed for the south end of Key Biscayne, which seemed enough of a margin for error.

Since I was keeping a weather eye on the weather to weather as *Mar Claro* buried her rail and charged shoreward, I was able to spot a line of white foam and a darkening of the water behind it as soon as it moved out from the beach. There was no curtain of rain with it, but it was moving rapidly in our direction and kicking up quite a fuss, and we wasted no time in getting sail off. We had just gotten everything furled and stopped when the squall line hit us with a blast like the blow of a fist.

The water was a froth of whitecaps and wind streaks at right angles to the daylong southerly chop. I've never been in a maelstrom, but this had to be what one is like, and just as it erupted all around us, someone must have looked out the window at the radio station, because there were now sudden high-pitched warnings about "possible tornadoes" coming over the air. Thanks a lot.

Mar Claro had a convertible canvas hood over her main cabin, a feature which earned her the nickname of "floating covered wagon" in some quarters, and this seemed to provide enough windage to act something like a storm sail. While Jane secured everything in the cabin that could possibly move, I sat at the tiller and held it to leeward, and the boat lay to the howling northwester at an angle, making some leeway and a little progress to windward, and handled

Mar Claro at the pier in Cat Cay before starting back

the jumping mess of sea beautifully by herself. She never took solid water on deck, though the motion of a light-displacement boat corking around on top had to be experienced to be believed. The clouds were low, black, twisting, and ominous in the dirty brown light, but there was almost no rain.

As we were hanging on patiently at the height of the onslaught, I was startled to see something bright blue leaping across the wave tops in the wildest kind of abandon, heading across our stern, and for a moment I thought it must be some marlin or sailfish gone suddenly berserk in the storm. Uncertainty changed to laughter when it came close enough in its hurtling, bouncing progress to be identified as a beach mat that the front had picked off the sand and was sending rapidly on its way to Bimini.

The radio was making noises about 55-knot winds, which I could easily believe, and still had tornadoes as a possibility, but the cool air behind the front didn't have the look of those conditions. (Actually, the tornadoes did hit up near Melbourne, in a mobile-home camp, as usual.) The temperature had dropped rapidly and there was a gradually widening band of gold in the west and a barely noticeable lessening of wind strength. After three hours or so, we were about seven miles north of where we had been hit by the squall, as we had not quite got out of the Stream, and finally I decided that she could handle the working jib and a reefed main. The wind had settled down to about 25–30 from the west, and by sunset, which now blazed yellowly on a clear horizon, we had beaten our way back to the spot we'd been in about 1430 when the front hit. Twenty minutes more at that time would have put us inside Government Cut before the front. Now, as we came into the lee, I tried to start the outboard in its well aft, but the bouncing around and slop of sea had been too much for it and it refused to cooperate.

So, for the finish of our adventure, we had to beat dead to windward up the four-mile channel of Government Cut, four hundred feet wide (and against an ebb tide to boot), before we could turn to port off the old Clyde Mallory piers (where SCTC had been located) and reach down Biscayne Bay to Dinner Key. I've never been happier to have a self-trimming jib than on that multi-tack session. We were both very hungry, but cooking was impossible in the constant flipping, so Jane handed up sticks of celery, raw carrots, and hunks of cold cuts to keep me going.

When we finally eased into our slip at the Coral Reef Yacht Club, it was close to midnight and the boat was a wet shambles that took two days to dry out, but we fell into the sack as we were. We had only been to Bimini and back, but it sort of felt as though we had been at least once around the world.

The Worst Goof

The episode of which I am least proud in all my sailing experience was also a Gulf Stream event. In 1970, I was loaned a stock thirty-foot sloop for the final week of the SORC. She was straight from the builder, and we had to commission her for the first time and get her ready for offshore competition in a few frantic days at a Miami boatyard.

To add to the usual complications, her sails failed to arrive, and we had to scrounge "seconds" from other boats around us to get her out to the Lipton Cup start. This meant we had to put press-on numbers on, and, since it was our wedding anniversary, we had the crew and friends come to our motel room for a number-pressing champagne party.

It all seemed a great success at the time, so it was a bit disconcerting to have the numbers blow off, one by one in rapid succession, as we cleared Government Cut in a fresh northeaster. As the first one went, there was a general cry of dismay, but as each one followed, the crew ended up like a high school cheering section—"Give me a 2!"—and the two would blow away amid great cheers, while crews near us eyed us with some concern for our sanity.

This was the last Lipton Cup with a "moving mark" in the Stream, one of the methods the sponsoring Biscayne Bay Yacht Club had tried over the years in an attempt to set a fair course despite the fact that there was no way of making a triangle by placing an offshore buoy in the deep, fast-moving Stream.

A Coast Guard cutter would be stationed in the Stream as a turning mark, and this makeshift had caused some of the most unusual mark roundings in racing history.

To keep station, the cutter would have to stem the 2.5-knot current, but she could never do this at an even, steady rate. Instead, she would idle for a while, then put on a burst of speed and move ahead. If this happened when you were approaching her, you might find her steaming right by just as you thought you were laying the mark correctly, and it was always something of a thrill to be just off her bow when a puff of black smoke would burst from her stack and she would suddenly have a bone in her teeth and be heading right for the boats in her way, scattering them like chickens fleeing a fox.

The old system for an offshore mark in the Lipton Cup had a Coast Guard cutter holding station in the Stream

No matter how much adjusting for position she did, she always seemed to end up farther to the north as each class got to her, and the last classes usually sailed a very different triangle from the leading ones. This was one of those days, and we had the longest beat out to her, while the bigger boats had a short beat and more reaching on the inshore leg—not the fairest kind of race.

With our borrowed sails, we were not exactly starring anyway, but the boat seemed to have a fair turn of speed and we felt somewhat organized as a crew as we got ready for the Miami-Nassau Race two days later. And it was encouraging when we found that our sails had arrived while we were out in the Lipton.

The wind was still fresh in the east for the Miami-Nassau start. The previous year, we had had a wildly exciting race in another borrowed thirty-footer, reaching fast across to Isaac in a fresh southerly, then picking up a howling northwester behind a cold front in good old Northwest Providence Channel. We had zoomed the 184 miles to Nassau in twenty-six hours (while *Windward Passage* was setting a course record of fifteen hours) in the most exhilarating sleigh ride of a run I've ever been on. With a reefed main and the No. 3 genny wung-out, we had surfed on the cresting, ink-blue rollers between wings of spray shooting up as high as our spreaders. This looked like a very different sort of race, and I decided, for the first time in my life, to take a seasick pill, one of the bonamine derivatives. I remembered my problems with "captain's stomach" in the SC and thought this might be another occasion for it.

The captain's stomach was made no less queasy as we cleared Government Cut, when the engine ground to a halt amid a horrifying clatter and we had to negotiate the narrow entrance between the jetties, both asmother in foam with the onshore seas dashing over them, under sail. It seems the ventilation hose in the engine compartment had not been secured well enough and had tangled in the propeller shaft, effectively making us a sailing-vessel-only until the mess could be laboriously cleared, a task that eventually took several hours in the calm of a marina, working around cramped corners and angles, and that would have been impossible to do in bouncy Gulf Stream conditions.

Our crew was exotically international. In addition to daughter Martha and me, we had one college-age friend of hers, Kip Lewis, from Florida, on his first ocean race (he was later to develop into one of the most sought-after crews in the sport); the sales manager of the boat's manufacturer, a Scot living in Canada; Bob Harris, an Australian living in the United States; and a young Finnish boy, also on his first ocean race, whose family Martha had lived with in Finland the year before.

Seasickness hit the sales manager almost immediately, leaving him helpless for the rest of the race, but the rest of us held together as we headed out into the steep lump of seas in the Stream. The weather was overcast with squalls, giving the water that black look instead of its bright blue shade in sunshine. Squalls brought frequent quick changes in wind direction, and it was hard to figure the correct tack and to keep a D.R., as we flipped frequently. As an example of how violent the changes were, the big Class A boats, which had started behind us, caught us just as one squall hit, and the seventy-three-footer *Ondine* crossed our bow by a few hundred feet. Soon after she did, the wind shifted again, giving us a lift on the opposite tack, so we flipped over and actually crossed *Ondine* the next time we came together.

This didn't last very long, though, as the big boats disappeared in the murk ahead of us, and soon we were alone in the deepening dusk on a very lumpy stretch of ocean. The wind had settled back in the east and was blowing harder, setting up a short, heavy chop on top of the bobble that the squalls had left, and the motion of the boat became violently jerky. It was almost impossible to move in the leaping, crashing bounce of the little thirty-footer pounding into it, and I found myself developing a peculiar indolent inertia.

I knew I should be plotting our course changes on the chart and keeping a running D.R., but I kept telling myself that our general heading was good enough to pick up Isaac, with its loom visible over sixteen miles, and I tried to keep a running D.R. in my head as I scrunched in one spot in the cockpit and occasionally took a wheel trick.

As the night wore on and Isaac didn't appear, I should have begun to worry, but the lethargy still held, and I did very little about anything. Martha realized that I wasn't doing what I should, and she began to needle me quietly, making sure the rest of the crew didn't hear. Finally, she became so perturbed that she took the direction finder herself and tuned in on a beacon, putting us directly offshore of West End on Grand Bahama, about thirty miles north of where we should have been. We had really been set by the Stream.

This jolted me into action with a horrified realization of how derelict I had been, and we came about and started beating along the southern shore of Grand Bahama Island. Out of earshot of the rest of the crew, Martha really let me have it, and then loyally spread the word around to the others, out of my hearing, not to rag me about it because I was upset enough already.

We had already ripped our No. 1 genoa, and shortly after sunrise, the No. 2 developed a split. With no headsails left—we had no repair kit on the newly commissioned boat—and no engine, the only thing to do was to turn back for West End, and it was a tricky business negotiating the narrow dogleg entrance through jetties while hard on the wind under main alone. Then, when we had finally made it safely alongside at the marina there, we found that the main halyard was jammed, and we couldn't get the main down until someone went up in a bosun's chair.

It was the first time since I was nineteen that I had made a navigational error, and it is the only time I have ever had that peculiar feeling of inert lethargy keeping me from doing what I basically knew had to be done. As an excuse, I can only assume that the seasick pill acted like a tranquilizer. I have only had tranquilizers twice in my life, both times to relieve muscle spasms in my back, and there was that same feeling of "so what?" about everything then. I've never taken another pill, and I've never goofed that way again either.

The Great Sheep Run

In contrast, one of the better days in the Stream, a happy memory with no big waves or flying spray, came in the 1971 Lipton Cup. There had been so many complaints about the "moving mark" that 1971 brought a change of course. The first leg was to be north, directly up the beach to a marker boat off Hollywood, and the return was a sort of slalom arrangement, a zigzag route through a bunch of marker boats and buoys in a staggered pattern. Some were just out in the Gulf Stream, where it was still shallow enough to anchor, and the rest were out of the current, closer to the beach.

That year, I had been loaned *Jaan*, a Hinckley Bermuda 40 with a new tall IOR rig, for the last three SORC races. Daughter Martha was married to Hank, the youngest Hinckley, and his father was generously letting us use his own personal B40. I had my own crew, with Marth and Hank naturally a part of it, and the Lipton was to be our debut.

The Tripp-designed B40 is a beautiful cruising boat, one of the longest-lived stock models in the history of the sport, and she sails well in that category, but by 1971 her days of ranking at the top among serious ocean racers were almost a decade behind her. The light-displacement era of the Cal 40s and the advent of stripped-out machines built under the new IOR Rule had obsoleted the B40 for top-level competition. Most boats fade from view when this happens, but she was so popular as a luxury cruising auxiliary, with good sailing qualities and solid construction, that she had achieved a whole new life and identity in this field. It was therefore the usual thing to load a B40 with every amenity possible, and *Jaan* had just about every one you could name, such as air conditioning, extra tankage, water maker, deep freeze, shower, and every electronic item imaginable.

With all this weight and a long-keeled hull with attached rudder, it was tilting with windmills to race against a hotshot collection of the latest fin-keel, spade-rudder IOR models, stripped out to such an extent that heads were not enclosed, standing out in the middle of the cabin like a birdbath, and bunks were canvas and pipes. We knew this, but we always enjoyed the whole atmosphere of the SORC and involvement in it, and we would race *Jaan* as hard as we could for the fun of it, without expecting too much.

Jaan on her way to winning her class in the Lipton Cup

Race day was ideal. There was a moderate southerly under bright skies, a spinnaker run for the first leg. The big boats were to start first, and we watched as they maneuvered for the line. My navigator was Jim Davis, a six-foot-eight giant with the most easy going, pleasant personality anyone has ever been shipmates with, combined with expert competence as a seaman and navigator. He located the starting marks, which were somewhat ambiguously described in the circular, and pointed out in some glee that *Windward Passage*, the monster seventy-three-foot ketch that made a habit of setting course records and was the scratch boat here, was not starting between them. She had mistaken one of the white buoys that mark a special pilot anchorage in the area for a starting marker, and she charged off under her mammoth spinnaker several hundred yards offshore from the correct starting line. Several other boats in Class A followed her in the same mistake.

When our turn came with Class D, we made the decision to play the inshore end of the line. There was a question whether it was worthwhile to slant offshore and get into the favoring current of the Stream, sailing a longer distance but getting a lift, or to stick to the rhumb line. Jim pointed out that the marker boat's position would be well in from the Stream, and we finally decided, after a confab, that it would be better to sail the shorter distance.

A B40 might have been outmoded for all-round hotshot competition, but it was still a good design down wind. Despite the extra weight of heavy construction and luxury amenities, the new tall rig and long waterline were still good qualities, and we were not doing badly as we headed up the beach under every stitch we could fly. No one was walking away from us, but the others were certainly on a divergent course. I concentrated on steering and keeping her under the spinnaker at the best trim, but I couldn't help but notice that our competition was tending well offshore, and that the bigger boats ahead of us were also farther out to sea.

"Why are they way out there?" I inquired to thin air, and Jim answered.

"I don't know, but this is the course."

We kept surging along with good speed well inshore of most of the fleet, eventually passing the Sunny Isles buoy at the north end of Miami Beach close enough aboard to spit on it, and by now I was getting quite nervous about how far offshore the other boats were. Meanwhile, the radio began to come alive with all sorts of chatter from the Class A boats about the location of the turning mark. There seemed to be a great deal of confusion, and, just about this time, we noticed a large white boat up ahead of us hard on the wind on the return course.

"Must be *Windward Passage* on her way back," I said, but the more I looked at her, the less she looked like *Passage*. She was in fact a yawl, not a ketch, and proved to be *Panacea* in Class B as she came closer. If she was the first boat around, something was definitely screwy, as she had started fifteen minutes after Class A and was naturally not as fast as the monster maxis. Also up ahead, numerous powerboats were anchored or trolling, making it difficult to pick out the correct marker boat, and the symmetry of disappearing spinnakers in the A fleet had broken down into a patternless jumble of boats milling about at different angles. *American Eagle* was actually heading in to the beach from the northeast. Meanwhile, the rest of our class was in a cluster well out to sea.

Again I made noises about where we were in comparison to everyone else—even the Class E boats astern of us were well offshore—but Jim stuck to his guns.

"If the marker boat's where she's supposed to be, she's got to be on our course just like the Sunny Isles buoy. It's two miles beyond that, and we should be running our distance out any minute now."

Skip Maguire had been using the binoculars to scan the odd action ahead, and when Jim made his statement, he began searching ahead and to port in the confusion of fishing boats.

"What identification is the mark supposed to have?" Skip asked, without lowering the glasses.

"Code flag M."

"Blue with a white cross?"

"Yep."

"Then that's it." He pointed to an anchored Hatteras a couple of hundred yards inshore, just as several Class A boats converged on it from various northern points of the compass.

"Are you sure?" I asked.

"Got to be," Jim and Skip agreed. Distracted by all this, I was letting the spinnaker break and was about to go into an involuntary jibe, but, finally convinced, gave the order to jibe and douse spinnaker, and we approached the Hatteras as *American Eagle*, *Nepenthe*, and *Charisma*, just clear of the mark, charged past us, crews grimly silent and looking mad enough to chew nails.

"Is that the mark?" one of our crew called out as *Eagle* swooshed by us, but all we got was a phalanx of stony stares, except for one guy who pointed off toward the northeast. No question. This definitely was the elusive mark, and the Class A boats were thoroughly upset to find a D boat rounding with them.

"Are you the mark?" we asked of the Hatteras, and a woman sitting on the bow laughed.

"Yes, we are. Where is everybody?"

Trimming sheets, we swept around and came hard on the wind amid whoops of amazed disbelief from the crew. Here we were right with Class A, and there was the rest of our class still surging north on the Great Sheep Run, blindly following *Windward Passage* to Jacksonville, or maybe even Nova Scotia. You can wait through years of ocean racing for a delicious moment like this.

Windward work has never been the forte of B40s, even in their heyday, and it was a long slug of beating to thread our way through the slalom of the return leg, but our adrenalin was flowing and we kept her at it with every ounce of concentration we could muster. A couple of Class E boats behind us had located the mark o.k. and were not far astern, but only A and B boats managed to overtake and pass us. Looking back, we saw that a blue Cal 40, *Williwaw*, being sailed by Jack Price, one of the most experienced local sailors and a frequent SORC prizewinner, had been the first boat in our class to wake up and turn back, and we knew we had our work cut out for us to stave off the surge of this much hotter and more modern machine. Playing every angle to stay out of the Stream until the very last minute necessary to round the marker boats anchored in it, we did everything we could to get the utmost out of *Jaan*, as *Williwaw* gained inexorably. She gave us time, but we wanted to beat her across and hear that soul-satisfying boom of the gun.

We barely made it, figuring the last tack to the inch, and staving

her off by a hundred yards, and the blast of the committee boat's gun
was greeted by gleeful shouts and a storm of backslapping. Jim was
the hero, with an assist from Skip, and, checking over his figures, we
decided that most of the navigators had plotted their course from the
white marker buoy. This was actually well outboard of the starting line
and was only cited as a reference point in the circular. The starting
line, marked by two boats flying Race Committee flags had been well
inshore of it, but when *Windward Passage* picked up the wrong marks
and started in the wrong place, everybody played that safe, easy game
of "Follow the A boats. They know where they're going," and the
Great Sheep Run resulted.

Later, when I compared notes with Jack Price, he admitted he had
seen us on our inshore course but thought we were crazy, and when
they saw us jibe for the mark they just thought we were having spinnaker trouble.

It was a great day on the water, and, since it was our anniversary
again, a great celebration ashore. I'm also absolutely certain that it was
the last time an air-conditioned boat ever won a class prize in an SORC
race.

PART II

"Olden Times"

The perspectives of looking backward are all so relative. To someone of my generation, the Depression, FDR, and World War II seem like only yesterday, while our children, now adults with fairly long memories of their own, regard them as dim antiquities. I remember putting such a perspective on when the Princeton 1935 football team was introduced between the halves of the 1975 Yale-Princeton game. I had been a freshman when they had an undefeated season, and to me this was a very fresh memory, and they still seemed like stalwart fellows in the prime of life. Then I realized that, had a comparable team been introduced when I was a freshman, it would have been the 1895 one, which to me was as dimly back in history (a different century even) as Genghis Khan or George Washington. And, a few years ago when my son was squash coach at Tabor Academy in Massachusetts, I happened to play (and beat) him in front of one of the boys on his team. The lad was aghast that some ancient party had beaten his coach, and afterwards he asked me, "Gosh, sir. How long have you been playing this game?" "Oh, a little over thirty years," I answered, and his surprised response was, "Gee, did they have it in those days?"

And so "olden days" are a relative thing, but here are some of my earliest "sea stories," prefaced by a really old one from my family's seafaring background.

An Unusual "Abandon Ship"

My paternal grandfather was a sea captain out of Hull, a port on the Humber River on the North Sea coast of Yorkshire. He had gone to sea as a cabin boy, and his first voyage away from home took him to Boston. In walking around the streets there, he saw a vegetable stand with a display of tomatoes, which he had never seen before and thought must be the reddest, juciest plums he could imagine. He bought one and took a big bite, and the strange taste was such a shock that he suddenly became so homesick that he sat down on the curb and burst into tears.

He kept at a seafaring career, however, and became a sailing ship master in his twenties. At first he made coasting voyages, but his commands grew bigger, and he ranged the trade routes of the world. Very few of his adventures have been passed down, though my father remembered his father telling tales of repelling pirates in the Malay Straits in hand-to-hand combat, and Dad was also full of stories of how stern a disciplinarian Grandfather was when he was ashore, and when he finally retired.

It must have been a help in his career to marry "the boss's daughter." My grandmother Susan Applebye's maternal grandfather Briggs was a shipowner in Hull, and Grandfather was soon commanding vessels under the Briggs house flag, including the pride of the fleet, a full-rigged ship named *Brunelle*. She was a graceful, slender vessel of over two hundred feet with a great turn of speed, once clocked at over 16 knots and often sweeping by the steamships of the day, but she had one failing.

There was some flaw in her construction that made her very loose and flexible. In any kind of sea or at any speed, her planks would "ripple," and it was the carpenter's duty to make the rounds of the chain plates and knock in the bolts as they worked loose. Although he loved her for her speed and handsome lines, Grandfather finally tired of this problem and asked to be transferred to another ship. A new captain would be assigned *Brunelle*, but no one ever stayed with her for long. After the unsettling sight of her rippling sides, they would sign

A painting of the rescue of *Brunelle*'s crew

off quickly. One captain only got as far as the Orkney Islands before jumping ship, and each time Grandfather, now reaping one of the disadvantages of being in the family, would be dispatched to take *Brunelle* on her way again.

Finally, the failing caught up with her on a passage from Canada to England in January 1874. She had a cargo of grain when she sailed from Halifax, and Grandmother and her oldest son, Billy, aged six, were passengers aboard. This seems odd for a winter North Atlantic voyage, especially since she was also pregnant, but passengers they were.

Brunelle suffered a series of gales, making heavy weather of it and taking a severe beating, until her hull worked so much that leaking couldn't be controlled. The grain soaked up water and began to swell, adding to the strain on the hull, until she developed a bad list and became almost unmanageable. Unable to heave to properly, she was swept by seas until her foremast was carried away and the mainmast damaged, and her condition was truly desperate.

Fortunately, help appeared in the form of a little Dutch brig named *Castle Eden*, half the size of *Brunelle* but undamaged and better able to handle the long, sweeping seas. The decision was made to abandon ship, as there didn't seem any way to correct the list or repair her rig, but the operation then presented the problem of getting a pregnant woman into the lifeboat.

Brunelle's ship's boat was launched, and the crew jumped into it one by one and maneuvered it under *Brunelle*'s stern. Breaking with the tradition of the captain being the last to leave, Grandfather handled the situation in an unusual way. First he helped Grandmother over the taffrail so that she was hanging on the outside of it, facing forward. Then, passing Billy down to the lifeboat, he timed himself carefully and jumped into the boat as it went by the level of *Brunelle*'s rail on one of its up-and-down swings with the waves.

Grandmother was still grasping the taffrail firmly as the small boat rose and fell past the stern, and Grandfather, braced at the coaming of the lifeboat, with sailors holding his legs, grabbed Grandmother around the waist as the boat lifted by her on a wave, shouted "Let go!," and tumbled back into the boat with her in his arms.

The transfer to *Castle Eden* was made without mishap, but Billy was quite put out, and told his mother so, because he had come into the small boat without his fishing line, and it would be much easier to fish in the low boat than from the high-sided *Brunelle*.

Grandfather later commissioned an oil painting of the scene, along with another painting of *Brunelle* under full sail, which have come down to me as prized possessions. The doughty ship never did sink. A battered hulk, she finally came ashore on the Brittany coast almost a year later.

As far as I know, Grandmother never went to sea again.

Uncle Billy and the Language of the Sea

My very earliest memory of a boat is at Bluepoint, Long Island, on Great South Bay, when I'm told I was three. Visiting friends there with my parents, I was taken to see the catboat of a family named Bannerman. She was tied up in a creek, and one of the Bannerman boys, college age, invited me aboard and tried to take me by the hand and help me over. I remember looking down at the gap between the boat and the bulkhead, with water gleaming darkly at the bottom, and then shying back and refusing to step across. Finally, Bannerman, in some impatience, picked me up and lifted me onto the deck, and the future editor of *Yachting* magazine, whining and kicking, boarded a boat for the first time. It was one of the few times I have ever shown reluctance to do so, at least until *J & B* in the 1976 Miami-Nassau Race.

Much more clear, though, are early memories associated with summers at Nantucket, Massachusetts, and dominated by Uncle Billy, the survivor of the loss of *Brunelle* and for whom I was named. He had not let that experience keep him from a seafaring career, and, as the oldest son of a sea captain should, he shipped out under sail as an apprentice at the age of fourteen. His thorough grounding in things nautical must have been helpful, as he had his officer's ticket when very young, and by the time he was twenty-eight he was first officer of the White Star liner *Majestic* in 1895.

He was qualified for command and this should have soon led to one at an early age, but his career ended, and his whole life changed abruptly, when he met an American heiress who was a passenger on the ship. Courtship of her brought a promise to retire ashore, which he did with the utmost grace, never to work again while ruling the family, as much in command as the master of any ship, with the benignly bluff manner of an old British sea dog.

His wife was a New Yorker, with a country place at Cornwall near West Point in the Hudson Valley, and they settled there and started to raise a family of three girls. The house was on a knoll surrounded by meadows, with Storm King Mountain rising to the eastward between it and the Hudson. Cornwall was in a valley that had once been the bed of the Hudson before some prehistoric geological upheaval had shifted Storm King Mountain, blocking the path the Hudson followed then and altering the river's course to the other side of the mountain. The house's knoll must have been high enough to be near the surface of the river as a shoal, and, far from the sea, Uncle Billy managed at least a small nautical touch by naming the place Knoll Shoal.

It was great fun to visit there, as it had a barn with chickens, horses, and cows, a brook with several pools, and wide fields to run in. The house itself was a large gray shingled one with high ceilings and heavy, imposing woodwork, and my main thrill in going there was to be lifted up and shown the model Grandfather had made of *Brunelle*. It sat in its case on the mantel of the great fireplace in the entrance hall, and Uncle Billy would point out, each time he showed her to me, various details of her rig and fittings. That model and Uncle Billy's Navy sword from World War I are now in my possession, and the model and the paintings of *Brunelle* add a touch of family history to our living room.

The knoll, which fell off steeply for perhaps fifty feet toward a

Uncle Billy   I'm in the stern of *Alicia* at a family picnic

brook that ran behind the house, gave rise to one of the long-standing quotes in my family. Our cook, Mary Flaherty, who had grown up in pancake-flat Elizabethport, New Jersey, came with us to Knoll Shoal when we took it over while Uncle Billy's family was on a trip. Soon after arriving, she stepped out the kitchen door, peered over the edge of the drop-off, clutched her ample bosom, and said, "My God! What a mountayne!" Anytime thereafter when any of us commented on any sort of hill, cliff, or whatever, Mary Flaherty's exclamation was usually invoked.

Knoll Shoal was fun, but it was Nantucket, where Uncle Billy and Aunt Edwina, known always as Auntie Ed, spent their summers from about 1912 on, that gave Uncle Billy the perfect setting for his role as retired sea dog, and where I remember him best and with the greatest fondness. The "family compound" consisted of a cottage and a bungalow under the brow of The Cliff on the north shore of the island just west of the jetties that formed the harbor entrance. With typical British whimsy that seems to have to name every type of

Jetsam

structure from henhouse on up, the cottage was called Ittldo, one of
the minor embarrassments of my youth, and the bungalow was
Jetsam. This was an apt name, since it had been built by a resourceful
Nantucketer out of odds and ends scavenged off the beach.

The beach was right in front of Jetsam, first a wild and undeveloped
one, but later, from the mid-1920s on, the site of Cliffside Beach Club.
This gave me a great choice of kids to play with, and, even better, the
famous Gilbreth family of *Cheaper by the Dozen* was right across the
street, all twelve of them. With one Gilbreth boy a year younger, one
my age, and one a year older, it was wonderful for me, as the only
child at Jetsam, to have such a lively neighborhood. I'll never forget
Dan Gilbreth's look of scorn when he came to get me to play one
morning and saw two bottles of milk that had just been delivered
on our back doorstep. "Is THAT all the milk you get?" he asked.
"We get twelve bottles every day."

Uncle Billy ran Ittldo like a ship. The time was kept by ship's clocks
that chimed the hours away on the eight-bell system, and a large
telescope was mounted on the front porch so that he could keep an
eye on the marine traffic in and out of the harbor. The flag was
raised and lowered with great ceremony each day, and for years,
before Nantucket's garbage service was extended that far out of town,
there was a unique family ritual known as the Garbage Parade. Twice
a week, Uncle Billy would put on some sort of mock uniform and
marshal the whole family and anyone else in the neighborhood who
happened to be around, and would lead a procession out into the
nearby dunes, with the garbage cans toted on long sticks like the bag-
gage of a safari. Youngsters would be beating pans and tootling kazoos,

Uncle Sam and Uncle Billy

and, when a sufficiently remote spot was reached, a pit would be dug and the garbage interred with suitable mumbo-jumbo. It was a sad day for the kids when a regular garbage truck began to service the area, but we probably would have run out of dune space if it hadn't.

As he paced the porch of Ittldo, stopping at the telescope now and then to identify a yacht or fishing boat negotiating the jetties, Uncle Billy had very much the look of a captain on his bridge. He was not especially tall, only about five foot ten, but was solidly built and imposing in bearing, and his gruff, strong voice had a ring of authority. Not only was it a strong speaking voice, but he also had a fine tenor and loved to sing. For many years he led the choirs at St. John's in Cornwall and St. Paul's in Nantucket, and he had an endless store of sea chanteys. We often had family singsongs around the piano in the evening, and family picnics, which were another favorite ceremony of his, were always enlivened by his chanteys. When I later went to Camp Viking, a sailing camp on Cape Cod where we sang chanteys as a formal part of the day's activities, the other campers were tremendously impressed that I already knew the words of most of them.

Uncle Billy could be imposing and stern, but he also had a droll sense of humor that was never far from the surface. His face was long, well lined, and ruddy, and a full-rounded lower lip rolled out beneath a long upper one, giving him the look of the English actor George Arliss got up to play Captain Bligh. It was a greatly expressive face for telling stories, for putting extra life and liveliness in songs, for

Nantucket Yacht Club committee boat

amusing children, and for turning severely dignified when the occasion warranted. As he got along in years, he became increasingly vague and would often stop in the middle of a sentence with a long-drawn-out "—aaaah," shake his head, and say, "Now where was I?" One morning, as he was musing over plans for the day and the things he had to do, he said, "Let's see now. I've had my breakfast—" and that became a family watchword to preface any discussion of plans.

The singing sessions became livelier than ever when Uncle Sam, a couple of years younger than Uncle Billy, and Aunt Jessie came to visit from Vancouver, where they lived. Uncle Sam had also gone to sea and got his ticket at an early age. He had also married an American, but she was not an heiress who could demand his retirement. She was a Sears from Searsport, Maine, who had been aboard her father's sailing ship in Hong Kong when she and Uncle Sam met. He was with the Canadian Pacific Line, commanding many of their ships, ending with their Pacific flagship *Empress of Japan* before retiring in the mid-1930s. If Uncle Billy was a fine figure of a sea dog, Uncle Sam was the absolute quintessence. He was half a head shorter, half a yard wider without an ounce of fat, with a craggy, deeply lined face; firm, clefted chin; bright blue, deep-set eyes; and a mane of iron-gray hair. If anyone ever had a seaman's gait it was Uncle Sam, a pronounced roll as he walked.

He too had a fine voice, though not as well trained as Uncle Billy's, and they would feed each other cues leading from one chantey to another in the family sings. Their reminiscences and "sea stories" went on for hours and I never tired of listening, and one of the better acts to watch was their joint effort at backing the car out of Ittldo's driveway.

Standing "astern" of it, Uncle Sam would direct Uncle Billy at the wheel with "Hard aport now—steady as she goes—look out to starboard—all clear aft—" until the drive was negotiated. Actually it wasn't an act. It was just the easiest way for them to communicate. Most of their conversation was carried on in nautical terms and it was hard for either of them to describe something in any other frame of reference. They were both extremely strong-minded men, accustomed to command and to having their own way, but their understanding of each other was so complete that I don't remember any obvious clashes. My father was eleven years younger than Uncle Billy, and he had hardly known either of them as a boy, as Uncle Billy had gone to sea when Dad was three, and Uncle Sam soon afterward. Dad signed up in the Army in the Boer War and never had gone to sea, calling himself the "farmer" of the family, so he was on the sidelines for all the nautical chatter, but he knew the chanteys and entered into the singing with gusto.

Another evening pastime was word games, and there was one spelling bee when "erysipelas" was used. Uncle Sam got it wrong, but refused to accept the verdict—I think he had an "i" in place of the "y"—even when shown the dictionary. "Too bad," he said firmly. "Your dictionary's wrong." No one crossed the captain when he had his mind made up.

My father had followed the family tradition of marrying an American, but not an heiress, and he had to spend much of the summer selling refrigerators and generators on West Forty-fifth Street in Manhattan, with only two weeks in August for Nantucket. Dad loved to fish, and much of the time he was there was spent out on the jetty rocks fishing, with the most memorable moment the hooking and landing of a six-foot sand shark that was the sensation of Cliffside Beach when we dragged it home along the water's edge.

For the rest of the summers, Uncle Billy, in his daily presence, was a strong influence. His daughters were college age by the time I was six or so, and, without a son of his own, he treated me almost as a surrogate son and the beneficiary of his vast store of nautical lore.

It was Uncle Billy who first took me out in a sailboat, putting me at the tiller of my cousin Marie's skiff *Alicia* and showing me which way to push it to make the boat turn, as he explained what the sail was doing. My favorite kind of excursion, though, was to go out with him in the Nantucket Yacht Club committee boat. As Fleet Captain, he ran the Wednesday and Saturday races for the club fleet of Rainbows, Baby Rainbows (Beetle Cats), Indians, Skiffs, Hottentots, and Interclubs. The two Rainbow fleets were so named because they had colored sails, a bright addition to the harbor scene and a great boon to the island's postcard industry.

The committee boat was an ancient, raised-deck cruiser with varnished sheer strake, run by a retired Portuguese fisherman named Harry, who was even saltier, if possible, than Uncle Billy. Usually there were other members to help Uncle Billy with the signal hoists (Harry always fired the brass cannon with great relish), but one day just the three of us were aboard, and Uncle Billy told me in solemn, ceremonious tones that I would have to work the hoists.

Never have I felt such a sense of responsibility, and all went well, if nervously, for a while. Then, somehow, I put up the wrong code flag for the next class. I knew it instantly and shall never forget the horror of that naked blue and white flag that should have been yellow and blue.

There was a natural, instantaneous reaction from Uncle Billy. I didn't pay much attention to the words, but the manner in which they were said left no doubt as to their import. I guess they were pretty salty, but the reaction seemed normal and thoroughly justified to me, and I was so red-faced with shame and confusion that I didn't think much about what had actually been said. I just knew I'd made a mistake. After we rectified it, the rest of the day went smoothly.

It was a surprise, therefore, when Auntie Ed called me up to Ittldo the next morning as I was playing outside Jetsam and said that Uncle Billy wanted to talk to me. Auntie Ed was a tiny butterball of a woman with sharp, wizened features and a forthright manner that did nothing to hide the fact that she found it difficult to tolerate small boys and the noise they made. In so many words, I was frightened of her and remained so until past adolescence. Uncle Billy was as abashed as I felt as he took me aside into the living room and mumbled his way through an apology "for what I said to you yesterday." I don't know whether he or I was more embarrassed, and we were both very relieved as he finished.

I was ready to dash back to Jetsam, but Auntie Ed stopped me and said, "Well, Bill, sailors will be sailors, and when they get excited they use strong language. I just don't want you to think you can use the same words."

As I nodded dutifully and ran back to play with a great sigh of relief, I wondered how Auntie Ed knew what Uncle Billy had said. He must have confessed to her without realizing how she would react. But what really bothered me was that I couldn't for the life of me remember what the words were that I wasn't supposed to use. Boy, if I only knew them!

Cousin Lulu

Although Uncle Billy usually ran the Race Committee, and the sailing in the family was done by my older cousin, Marie, there was one memorable day when Marie had a conflict of some sort and Uncle Billy agreed to race her skiff *Alicia* for her. The Nantucket skiff was a clinker-built, hard-chine, low-freeboard catboat, sixteen feet, with a low-aspect gaff rig that had a long, low boom. Marie had taken me sailing (not racing) a few times, and I was always being told to "mind your head" when the low boom swept across the cockpit.

For crew, Uncle Billy had signed up his wife's first cousin, Lulu, and, both being in their fifties at the time, and no longer sylphlike, there had been some good-natured conjecture about their ability to handle the skittish little boat in a race.

Alicia sat on a mooring off Brant Point, and they rowed out to her in a dinghy to get ready to race. Up went the main, and Uncle Billy then inched up to the narrow foredeck to make the dinghy fast to the mooring buoy and cast *Alicia* off. While he was perched precariously, leaning over to the buoy, he felt the boat begin to gather way and realized that the sail, which had been swinging back and forth while luffing, must have filled. He was having trouble freeing the mooring line, especially with the boat moving, and he called back, "Free the mainsheet, Lulu."

No answer.

"Lulu," a little more insistently, "free the main!"

Still no answer, and the boat was moving faster. Starting to shout again, he looked over his shoulder, and the cockpit was empty.

"Lulu!" he bellowed. "Where are you?"

From back in the wake, as he scrambled awkwardly down to the cockpit, came a faint cry.

"Here I am, Billy!" Cousin Lulu called as her head emerged from the water.

Eventually, once he had things under control in the cockpit and could jibe back to where she was placidly treading water, he managed to manhandle her back aboard, thankful for the low freeboard, and she insisted on going through with the race despite her soggy condition. It seems that she had been leaning over the gunwale fending the dinghy off when the boom came across with a good swing and caught her a solid thwack squarely on her ample exposed area with enough force for her to take a header.

Kaiwonkigongs and Irving Johnson Too

All this had been in the 1920s, but the '30s brought changes. Marie had married and was raising a family of her own. They took over Jetsam, and in the depths of the Depression my family could not swing their own summer place. They did, however, scrape enough together for me to go to camp, and while I missed Nantucket, Camp Viking on Pleasant Bay, right at the "elbow" of Cape Cod, was a great place to build on the minimum introduction I'd had to sailing.

It was run by a retired Navy officer, Norman White, known inevitably as The Skipper, an ebullient, bucko man with a loud, Ed Wynn–type laugh and a sense of humor that appealed perfectly to camp-age boys. There were all sorts of local jokes and gags at Viking, starting with the trip up from New York on the Fall River Line steamer. When new boys wondered at the phosphorescence in the wake of *Commonwealth* as she steamed through Long Island Sound, they were told that the ship was going so fast that sparks were coming off her keel. At camp, the community privy was known as the White House, always good for a giggle, and each summer there was an elaborate mystery or special plot. One year, the Crown Prince of Sweden was supposed to be incognito as a camper, and we were to watch out for foreign agents trying to kidnap him. The result was that parents arriving for a visit or innocent tradesmen making deliveries would find campers pointing at them, taking down license numbers, and otherwise acting strangely.

The longest-running and most classic Viking gag was the Kaiwonkigong (spelling arbitrary). One of the features of camp routine was the overnight trip, in which we were taken in Viking's motor sailer to Chatham Bar, a barrier beach that separated Pleasant Bay from the ocean. It was undeveloped, a wonderful place of pounding surf, sand

Getting set for Kaiwonkigong watching on Chatham Bar

dunes, beach grass, tidal pools, and a mammoth tern rookery. In daylight we would explore all this, skinny-dip in the surf, net for marine life in the pools, and generally have a fine time, followed by supper cooked over a driftwood fire, singing, and a night of sleeping under the stars, blanketed down amid the dunes.

New boys, puzzled by the isolated pools that were tide-fed only during extreme spring tides and were landlocked the rest of the time, were told that these depressions were Kaiwonkigong wallows. The Kaiwonkigong was said to be a mammoth sea beast who swam by day in the ocean but came ashore at night to hunker down in the sand to sleep. He was so big that the places where he "wallowed" filled with water—hence the pools.

As an old Nantucket veteran of twelve, used to the tall tales of Uncle Billy and Uncle Sam, I was much too sophisticated to buy the Kaiwonkigong routine, but it went over big with the Midget set—the camp was divided into Midgets, Intermediates, and Seniors—and the counselors made a big thing out of stationing boys in good spots for Kaiwonkigong watching.

"You have to stay awake, now," they would caution. "They don't come ashore until pretty late."

In the morning, around the breakfast fire, counselors would start talking to each other in front of the boys who had been put on Kaiwonkigong watch.

Irving Johnson

"I think he was the biggest one I've ever seen," one would say.

"Well, maybe," another would answer, "and he sure made funny noises, but I think I saw a bigger one last year."

"Well, he was big enough," the act would go on. Then, turning to one of the campers who'd been on watch, "Didn't you think so, Johnny?"

Johnny would mumble and hang his head.

"Didn't you see him?" the counselor would ask in amazement.

"I thought I stayed up late enough, but I guess I went to sleep."

"Gee, Johnny, that's too bad. You missed a good one. Well, maybe next time," while all the "old boys" smirked in glee at Johnny's embarrassment. Even though I knew the gag, I couldn't help fantasizing what a Kaiwonkigong might look like whenever I went on an overnight to Chatham Bar.

An extra dividend at Viking was the advent of Irving Johnson as a special counselor, sort of like the added attraction on a vaudeville bill. Later to become famous as master of various *Yankees* on several circumnavigations and other publicized adventures, he had just returned from rounding Cape Horn in the square-rigger *Peking*, the same ship that is now part of the exhibit at New York's South Street Seaport.

He had wonderful movies that he had taken aboard her, and his commentary was enthusiastic and salty, with "roaring" as his favorite word, and his "sea stories" were great too. Even more fascinating was his physical strength and his ability to perform fabulous feats. He had done body-building to toughen himself for sea, and he would amaze us by such acts as suspending himself horizontally in the air from a fence post or balancing against a wall with all his weight on his thumbs.

He could tear up phone books, and, lying next to a two-hundred-pound man on the floor, would pick him up and walk away with him in a fireman's carry across the shoulders. He was a fantastic seaman, helping us with knots, splices, and marlinspike work, and he was far and away the most exciting thing that had happened at Viking, at least since the Swedish Crown Prince caper was exposed as a hoax. We did, however, finally find a weakness. His musculature was so over-developed, especially around the upper torso and shoulders, that he was muscle-bound for such a simple act as hitting a baseball. Although he wasn't too happy, we would lure him into softball games just to see his mighty but very restricted swing result invariably in a little dribbler to the pitcher. Somehow it made him more human, and it didn't do anything to diminish our awe at his other accomplishments. After my encounter with him at Viking, it was no surprise to me the way his career developed in later years.

The most exciting thing about Viking for me, in a personal way, however, was that magic moment when I first realized that I really

Part of the Camp Viking fleet

You can see how confident I've become as a
skipper at age twelve

knew how to sail. Later, I won the camp racing championship, greatly
satisfying and rewarding, but that wasn't as important as that first
critical turning point. It came in a "distance race" down Pleasant Bay
in the camp sharpies, flat-bottomed skiffs with leg-o-mutton sails, on
our way to a camp picnic on a typical Cape Cod summer day of a
fresh, puffy southwester. I must have been doing well enough in the
sailing lessons to be named skipper of one of the boats.

As we headed down the open bay, I suddenly realized that I had the
"feel" of the boat. I was reacting to lifts and headers, holding her
flat in puffs, tacking on favorable shifts, and playing the waves right,
as everything hit a rhythm I could sense, almost like catching on to a
dance step for the first time. A wonderful glow of confidence developed as the pattern fell together, and it was a real thrill to work
out ahead of the other boats, gaining each time we tacked.

When we reached the island with a lead of over a quarter of a
mile on the next boat, there were cheers and yells from the whole
camp, and The Skipper made the day complete by patting me on the
head and saying, "Boy, Bill, you really had that boat flying. That was
a great race!"

And that was it. From that sail onward, I knew that I had something that was special for me—sailing, and I was a sailor.

Nantucket Again—Wetly

By 1933 I was getting a bit elderly for camp (and I had discovered girls), and it looked as though a sweltering summer in Elizabeth, New Jersey, was in prospect. There was very little for a fourteen-year-old to do, jobs were unavailable to the undeserving middle class, and I managed a 1933 version of "getting in trouble" when my best friend, Hank Weeks, and I crashed a Saturday-night adult dance at Elizabeth Town and Country Club and were seen taking a drink by some friends of my parents. To save me from ruination in the fleshpots of New Jersey, Mother decided that we somehow had to get back to Nantucket as the only solution, and she began some desperate planning.

The B. Robinson house, 37 Fair Street   The W. Robinson Baby Rainbow

In the Sunday New York *Herald Tribune*, she came across a classified ad that read "Nantucket: apartment in private house; $75 a month" and was galvanized into persuading Dad that we could manage this staggering (for 1933) expenditure.

She answered the ad, and an acceptance came back very soon. So, come August 1, our 1930 Nash was trundled aboard the S.S. *Martha's Vineyard* at Woods Hole after a two-day trip from New Jersey, and, following the familiar three-hour voyage across Nantucket Sound and the traditional landfall as the Miacomet Water Company standpipe popped over the horizon, we disembarked and descended on 37 Fair Street, a wonderful tall old Nantucket house of yellow clapboard with a widow's walk. Typically, its front steps led directly onto the sidewalk, the yard was on the side, and the "basement" was really at ground level.

When I saw the doorplate, I let out a yelp of delight. It was a heavy brass one and read "B. ROBINSON." As it turned out, that was the reason we had ended up as tenants at 37 Fair Street. The landlady had received over fifty answers to the ad, and, not knowing how else to choose, decided on the Robinsons, as that was her maiden name, and it was her grandfather, Benjamin, who had built the house and whose nameplate was on the door.

We had the whole house except for two rooms in the "basement" which the landlady lived in, and, aside from the fact that she had once entertained operatic ambitions and sang loudly—in fact, piercingly— and off-key for most of her waking hours, it was a great arrangement.

Although Jetsam was three miles away from our midtown location and was occupied by cousins, Uncle Billy was again a dominant figure and made my summer by arranging a junior membership for me at the Nantucket Yacht Club. He also staked me to the charter (at the magnificent sum of thirty dollars a month) of a Baby Rainbow so that I could race in the club series.

It seemed almost too much of a coincidence that her owner was W. Robinson. He was a Nantucketer named Wallace, no relation to Benjamin as far as I knew, a breezy, friendly guy about my age who also took great delight in the coincidence of names. He was especially tickled when I would occasionally place in the races and the name "W. Robinson" would appear in agate type in the Boston *Herald* and Nantucket *Inquirer and Mirror*. His friends all accused him of going fancy and consorting with the summer people at the Yacht Club, and he took great relish in letting them think what they wanted. And I thoroughly enjoyed sailing W. Robinson's boat and then walking in the front door past B. Robinson's nameplate. I felt I really belonged.

The first day of my Yacht Club membership, before I had arranged the charter, was a race day, and I went timidly to the club, not knowing a soul, to see what was going on. Standing on the bulkhead watching the bustle of preparations and feeling very much the outsider, I was surprised when a tall boy came up to me and somewhat diffidently asked me if I'd like to crew for him in the race.

Trying to be nonchalant about it instead of jumping for the joy I felt, I allowed as how I might be persuaded. His boat was an Indian, an eighteen-foot sloop that usually had a crew of three, but the wind was fresh from the northeast on a day of gray overcast, and he felt he needed extra weight.

"I have a girl and a little skinny guy," he said, introducing himself as Bill Weidersheim, "and they're good, but they're just not heavy enough."

I felt I had to admit to a complete lack of spinnaker experience, which hadn't been on the Camp Viking curriculum, but he said the others could handle it o.k. The girl was a glamorous brunette, carefully made up and with bright red fingernails, adding an exotic touch I hadn't expected, and we all worked together to get the sails on and head for the starting area. I did my best to keep my excitement under control as we swooped through the fleet, concentrating on which line was which and where they led.

It was a close, exciting race, with action every moment, and I had my head down and my eyes in the boat doing my jobs as carefully as possible, but I couldn't help but look up every once in a while at the spinnaker, the first one I'd ever been shipmates with, awed by its power and the feeling it generated of being constantly within an inch or two of disaster.

As we approached the leeward mark under spinnaker, there were boats close in on each side, locking us in and forcing us a bit by the lee, with no control on our course or actions for the moment. We just had to hang on and go with the pack, but the whole situation was taken out of our hands when a boat charged across our stern and took our wind. The main went slack and came amidships because of our speed through the water (this was before boom vangs), and when the boat astern cleared past, a sharp gust caught the main and jibed it against the spinnaker. We screamed around in a broach, and before I knew what was happening, I was being thrown out in a good imitation of a racing dive to land with a loud *splat* on the sail, joined by the rest of the crew, and there we were, capsized, as the rest of the fleet sped on.

After some gurgling and gargling and a few four-letter words, and checking that everyone was in one piece, we wallowed around in the ignominious routine of post-capsize organizing. We were just inside Brant Point in the main harbor anchorage, and before long the launch of a glossy steam yacht came over to us and offered help. The two young sailors in the launch only had eyes for our girl crew, whose figure in her wet, clinging clothes made up for what had happened to her makeup and hair, but they did take us in tow, depositing us on the beach in front of the White Elephant Hotel, Nantucket's fanciest. Ladies in chiffon dresses and picture hats having tea on the terrace looked at us in amused horror as we went about our bedraggled way, bailing the boat out with garbage cans scrounged from the White Elephant kitchen.

To add to the show, the launch, with the eyes of her crew perhaps still on our girl, managed to get the White Elephant's swimming lines wrapped around the propeller, and the sailors ended up in the water beside us disentangling the snarl on the prop. They were there even longer than we were. My main memory of the whole episode is the sight of the blood-red, beautifully manicured nails of our girl valiantly wielding a greasy garbage can as we bailed. Before long we were all in high spirits, splashing and horsing, and by the time we were finished we had the whole terraceful of tea drinkers cheering us on. In our splashy camaraderie, I felt as though I was among old friends.

It was a great day for tea drinking on Nantucket, because I arrived back at 37 Fair Street to find Mother entertaining a group of ladies at the same activity, and I caused quite a stir as I staggered soddenly in. At least I wasn't forced to shake hands all around, and was quickly sent to my room to dry out.

Emptying my pockets, I checked out each soggy item and ended up with an agonized cry of dismay when I came to the money that had been in my pocket. This was almost our first day there, and I had my entire allowance for the month, seven dollars in the form of a five and two ones, with me when I'd gone out in the Indian. Now I found just one wet, sad-looking one-dollar bill, and I faced disaster. I knew how closely everything had been figured to make the month in Nantucket possible, and I didn't see how I could reasonably expect any replacement of my loss.

I spent a miserable Saturday night contemplating how I was going to get along for a whole month on one dollar, so imagine my joy the next morning when I checked the money on my bureau and found seven dollars there again, perhaps the pleasantest surprise of my life. The ones had been on each side of the five, and all three had been plastered together when wet. When they dried out, they separated again. So I had two friends, I knew a pretty girl, and I was rich again. What a month it was going to be. And it was.

Dad in a Sailboat

The episode of the vanishing and reappearing allowance increased my financial awareness to the point that I was acutely conscious of the dollar a day that the Baby Rainbow was costing. I didn't need a special prod to go sailing in the stubby, beamy miniature Cape Cod–type cat, twelve and a half feet long, with a gaff-rigged sail of bright orange, but knowing that any day she remained idle was a dollar down the drain was an added incentive, and I sailed all of August except for a three-day northeaster.

During it, there was a joint effort in the Rainbow fleet to haul all the boats out on the beach while the wind blew over 50, and gray, foam-streaked whitecaps made the harbor look like the open sea. Nantucket is no place to be in a northeaster. The boats sat up there, high and dry, and I took it as a personal thing that the northeaster was depriving me of three dollars' worth of sailing. It was like getting out of school when the weather finally turned bluebird and the boats were bobbing on their moorings again.

Dad liked to do his fishing from the solidity of the jetty

A not very enthusiastic scup fisherman

Except for the interruption, I sailed every day. There were races Wednesdays and Saturdays, and on other days I went fishing for scup, explored up harbor toward Wauwinet along the scalloped beaches of Coatue, the long bar that separates the harbor from Nantucket Sound, or made "speed runs" from Brant Point to the jetty entrance and back, trying to break my own record. Various friends (boys) came with me, sometimes I could get the girl of the red fingernails to come along (they were fascinating putting bits of quahog on a fishhook), and often I was alone. No matter what, I had to be out there.

When Dad came for his vacation and made noises about going fishing, I wanted to keep using the boat, but he preferred the jetty rocks. I don't think he trusted anyone in a sailboat, even Uncle Billy, much less his fourteen-year-old son. Dad, a thinner, younger, handsomer version of his two seafaring brothers, was not a sailor and took pride in not being one. He loved to putter around the house, fix broken things, tune the engine of his car, or work in the garden, and he had a very low (and, I must admit, partially correct) opinion of my practical capabilities. He had a favorite description of them; when I loused up on some simple mechanical thing, he would shake his head and say, "You couldn't pour piss out of boot if the instructions were on the heel"—changing the liquid to "water" when Mother was within earshot.

While I admit this lack, sailing was something that I felt confident in, a skill I was proud of, and I wanted to impress upon him that I did have at least one competence by taking him out in the boat. Finally, I must have caught him off guard, because he agreed, probably at Mother's behind-the-scenes urging, to try a fishing trip in the Rainbow.

There was a good breeze, and the harbor was choppy enough to kick some spray over the Rainbow's bluff bows. I did everything I could to steer around the waves and keep the spray down, but there were a few waves that caught me in a one-two punch before I could take evasive action, and Dad, hunkered down on the cockpit floorboards, would wince and groan as the wet stuff hit the back of his neck. He didn't say anything, but I could see that he was already regretting the decision and reaffirming to himself what he basically felt about sailboats.

My favorite spot for scup was out near the end of the jetties. When we reached it, I rounded into the wind, dropped the anchor over the bow, and lowered the sail. I was tying the last stop on the sail when I happened to glance up just in time to see the loose end of the anchor line slide over the bow and into the water. I had forgotten to cleat it. A desperate leap for it across the deck just missed.

Dad had been busy baiting a hook and hadn't noticed the disaster until my violent action made him look up. He realized something was wrong, and I had to tell him what had happened. He didn't say much this time either, but the look on his face told all I needed to know about his continuing opinion of my boot-pouring abilities.

With the sail back up, I jumped in and tried surface-diving for the anchor line between shouted instructions to Dad on keeping the boat near me, but, in water too deep and tide too swift, I had no luck.

It was a glum, fishless, anchorless sail back to the mooring, and I never got Dad out in a sailboat again.

Kidnapper?

One of my favorite pastimes at Nantucket was boat-watching in the harbor. Every afternoon a new fleet of cruising boats would round Brant Point and anchor beyond the steamer channel off the Island Service Company wharf. The great luxury yachts of the 1920s were gradually being laid up, but there were impressive ones still in commission, and I loved to sail through the anchorage amid the big gleaming motor yachts and the smaller auxiliaries and cabin cruisers, skimming as close as possible, and rubbernecking up at the fantails of the fancy ones, where stewards in white coats served formally dressed people sitting in wicker chairs. It was also fun to sail near the daily steamers as they rounded Brant Point, waving to the passengers and looking for friends on deck.

In the evening, after supper, I often used to walk the mile or so down to the Island Service Company, whose long pier jutted well out into the harbor. The company dealt in oil and coal, and the local trawlers also tied up there. It was the nerve center of the harbor and a colorful beehive of activity, and the company had thoughtfully placed benches along the bulkhead at the outer end of the wharf for those who liked to sit and look at the water and the anchorage.

I would sit on a bench and look at the riding lights of the yachts at anchor casting paths across the darkening water, while inhaling the mixed, heady aromas of the waterfront. To me, it was as pleasant and romantic a spot as I could imagine, and I remember my horror in overhearing a conversation between a young girl and an older woman who were sitting at the other end of my bench one night.

"Isn't this nice?" the woman said.

"Yeah. It's o.k.," came a flat answer from the girl. "But I know where I'd rather be."

"Where?"

"Can't you guess?"

"Well—Hawaii?"

"Nope."

"Bermuda?"

"Nope. Guess again."

"Maybe Havana?"

"Nope. Give up?"

"I guess I do."

"I wish I were in Port Jervis."

Having been in that grubby railroad-switching center where New York, New Jersey, and Pennsylvania come together, I had to leave the bench to keep from whooping with laughter.

One night as I sat looking at the harbor, the lights, and the play of twilight colors across the water, a short man wearing a beret and walking a fox terrier paused in front of the bench and looked out where I was looking, then turned and said, "Lovely evening, isn't it?"

"Sure is," I answered, and thought nothing more of it as he wandered along the bulkhead.

The Island Service Company wharf was the atmospheric center of
Nantucket Harbor

In a while, I started home, walking up the pier toward the town, and I happened to see the man with the dog drive by in a Chevrolet coach (like all teen-agers, I was very conscious of car brands). When he got a bit beyond me, the car stopped and pulled over to the side, and I walked by it. When I'd gone a short way past him, the car started up. I was still only peripherally conscious of it, but the second time it stopped and then started again after I had gone by, I began to take real notice. As I made my way up the narrow streets toward Fair Street, which was up the hill beyond the head of the cobblestoned double-width section of Main Street, the performance was repeated several times, and I suddenly became really scared.

This was shortly after the great mass of publicity over the Lindbergh kidnapping, and that was the only thing I could imagine about the mysterious, now thoroughly sinister, actions of the man in the Chevrolet. I took the license number of the car (New York plates) and, when he followed me as I turned into Fair Street, I broke into a run and sprinted to No. 37. As I got there, he drove by and parked on the other side of the street, got out of his car with the dog on a leash, and walked back toward the house on that side.

I was hiding behind the front door, peeking out at him, but, secure in being home, and now more curious than scared, I stepped out onto the front porch, which was high above the sidewalk, to see what would happen. The man and dog crossed the street and came back along the sidewalk on our side, and, my heart beating rapidly, I decided to stand my ground.

As they came by the steps, he looked up and said, "Good evening. I'm walking my dog."

"Oh," was all I could manage, as I retreated inside and closed and bolted the door, now thoroughly mystified.

The next day, I told Mother and Dad about the "kidnapper," and Dad, looking a bit grim, asked me a few questions about what the man looked like. I proudly came up with his license number, fully expecting Dad to call the police with it, and it was a real disappointment when he didn't do anything about it.

The next Sunday, we went to church, and there, singing a solo in the choir, was the "kidnapper." Excitedly, I pointed him out, and Dad just murmured "Hmmmm" and shushed me. Later, when we got home from church, Dad squared his shoulders and we had a little talk. He had already told me about girls. Now he had to tell me a few more facts of life.

And I had been wondering what the ransom would be and whether Uncle Billy would pay it.

Learning to Cruise

Two Augusts of Baby Rainbowing at Nantucket completed my preppie days, and the next three summers saw me working at summer jobs to help finance college. Uncle Billy was my tuition angel, but I had to work to earn spending money and I spent two fascinating summers as an office boy at the McGraw-Hill publishing company on West Forty-second Street in New York. I learned a lot of things that have nothing to do with this book, but I had no chance to do any sailing.

At the end of junior year, I had made enough money from student employment jobs to convince me that I didn't have to spend what loomed as the last free summer of my life working in New York. I figured I would never have the whole summer off again, and this was my last chance to do some real sailing for quite a while. Dad thought I was crazy, but Mother, romantic enough to go along with the idea, overrode him, and I went ahead with plans.

I signed up two classmates, Gordy and Frank, to split the month of August in ten-day and twenty-one-day stints, and then went looking for a boat. Through a broker in Mamaroneck, New York, at the western end of Long Island Sound, I found *Bona*, a sturdy twenty-six-foot gaff-rigged sloop of indeterminate age for the sum of $105 for the month (including broker's commission). She had been bought on the strength of a bonus the owner had received, and his son, who was taking Latin at the time, had insisted on feminizing the word for a boat name.

I was checked out by the owner and family on a Sunday afternoon, and the poor man looked as though a potential rapist was taking off with his daughter, but he still was pleasant and helpful. Gordy arrived the next morning, and, eager to be off, we threw luggage, groceries, and odds and ends of gear down the hatch helter-skelter and chugged out of the harbor into a placid Sound. As we cleared the entrance buoy, a whisper of a southwester ruffled the oily surface, so we made sail and settled back with all the confidence of Ferdinand Magellan, even though I had never handled a boat this big and Gordy had hardly sailed at all.

Bona

Throughout the warm, hazy day, the southwester built beautifully, and we swooped eastward, enjoying ourselves to the hilt on a glorious sail. I had no plan on a destination. The sailing was too great to worry about that, and we would just keep surging down the Sound, munching peanut-butter sandwiches and drinking beers. What a life!

What a life until the sun began to lower into the coppery smog on the western horizon, and I came to the realization that, as captain and navigator, I should have a port picked out for our first night's stop. By now we were passing New Haven, and I became aware, as I scanned the chart, that we had just about run out of good harbors. We had to get into some harbor before dark or sail all night, and I didn't think we were quite ready for that.

Finally I found Branford on the Connecticut shore, and that seemed to be it, though the channel was tricky-looking, winding through rocks and reefs, and it was dead downwind. That would mean several jibes, so I decided that we had better get sail off and power in. Gordy was very firm about the fact that he had no idea what "all those strings" were, so I gave him the tiller, told him to head straight into the wind, and went forward to work the halyards.

At full throttle we rounded into the seas that had been curling nicely under our transom all afternoon, and suddenly they were monstrous, steep cliffs, crashing down on us in close order in the shallower water near shore. We rose high over the first one, crashed down on the second, and went right through the third, almost washing me overboard. I shouted to Gordy to throttle her back, and started fighting the sails down as spray followed by green water continued to sweep across me. With two jibs and a gaff-rigged main, there were all sorts of strings to handle, and, between holding on as we charged over and into the seas and fighting the flailing sails, I managed to let about half of their ends go to tangle around the lazy jacks.

Somehow I managed a semblance of a furl, and we turned back toward the harbor entrance, almost rolling our bottom out as the seas came abeam, then yawed our way in past Cow and Calf and made the turn hard to starboard by Blyn Rock. The seas built higher against an ebb tide, threatening to poop us, but finally we made the entrance to Branford River and breathed a great sigh of relief in calm water, the turmoil behind us on the other side of Indian Neck.

We were inside, but there was still a tricky fore-and-aft moor to make between stakes along the edge of the channel, and it was pitch-dark by the time we had backed and filled enough to get our lines out and secure everything. It didn't help to have people on other boats watching us in tolerant amusement.

Ravenously hungry, we finally fell below to find disaster personified. The ports had never been shut, and we had not stowed our clothes or provisions. The lights didn't work, but one glimpse in the beam of a flashlight was enough. Clothes, bread, eggs, binoculars, charts, shaving cream—the works—made the most ungodly jumble imaginable. I snapped off the flashlight and we collapsed onto the sodden bunks.

As I fell asleep, I had to admit to myself that there was more to this cruising than I had realized.

Pinpoint Navigation

Eventually we became a bit better organized and managed to find our way to Nantucket without further mishap. Gordy's ten days were up, and Frank arrived on the steamer to replace him.

Uncle Billy, who was delighted to hear of our adventures in *Bona* when I checked in with him, set up a guest card so that we could use the Nantucket Yacht Club, where the social life was active, and, between friends from four years ago and college connections, we had continuous blast of dates and dances as well as beer parties on sails in *Bona*.

One day, as we tacked around the harbor with a party group aboard, we discovered something new had been added to the scene in

Salvage efforts on the wreck of the powerboat

The schooner *Alice Wentworth* took over the salvage

the form of the half-sunken wreck of a glossy power yacht of perhaps
eighty feet. She was parked on a shoal on the Monomoy side of the
harbor, lying at an angle, with the deck just about awash. This naturally
caused quite a stir in the harbor, and we sailed around the forlorn sight
agog with curiosity. Eventually we pieced together an approximation
of what had happened from gossip around the club and waterfront.

The yacht had been on her way from Edgartown to Nantucket,
and the entire complement of two couples decided to play bridge. The
owner set the automatic pilot on a heading for Tuckernuck Shoal
Buoy, where the course changes halfway between the islands, and
settled down to the game. It must have been an absorbing one, an

the course had definitely been accurate, because, with the bridge fiends dealing and bidding away obliviously, the vessel slammed spang into the big offshore buoy at full tilt, with a crash that sent the card players flying.

It also cracked open the bow, and a hasty SOS on the radio and panic-party abandon-ship drill followed. The four "survivors" went off in the ship's boat, with the owner's wife clutching her jewel box, the only item they had salvaged. The yacht was taking on water, but slowly, and was still very much afloat when a Coast Guard surfboat from the Great Point Station on Nantucket arrived at the scene. The yacht's party, still in the dinghy, was taken into the Coast Guard boat, which then proceeded to tow the damaged vessel toward Nantucket.

As the tow progressed slowly, the Coast Guard crew realized that they didn't have enough gas to make it to port and radioed to another Coast Guard boat to come out with more fuel. Unfortunately, this Good Samaritan ran hard and fast onto the Nantucket breakwater, so the towing boat did, as they had predicted, run out of gas, and the little convoy was left wallowing helplessly, with the damaged yacht gradually sinking lower.

Finally, another Coast Guard boat arrived to unscramble the mess and complete the tow, but the yacht was by now so far down in the water that she barely made it into the harbor and had to be grounded on the shoal to keep her from sinking in a deeper spot.

That's how we heard it, anyway, and we watched with interest each day as the derelict was salvaged by a work party based on *Alice Wentworth*, a beamy, rugged-looking coastal schooner that came alongside her and acted as a stable steadying force, while the wreck, lashed securely alongside, was pumped out and raised.

Whether the owner's wife had to hock her jewelry to finance all this we never heard, and who did what to whom in the aftermath among the Coast Guard boats we could only imagine.

Clean-Cut Kids

One of the joys of *Bona's* Nantucket period was renewal of old acquaintance with a girl named Suggie, whose family I had known for years. Their house on Brant Point was a center for the college group, and we had a great time practically living there while *Bona* rode at anchor off the beach.

Sug was gay and full of life, and there was always something doing, but she had been going through an experience that was a bit beyond the usual college-age involvement, very much entangled, now unhappily, with an older, divorced man. Her mother, Mag, was a recent widow with one of the most forceful personalities I've ever known, intensely human, short, wiry, with a deeply sunburned complexion and a voice like a tired tobacco auctioneer, and she was not happy about her daughter's situation.

As an old family friend, I ended up on the receiving end of Mag's concern, and she poured out her troubles at great length.

"If my husband were still alive, he'd know how to handle that louse," she'd say, "but I don't know what to do about it."

Finally she talked herself around to a solution. Frank and I were talking about taking off for Martha's Vineyard and the Cape, and Mag latched onto an idea.

"You know what would be great for Sug? She should go off with you guys on that boat for a few days. Some fun with some good clean college-boy types would take her mind off that son of a bitch. That's just what she needs. Would you take her with you?"

This was the first time I'd ever had a mother proposition me in just this way. Usually I had spent hours trying to convince parents that it was safe for their darling daughter to go sailing with me, and here we were being handed Sug on a silver platter.

"You'll have to find her a place to sleep ashore every night. I'm sure you can do that," Mag said, "and this will be just great."

So, when *Bona* reached out between the Nantucket jetties on a lively southwester, there was Suggie on board. She came in a rubber bathing suit, a figure to fill it in just the right away, a smile, and guess some dress or something to wear ashore, but all I remember is the bathing suit.

She was fun and we had fun, and we dutifully found her a bunk ashore in places like Edgartown and Harwichport, where we had friends with summer houses. We would come ashore and look them up and I, feeling like a kid on the first day of school, would introduce Sug to the mother of whatever friend it was whose house we had targeted on, saying, "This is my friend Amy Ann." (That was her real name.) "She's sailing with us but she's supposed to sleep ashore, and I wondered if you had a bed."

As the mother-type would raise eyebrows slightly and ponder the situation, Amy Ann would say, "Oh, just call me Suggie. That's what everybody does." The eyebrows would go higher, and I'd be ready to hide in the bushes, but she did get a bed every night.

I don't think she ever let herself be alone with either of us at an

Suggie in her formal going-ashore clothes

ime, and Frank and I, goggling and drooling, with all sorts of visions
dancing in our heads, were, despite ourselves, the perfect chaperons.
It was a joyous, completely innocent cruise, even considering the
totally thwarted dreams of the two male crew members, and in
retrospect I've always gnashed my teeth at how Mag could be so
goddam right about those "clean-cut college-boy types."

Night Navigation

As the end of August neared, it was time to get *Bona* back to
Mamaroneck, but we were having such a good time in Nantucket that
we waited until the last minute to leave. We only had three days to
make it, but we planned on pushing through hard.

The first day went well, with a fresh, clear northeaster giving us a
fast reach to Edgartown. We weren't the fastest boat out there,

though. The big seventy-two-foot yawl, *Baruna*, glossily black and the center of all admiring eyes after winning the Bermuda Race that year, had been at anchor in Nantucket when we left. We took the Tuckernuck Shoals route, and halfway across we saw her tall sails appear on the horizon behind us and rapidly sweep by to the eastward on the deep-water course via Cross Rip Lightship. When we surged into Edgartown, going about as fast as *Bona* could, *Baruna* was already snugged down at anchor looking as though she'd been there all summer.

When we left Edgartown, the motor refused to start. My father's opinion of my mechanical abilities was all too valid when it came to fixing engines, and Frank, although he had passed an ROTC course in engine repairs, had no better luck. There was a good breeze and we had no money left, so we figured we would just have to sail through, standing watches at night. I'd never done any night navigation, but I was feeling pretty salty after a month as skipper and didn't expect any trouble.

A southeaster took us around the Vineyard, and late in the afternoon we passed Vineyard Lightship and began the twenty-five-mile open-water passage to Point Judith. I decided to hit the sack for a while before starting night watches, and I went below without telling Frank the course change to make at the Lightship.

We should have come right about 25 degrees but never did, and the resultant confusion when I came back on deck soon after dark was classic. It was a very clear night, and we were headed right for a long string of lights that stretched well to seaward of our course. I thought that it was Point Judith and that we were heading well inside it. This prompted those classic words, "This compass must be off," and we corrected course to port to head outside the last of the lights. From then on, I couldn't make anything work right. No light or buoy agreed with any identifications I wanted to make, and I was too inexperienced to backtrack to a known spot and figure out what might have gone wrong.

Also, I never gave Block Island a thought. On our way up, smoky sou'wester weather had kept Block Island hidden as we passed between it and Point Judith, and I mentally placed it far out to sea like Nantucket.

It was a long night's sail as the breeze lightened and we headed a bit south of magnetic west into "mystery land." As far as I knew, we were anywhere between Providence and New Haven and I was completely lost, but we just made sure that there was nothing ahead of us that we could bump into. Visibility turned bad in the small hours as damp haze settled over the ocean, and it was something of a shock when the sun came up and burned the stuff away to find ourselves outside Montauk Point on the open Atlantic. It was Block Island whose lights had confused me, and we had gone to seaward of it.

With the dawn, the breeze stopped, and it took us a full twenty-four hours to drift around Montauk and across Gardiner's Bay to Plum Gut and into the Sound. We were just off Horton's Point at the next dawn, barely stemming the tide. Since we had planned to stop at night originally, we hadn't stocked up on food and had intended to buy just what we needed for the last days, so sustenance was now a real problem. In fact, all we had aboard was strawberry jam and Rice Krispies, and we had three meals of a mixed glom of them, made all the more unappetizing by the sight of an Eastern Steamship Lines ship on her way in from Nova Scotia steaming serenely by while visions of the meals being served in her dining saloon tantalized our minds.

It was a long, slow, muggy day of drifting westward until a southerly came in late in the afternoon and we began to make some

Morning found us to seaward of Montauk Point

knots. Through the evening, it headed us gradually and became stronger, until we were skinning along the Norwalk Islands hard on the wind and pounding. The inshore waters were full of oyster stakes, and, though we kept the best lookout we could, most of them only appeared when they were abeam and could be seen against the shore lights. Fortunately, we avoided being impaled.

Midnight brought a series of thunder squalls, with lightning bouncing around us and thunder filling the air. They lashed us briefly with torrents of rain and enough wind to have to shorten down to a reefed main for a while. Midnight had also brought the legal end of the charter and the end of the insurance coverage on it, and it was an anxious time of slugging into a nasty chop and keeping track of where we were. Sleep was forgotten and even the Rice Krispies were gone, so it was a bleary, weary crew that finally brought *Bona* into Mamaroneck on the failing breeze of a humid dawn.

Sounds terrible, doesn't it, but would you believe we'd had the time of our lives?

June 1939 — Eras Ending and Starting

As a farewell to college, four friends who had listened to and believed my stories about the joys of cruising joined with me in chartering forty-three-foot sloop for the week following Commencement. She was a lovely old boat named *Sally R* out of Manhasset Bay at the western end of Long Island Sound, and we thought it would be great to head for New London and the Yale-Harvard crew race. We'd heard about the parties that went with it, and we thought that five Princetonians could misbehave anonymously in fine style.

Fortunately for *Sally R*, we were invited on another boat with professional captain to go up the Thames and watch the race, as the jam of spectator craft was quite something, and I was glad not to have the responsibility of handling the boat. Dominating the scene as we found an anchorage in a great jumble of boats was J. P. Morgan's large *Corsair*, her great black 343-foot bulk looming high above any other vessel there, with a giant Harvard banner suspended between her masts, and her bowsprit flaring proudly above everything anchored near her. This, in 1939, was her last appearance as a yacht in American waters, as she went into the British Navy when war broke out that fall.

The fleet was anchored from noon on, and, as the race wasn't held until late afternoon, it was a long day of partying. It might have been reassuring to have a professional captain, but he got drunker than any of the college boys and girls and smashed the boat into the piering of the drawbridge in the traffic jam after the race. The race, barely visible in the twilight by those who could still see at all, was not half as dramatic as all the whanging and banging in the spectator fleet in the mad dash for the draw.

The traditional post-race rites always took place at a great rambling hotel called the Griswold on Eastern Point in Groton, across the river from New London. Its wide porches and high-ceilinged public rooms, where old ladies genteelly rocked the summer away and drank tea, were taken over for that one night for the wildest shambles of a mass drinking party we poor innocent Princetonians had ever seen. We came to "misbehave" and we stayed to cringe in corners trying to avoid the flying glass, the fistfights, the upchuckings, and the spilled gore.

There were quieter retreats amid the mayhem where guys with dates tried to keep them from the madding crowd, and one of these was on a long porch overlooking the Sound. Couples balanced on the rail, swinging their feet and chatting in semi-darkness. It was a peaceful scene until a small, stocky figure, impeccably dressed in tweed coat and gray slacks, started down the row. He would stop in front of each male and inquire in a soft, polite voice, "Are you Yale or Harvard?" If the answer was Yale, the young man would throw a swift, solid punch, and the surprised Yalie would tumble off the rail backward onto the lawn.

All this was done so quietly that each one was caught by surprise, and the intrepid Cantab seemed to be getting away with it without reprisal until his course brought him to a set of steps leading up from the lawn. Here the Yalies had gathered forces after picking themselves off the grass, and they met him as a committee and gave him back what he'd been handing out, plus a few more. The last we saw him, he had escaped into the darkness of the lawn just before the end of his time on earth might have come.

We picked no fights, wolfed no girls, and, at least, stuck to our intention to remain anonymous, and we were happy to get back to *ally R* in one piece. We had seen some moderately rugged parties at Princeton, but this was a new level of mass debauchery in public as far as we were concerned.

Sally R

Putting on a Captain Bligh act at the wheel of

We had our own mild debaucheries in bars in the ports we visite
on the way back, but nothing like the blood and gore of the Griswold
It was a great week of shifting gears from the college world to th
"real world" that lay ahead, a world coming out of the Depressio
and facing the threat of Hitler.

As we approached Manhasset Bay on the last few miles of the cruis
we could see a great gathering of vessels ahead of us just outside th
entrance to the bay. We couldn't figure it out until we came close
and could see that they all centered on a giant seaplane wallowin
along at slow speed. It was Pan American's Dixie Clipper about t

Pan Am's Dixie Clipper taking off at the start of the first transatlantic flight with a passenger payload

take off with the first transatlantic payload in the history of heavier-than-air aviation.

Just as we came abreast of her, her engines revved up with a mighty roar, her hull lifted, and great plumes of spray shot out behind her. Gradually she gathered speed and thundered down the Sound until a thin line of daylight appeared beneath her hull, and she was off. Climbing very slowly, she was soon a speck on the eastern horizon. An era was ending for us; another era was beginning.

Emergency in the Fog

Fortunately, the end of college did not mean the end of sailing, despite my fears. In college, I had managed the Princeton Travel Bureau as my student employment job, booking plane and ship travel for undergraduates and townspeople, and three airlines offered me jobs when I graduated.

None of them had a definite starting date, but Eastern had offered seventy-five dollars a month (yes, a month) and the other two were only at sixty-five, so I said I would accept Eastern's magnificent offer, and then took off on *Sally R.* Halfway through the week, a man from Eastern called up my family's house and wanted me to come to work the next day, and I got the word when I called home from New London to check in as promised.

"You come right home, Bill," Dad said. He had had two companies fold out from under him during the Depression, and the offer of a job was not to be sneezed at. "When people offer you a job, you don't mess around."

"Can't, Dad. I'm the only one who knows how to navigate."

He muttered and grumbled and acted as though I were doomed to unemployment for the rest of my life, but I finally convinced him that I had an obligation to *Sally R* and that I would check with Eastern the next morning. Fortunately (at least for my relationship with Dad if not my pocketbook), I could still have the job by reporting for work the next week.

The best thing about the job was that I worked shifts at Newark Airport, often with daytime hours off, and I managed to find a beat-up sixteen-foot sloop for sale in Perth Amboy, New Jersey, on Raritan Bay, for thirty-five dollars. She never remained afloat overnight, so the first duty on going sailing was always to pump her out, but Raritan Bay is wide and breezy and a fine place to sail if you look seaward instead of at the oil tanks and factories along the western shore, and she gave me some very pleasant hours. I also sold her at a profit, getting forty-dollars for her two years later, so I have a fond spot for the first boat I ever owned.

Through a teacher at Pingry, my old prep school, who was a member, I also joined the Corinthians, a unique organization designed to bring boatowners and willing crew members together for mutual benefit. The modus operandi is the "crew call" in which an owner tells a central club crewing office in New York what berths he has available for a given period, and the crewing secretary matches this with a list of available hands from the membership. In 1941, my first summer, I had left Eastern to await a commission in the Navy, and between my unemployment checks, free flying lessons under the CAA, and a Corinthian crew call every weekend, I really had it made. Borrowing a joke from the play *You Can't Take It with You*, I used to complain about having to come back from my yachting weekends on vessels like *Blitzen* and the New York 40 *Mistral*, and the Block Island and Cornfield Lightship races, so that I could pick up my unemployment check. "It really breaks up my week," was the way the punch line went.

Block Island was something special in those days. The big be-porched and gabled monstrosities of hotels that perched on its grassy hillsides were loaded with girls. This was where most of the factory girls and stenographers in southern New England came for their vacation, and the pickings were usually good for someone off a yacht. In fact, a few summers before, several enterprising Brown undergraduates had "chartered" an impressive-looking power yacht and tied her up at one of the piers in Great Salt Pond. Every night they would round up girls from the hotel crowd for a party, and the females, awed by the vessel's size and appointments, would flock aboard. Thinking they would be invited to go yachting the next day, they would willingly accept an invitation to retire to one of the numerous cabins, but the compliant dames didn't know that the vessel had no engines and was incapable of going anywhere. The Brown boys had paid a hundred dollars for a summer's charter and fifty dollars to a fisherman to tow their floating love-barge to its strategic location, and she had just that one function.

When I came in there as crew in a long-ended, skinny Swedish-built 30-Square Meter, forty-seven-feet overall and seven-foot-seven beam, after a race from City Island in which we had been scratch boat but dead last in a light-air downwind affair, we were not as well set up to impress girls as the Brownies, but we did repair to Deadeye Dick's Saloon "where the girls are" for post-race activity. In two-day beards and scruffy sailing clothes, we evidently did not fit a Pawtucket factory girl's image of yachtsmen, however. Our skipper, a distinguished New York lawyer, while dancing with one, was asked how he had got to the island and said he had come in his yacht, and her answer was, "Oh yeah? Well, my old man owns the *Queen Mary*."

No girls were inveigled aboard our sloop that night, which was just as well considering the condition of most of the crew and the size of the cabin. One man, as equally distinguished a lawyer as the skipper and at the time a commander on active duty in Naval Intelligence, ended up a post–Deadeye Dick basket case in the head. When his upheavals finally subsided, he crawled out on the fantail to lie down. In checking to see if he was still alive and hadn't fallen overboard, I found him shivering uncontrollably in the cool night air. He refused to come below, so I fetched a blanket and put it over him, for which he was pathetically grateful, and then, when I asked him if there was anything else he needed, he said in a low moan and the best of Harvard accents, "Oh, yes, old man. Could you possibly flush the head for me?"

All this evidently so impressed him with my competence that he called me a week later and asked if I could come with him in September on a cruise from Three Mile Harbor to Port Jefferson. He had the use of a thirty-six-foot Coastwise Cruiser sloop, wanted to bring his two sub-teen sons along, and felt he needed extra help in handling the boat.

In effect, I was sailing master and navigator, and we had a fine, relaxed cruise until the last night, when, while anchored in the Thimble Islands, one of the boys developed a severe stomachache. By the next morning we were all but certain that it was appendicitis. Connecticut ports were nearer, but since the father wanted to get to his own doctor on Long Island, we decided to get over there as quickly as possible.

The wind was on the nose and the boat's auxiliary was low-powered, so the best way to make progress would be to beat to windward under sail, with a boost from the motor. This was no longer relaxed cruising, as the thoroughly·miserable youngster was moaning in his bunk, with his father sitting anxiously by, and the other boy and I made sail and started out. Remembering my *Bona* fiasco, I was meticulous in my dead reckoning, a difficult job while going to windward in a cross-current, and soon after we hit the open Sound, dense fog added to the problems.

Not much was said, but I could feel the eyes of the anxious family on me as I plotted D.R. and timed our tacks. Heavy tension increased each time the boy cried, and we were a taut, silent crew as we made our way through the swirling fog. There are anonymous-looking beaches on each side of the entrance to Port Jefferson, and if I missed it, we would have trouble figuring out which side we were. Now and then a deep whistle from the traffic lane in mid-Sound added to the sense of urgency, and I had the boy on deck with me give the fog signal for whichever tack we were on. The mournful bleat of the horn seemed lost and ineffective in the void around us.

As time for the landfall neared, I checked my calculations repeatedly, trying to appear confident, and it was with a tremendous sigh of relief that I saw the Port Jeff breakwater looming darkly through the gray exactly where it should be. We tied up hurriedly and phoned right away for an ambulance, and twenty minutes after the boy reached the hospital he was under the knife for an emergency appendectomy.

That was my last cruise for a long time, as I went on Navy duty two weeks later.

PART III

~~~~~~~~~

Earthquake at Yokohama

My "involvement" with the Japanese was about to begin, but long before, in 1923, Uncle Sam had had a different kind of involvement in Japan that was without a doubt the most dramatic and unusual "sea story" of any of our experiences. By then he was a senior captain in the Canadian Pacific Railway steamship service, short, stocky as a bear, with firm, clefted chin, piercing blue eyes, and a rolling sailor's walk. Before the war he had commanded *Empress of China* and *Empress of India,* graceful yacht-like liners with white hulls, clipper bows, and raked funnels, almost like clipper ships without sails, and a lovely addition to the scene in Pacific ports.

In World War I he had done troopship duty on converted CPR ships and was Exec on a CPR liner which finally trapped the German raider *Emden* in the Cocos Islands in a highly publicized episode of the early days of the war. His first postwar assignment was to go to Hamburg to take over the German liner *Tirpitz,* which the Kaiser had planned to use as his royal yacht for the expected surrender of the Allied fleets. She had gone to the British as reparations and was sold by them to CPR and renamed *Empress of Australia.* He was her captain on September 1, 1923, and she was in Yokohama, a regular stop on her voyages between Hong Kong and Vancouver, British Columbia. The following account is taken from his personal papers, reporting on what happened on that and the next few days.

Ordeal of Peril

September 1, 1923, was a close, muggy day in Yokohama. It was typhoon season, and there was one churning northward some distance inland, sending a strong southwest wind across the harbor of the seaport city of 400,000.

Empress of Australia, an imposing 21,850-ton twin-screw liner with three tall stacks, 615 feet over all, 550 in crew, and the largest vessel to transit the Panama Canal up to that time, was berthed at the 1,800-yard long Customs Pier, which extended northward into the harbor in its southeast corner. This inner harbor was formed by a breakwater that separated it from Yokohama Bay, an arm of the Gulf of Tokyo. Its shoreline lay in a general east-west direction, and the breakwater ran north and then northwestward from the harbor's eastern end. The big-ship anchorage was a dredged area in the southeast part of the harbor off the Customs Pier, and a gap in the breakwater to seaward of this, marked by two small stone lighthouses, was the main entrance channel.

The *Empress* was on the east side of the pier, starboard side to the inner berth, forward of the large freighter *Steel Navigator*, and a French liner, *Andre Lebon*, was berthed on the west side undergoing engine repairs. Normal procedure for departures was for ships to back away from the pier to a turning basin, where tugs assisted them in swinging, in rather tight quarters, onto a heading for the entrance.

Empress of Australia, or, as Uncle Sam referred to her throughout his reports, E/Aus, was due to sail at noon. Her decks were alive with most of her four hundred and fifty passengers, and the friends who had seen them off were on the pier, standing on a twenty-foot-wide strip of wharfage between the ship and large sheds that covered its outer end. The first 1,200 feet of the pier out from the shore consisted of a roadway on top of steel pilings, and the sheds were on the outer end, which had heavy concrete bulkheads along the sides. It was the usual gala scene when a big liner is about to sail, with everyone calling and waving, and paper streamers festooned between ship and pier, Lines had been singled down to one each at bow and stern, led to bollards on the pier, and the gangway had just been removed.

Uncle Sam was on the bridge at 1159, ready to give the order to cast off the last lines, when he heard a great screeching roar and felt the ship shake and tremble. His first instinct was that something had happened to her main steam pipe, and he looked up at the stacks for some sign of trouble, but nothing was amiss there.

Then he looked over the bow toward the city. Yokohama's "foreign section," known as the Bluff, was strung out along the waterfront and for several blocks inland toward low hills, with streets running in a gradual incline from the hills to the water and a seafront avenue called the Bund. The buildings were of Western construction, solid brick and stone hotels, clubs, offices, warehouses, plants, and shops.

And there, to his shocked amazement as his glance turned from the ship to the shore, was the incredible sight of the entire area heaving in a succession of waves that undulated like the open sea. Down a broad avenue off the head of the pier, the pavement was being cleaved in a furrow like the bow wave of a big ship going fast, and behind the waves a great cloud of dust and smoke billowed into the humid air. As he watched, all the buildings along the Bund and on the inland incline crumbled to the ground in one instant, as though a giant hand had brushed against a house of cards. Over everything was a crashing, crackling, thundering roar of unbelievable intensity, and the wind quickly picked up to gale force. It brought the smoke and dust out across the pier in great, swirling gusts as the quake waves advanced from the shorefront to the pier, moving along it like a giant caterpillar, collapsing the roadway as they came and then shaking the pier and its sheds.

As the passengers who had been waving to friends and relatives just a moment before stood and watched in helpless horror, the pier and sheds heaved up and down and split and came back together in yawning, quick-closing gaps, tossing people like puppets. They were thrown into the water or slid into cracks, grasping desperately for something solid, and screaming pandemonium took over.

Crew members began to lower rope ends and ladders to the pier, which produced a scene of panic as people fought to grab them, clawing at those already trying to climb and even pulling them off. Uncle Sam feared that this would produce more casualties than the situation on the pier itself, and he ordered all ropes and ladders pulled back aboard until the gangway could be run out again.

It was an ugly scene as dazed, bleeding people milled about, fighting each other, while some, who had fallen into cracks, were trying to climb back up the pilings, but it was only one small corner of the general holocaust that had enveloped all of Yokohama. The ship and pier were now in dense smoke and heat, blowing on the gale. Through rifts in the smoke, the whole waterfront could be seen blazing

Empress of Australia

Uncle Sam as captain of the *Australia*

furiously, and sparks and burning debris began to rain down on the ship. Through it all, the gangway was run out and survivors and the injured were brought aboard from the pier, while the deck gang rigged hoses and played them over the burning debris as it landed on the ship. Making a hurried trip along the promenade deck to try to find out what the situation was at the stern, where *Steel Navigator* blocked any chance of escape from the dangerous situation, Uncle Sam was surprised to see a Chinese deck steward going about his normal sailing-time routine of setting out deck chairs and blankets. When he asked the man why he was bothering with that, the answer was that it was his job and no one had told him anything different.

Along with the airborne menace of flying debris, the ship was also being assaulted by a stream of lighters, junks, and other small craft, most of them on fire, being blown away from landings and loading basins along the Bund, scudding along with the 70-knot gale and bumping along her sides. Some were hosed down and fought off without too much trouble, but others lingered while burned or wounded people scrambled aboard the haven of the big ship. While this was going on, a large Japanese freighter named *Lyons Maru* suddenly loomed out of the reek, heading for *E/Aus* at a good clip while evidently trying to make a turn for the harbor entrance. She let go her anchors and backed down soon enough so that the collision did little damage, and reversed back out of sight into the smoke, but then, a few minutes later, came charging back again at a faster clip. A serious collision seemed inevitable, but, just at the crucial moment, a burning lumber lighter adrift on the gale came between the two big ships and acted as a fender. The lighter was demolished and her burning planks scattered into the air like matchsticks, and, most miraculous of all, a cargo coolie, squatting on the load of lumber as far from the fire as possible, was tossed into the air like a diver off a springboard, grabbed a line on the *Lyons Maru*, and scrambled aboard as that ship backed away and disappeared for good.

The two tugboats that had been standing by *E/Aus* to aid in her departure had evaporated at the beginning of the quake, and the great ship was now in a very difficult position. With the pier ablaze and burning material continuing to land on her, her situation was desperate. The gale had her pinned against the pier, preventing any attempt to swing her stern out, and *Steel Navigator* blocked a direct reverse course along the pier. The latter ship had been bumped well off the pier by the quake shocks, pulling her bow-line bollard loose, and had dropped both her port and starboard bow anchors. These effectively prevented *E/Aus* from moving.

An officer was sent along the pier to try to communicate with *Steel Navigator*'s personnel, but he fought his way back through the

iew from *Empress of Australia* of the collapsed pier soon after the earth-
ake struck, with buildings along the Bund burning in the background

Empress of Australia making her way through typhoon-like conditions

smoky gale with the report that he could raise no answer aboard. She was well out from the pier, and her crew was occupied with fending burning lighters away from her port side.

If *E/Aus* remained alongside the pier any longer, there was no way that she could be kept from catching fire, as the flames were spreading rapidly along the shed at the level of her promenade deck, and Uncle Sam came to the only decision possible. He would get good way on his ship, ram *Steel Navigator*, and hope to carry both ships clear of the pier, or the great number of lives now in his charge would be lost. With the last lines cast off from the blazing pier, he signaled for full astern, and, with her whistle going full blast at short intervals to blend with the roar of wind and flames around her, all 21,000 tons of *E/Aus* began to surge astern toward the high bow of the freighter.

Uncle Sam, standing on his bridge and feeling fully justified in this action, but "pretty sick about it" too, braced for the crash of the two big hulls, only to realize in amazement that the stern of *E/Aus* was swinging away from the pier and clear of *Steel Navigator*'s bow. The mass of wreckage from lighters, barges, and junks that had drifted between the vessels had again acted as a buffer. Instead of ramming the bow of the freighter, the liner slid along her side, crashing and bumping but doing no serious damage.

She didn't make it all the way, though. Trying to swing his stern farther out, Uncle Sam signaled for a short burst ahead on the port propeller with helm hard over, only to feel it fetch up on an obstruction and bring the vessel to a halt. The screw had fouled on *Steel Navigator*'s port anchor cable, and the ships were locked in an immobilizing embrace.

They were about fifty feet out from the wharf by now, however, and far enough away from the flames so that continuous hosing of the bow section prevented anything from catching fire. This was about 1400, and there was an hour of intense anxiety as the hoses fought the blaze. Finally, at about 1500, the warehouse collapsed into the harbor and the fire was out. Temporarily, the ships were safe. The immediate danger of this fire was past, and the gale wind had eased off to a calm, but the two ships were still held together in their fouled fraternization, and getting away from Yokohama was still a serious problem. In fact, it involved more perils than Pauline ever faced.

In the comparative calm, communication was established with *Steel Navigator*. From the afterdeck, Uncle Sam talked to an officer on the other ship who said that he had been chief officer but was now acting master, as he had received word from a crew member who had managed to get back aboard that his captain had been crushed to death in the collapse of the company office during the first shock of the quake. Many of his crew who had been ashore were also missing.

The ships remained there through the night as fires and explosions continued to fill the darkness. The port gangway of E/Aus was opened, and a steady stream of small craft and ship's boats came to it all night long with survivors picked from the water or the shoreline. Some had been standing in water up to their necks for hours to escape the fires on shore. By morning over two thousand bleeding, wounded, burned survivors filled her passageways and public rooms. The ship's personnel, passengers, and unwounded survivors worked through the night tending to the injured and sorting out the confusion of lost and missing people as best as possible.

The acting British consul found his way aboard and reported that a big park half a mile in from the water was the refuge spot for thousands of residents, who were without water, and boats from E/Aus were sent ashore to supply them with it. They queued up peacefully at the waterfront, bringing whatever containers they could find, and several thousand were served by morning.

Uncle Sam had been up all night checking on the craft coming alongside and on conditions in the ship's emergency sick bays, while keeping a careful watch on the fires and explosions on shore. His eyes were painfully swollen and red from smoke irritation, and he found that washing them in a boric solution gave some relief. By dawn, he was able to lie down in his cabin for a short nap, but the staff captain woke him at 0700 with the word that a serious-looking fire had broken out on the Bund about a quarter mile east of the Customs Pier. It was working its way through wreckage littering the shoreline and feeding on oil on the water seeping out of wrecked depots, and the position of the two ships at the end of the pier no longer seemed tenable.

The two captains had a conference across the rail aft, both agreeing that they had to get out of there as quickly as possible. Since E/Aus's port propeller was fouled and there was considerable wreckage jammed under her starboard quarter, while Steel Navigator's single screw was well clear of the mess, it was agreed that, with the ships lashed together, the freighter would tow the liner clear of the pier. They would then anchor in the turning basin and decide on further action. First, Steel Navigator's port anchor cable, which was fouled on the liner's propeller, would have to be slipped. Three blasts from the freighter's whistle would signal her readiness to start moving.

The E/Aus crew stood at stations and the officers waited anxiously on the bridge, watching the flames eating their way out from shore through the oil-soaked wreckage under the Customs Pier. Closer and closer they came until their roar could be heard as they flared up with each fresh supply of oil, and the heat could also be felt. Still no signal came from Steel Navigator, and soon the flames would be at the bow. The deck officer aft reported that the shackle seemed jammed on Steel Navigator's cable, but finally, just before the fire reached the ships, the freighter's whistle roared out with three blasts and the ships slid away from the onward-licking flames.

The reverse course turned them a bit to the westward, and there, right in their path, was *Andre Lebon*, which had dropped away from the pier and was anchored just off it. There was a grinding of steel as the pair of ships raked along the French liner, but they slid past without serious damage and were finally in clear water. When far enough out at what seemed like a safe distance, *E/Aus* dropped her anchors, the lashings between the two ships were cast off, and *Steel Navigator* steamed away for the harbor entrance.

A test was made of the liner's engines, and it was confirmed that the port propeller was jammed, while the starboard one and the rudder were free. It would be difficult to swing her with no tugs and with the port propeller not working, but plans were made to run lines to mooring buoys in the area, and Uncle Sam saw no real trouble in pulling the ship around and getting her headed for the entrance.

The sense of safety at being away from the pier was very short-lived, however. Oil gushed from fractured lines on the Customs Pier, surrounding *E/Aus* and covering most of the anchorage area, and, instead of petering out at the end of the pier, the flames, fanned by an increasing land breeze, started racing out toward the ship, feeding on the surface oil. Their vanguard was a ribbon of flame several feet high on the surface of the water, topped by clouds of dense black smoke. When the smoke thinned out, whirling columns of white fire would rise high in the sky and then fade down as new areas of low flame formed on the surface. Three separate masses were moving out rapidly on the breeze, all headed for the anchored ship. The swing to the westward when lashed to *Steel Navigator* had put *E/Aus*'s heading somewhat to the eastward of the most easterly mass of flames. The southeast corner of the harbor was to windward of the flames and seemed to be clear of oil, so her anchors were hurriedly lifted, and she charged ahead at full speed on her one engine, dragging the cable on her fouled propeller, racing diagonally across the path of the flames.

At their nearest point, the flames were perhaps three hundred feet from the ship, and their heat seared the faces of personnel high on the bridge as hoses played along her decks and sides. Wreckage littered her course, but she smashed through it, fortunately without fouling the one operating propeller, and brought up a few hundred feet from the breakwater, which was now awash because of subsidence of the harbor bottom during the quake. Ten minutes after clearing it, her former anchorage was engulfed in flames at masthead height, and a coasting schooner and several small craft that were seemingly abandoned there were swallowed in fire and destroyed.

With the wind on her starboard beam, and the starboard propeller's action aiding in turning, the ship was gradually worked around to a northerly heading, parallel with the breakwater, and then moved slowly toward the entrance, fourteen hundred yards distant, where the little lighthouses were now half submerged. She had to dodge wreckage and mooring buoys, and literally scraped past the semi-submerged light-houses into the outer bay, using her engine ahead and in reverse with radical rudder action to make the tortuous passage. All this had taken about three hours since *Steel Navigator* had pulled her away from the pier.

E/Aus had escaped the burning oil for the time being, as had *Andre Lebon*, according to information they received later, but the Perils of Pauline were far from ended. *E/Aus* could not be made to turn to starboard against the drag of the cable on her port screw and the torque of the starboard one, and her course after easing through the gap in the breakwater would put her hard aground in shoal water on the northern side of Yokohama Bay if she continued on it. She was there-fore allowed to come to rest riding to the cable on her port propeller, with the southerly wind on her stern, but it was not a good situation. A stronger wind would drive her onto the shoals before she could swing to her bow anchors properly, and there was a quantity of oil on the water just to the westward of her that blazed fitfully now and then. It posed no immediate danger, but its presence was a threat, and the great 615-foot length of the ship had to somehow be coaxed around about two and a half points so that she could negotiate the deep-water exit to the safety of the Gulf of Tokyo outside.

Uncle Sam tried time and again to snub the bow around with the starboard anchor, but it would not hold, and each attempt brought her nearer the shoal water to the north. Any change in wind or in the action of the oil to port would again mean the end of the ship and the negation of all the emergency makeshifts that managed to get her this far. She was, of course, jammed far beyond capacity with refugees as well as her regular complement, with more than three thousand persons aboard.

Just one tugboat would have been the answer, but none had been seen since the quake struck. While Uncle Sam was busy with his repeated attempts to swing the bow to starboard with the anchor, an agent of the Rising Sun Petroleum Company, which supplied Canadian Pacific ships with fuel, visited the bridge to offer a suggestion. He had come aboard as a refugee and was aware of the difficulty in swinging the big ship onto a safe heading. Anchored nearby was a small tanker owned by a subsidiary of Rising Sun, and the agent thought she might be used as a tug to swing the bow. While Uncle Sam continued his struggle with the anchor, the agent and the ship's staff captain went to the tanker, *Iris*, in a small boat and arranged for her to attempt a tow.

Iris came alongside to starboard, contrary to Uncle Sam's suggested plan, took a line, and eased out off the starboard bow, but as soon as the big ship began to move, the little tanker was "hung up," in towboat parlance, and started swinging into the bow of the liner. She had to cut the line quickly, tried once more with the same technique and same results, and, it now being dark, pulled away and anchored.

It was an uneasy time aboard the immobilized ship, made even more so by word from shore sources that several large warships lying off the nearby Yokosuka Naval Station had been destroyed by burning oil. This news coincided with the sight of a blazing vessel drifting into the oil spill to port and starting a fire. Fortunately, it failed to spread, but Uncle Sam and the Rising Sun agent felt that something had to be done and that *Iris*, with the proper technique, was the only answer. They went over for another conference with her master, Captain Konings, who agreed to try again after hearing of the latest developments, and a plan was worked out. *Iris* would cross the stern of *E/Aus* and maneuver out on her port side so that she could come in across her bow, take a line, and run it out to starboard about sixty fathoms before *E/Aus* would take a strain on it.

When all arrangements had been made, Uncle Sam thanked Captain Konings, saying, "Of course you have to be careful with your cargo of fuel oil."

"It isn't fuel oil," Konings answered quietly. "It's benzene."

This caused Uncle Sam some concern, but the other two assured him it was no problem, and the maneuver began as soon as he was back aboard his ship. *E/Aus* was lit up like a carnival, with all the deck and lifeboat lights, cargo light clusters over the bows, and a powerful cable light, as *Iris* maneuvered into position. It was a clear night of almost no wind, and, at 2300, *Iris* came close across the bow, her yellow funnel standing out in the lights as she took the line and ran her distance. When a strain was put on the line, the bow began to come round, slowly, slowly, one point, two points, and finally three points before the line was let go and the engine started.

At first, the cable on the port screw held her and the bow came back a point, but, as she gathered way, the helm took hold, and the bow came gradually to starboard, headed for the open waters of the Gulf of Tokyo. By 1145 she was anchored in eight fathoms outside all the shipping, free, finally, of the multiple perils of Yokohama Harbor and Bay.

She remained there for a week acting as relief headquarters for the ruined city, which had been completely wiped out in the space of four hours. Gradually refugees and survivors were transferred to other ships, and a Japanese battleship provided a diving team to remove the cable from the port propeller. A speed trial at sea on September 5 showed her engines and screws to be performing almost normally, and the divers reported only superficial damage to the propellers. They were driven by two sets of steam turbines coupled to the screw shafts by hydraulic transformers patented by a German engineer named Foettinger, an arrangement similar to modern hydraulic drive in automobiles, and the flexibility and give of this equipment probably prevented more serious damage from all the beating taken by the propellers.

After transferring the rest of her refugees ashore and picking up water and stores at Kobe, *E/Aus* made an uneventful crossing to Vancouver. She remained in service until 1952, doing heavy duty as a troopship in World War II, and Uncle Sam, who was eventually decorated by every country whose nationals had been saved by *E/Aus*, went on to be CPR's senior captain, commanding *Empress of Canada* and finally the flagship and largest and fastest vessel in the Pacific, *Empress of Japan*, until he retired in the mid-1930s.

PART IV

~~~~~~~~

The Navy—Atlantic

As earlier anecdotes have revealed, I was in the subchaser Navy in
World War II, the original source of the phrase "sea stories" for me,
and an unending source of them for all who served in the 110-foot SCs
and 173-foot PCs. All my duty was in the former—long, narrow
wooden vessels turned out in great numbers early in the war as the
quickest way to set up some form of convoy system. German U-boats
were sinking shipping with impunity all along our shores in early 1942,
as most tankers and freighters had to go unescorted, but the hastily
assembled SC Navy, while not offering much of a threat in any one
ship, was the quickest "fleet-in-being" that could be achieved, and the
formalization of convoys did force the U-boats to operate elsewhere.
Eventually, subchasers were sent to all theaters of war and did all sorts
of duties that had never been imagined when they were ordered. I
originally got in the Navy with a specialist's commission in communications and eventually qualified for sea duty via a session at a "Ninety-
Day-Wonder" course and then SCTC in Miami. I had also changed
from bachelor to benedict in February 1942. These tales of Navy duty
are not intended to show how SCs were the secret weapon that won
the war, nor is there any "there I was flat on my back at 30,000 feet"
sort of thing. I can go for months at a time without thinking of the
war, but when the "sea stories" start to come back, they do recall a
forced interlude in life that was not devoid of laughs and excitement.

The Route to Sea Duty

The transition from civilian life to the deck of an SC was not a direct one. In fact, it was rather devious.

My first duty was with the code board of the Communications Department of the Fifth Naval District in Norfolk, Virginia, which handled all the classified communications of the command, and, in one of those accidents of a rapidly developing military situation, I ended up in charge of the board on November 1, 1941, one month to the day after first reporting for duty as an untrained ensign. I even pulled the old horse chestnut of saluting a senior CPO, covered with gold hash marks, thinking he was an admiral, on one of my first days.

I was just beginning to feel confident in the strange new work when Pearl Harbor, a month later, threw things into utter turmoil, and we were hard at it for sixteen hours a day, seven days a week. Codes no one had ever seen would come popping onto my desk, and I would have to figure out how to handle them. One day a message came in that was all numbers (our codes were all letters), and by some digging around I finally figured it was British.

While I was working on it, I happened to look out the window as some strange, flappy-winged, piano-wired biplanes floated in for a landing on the station airstrip, then went back to my work. Some minutes later, I put the numbers all together, and found that the message was from a British carrier approaching the Virginia Capes. It read, "Aircraft have left."

My first break in two and a half months was to get married (on two weeks' notice, which caused a considerable tizzy among the females of both families). It could have been sooner, but I had to finish paying for my Navy dress overcoat, and I also had to find a place to live amid one of the monumental housing shortages in history. I had been in bachelor quarters in a cousin's house. Jane was an excellent catch, since she had a 1940 Hudson Terraplane with four new tires and the ones on my 1933 Olds were getting a bit threadbare, so I sold the Olds to finance our start in married life.

Each morning I scanned the For Rent classifieds with no luck and was beginning to think we would have to live in the Hudson, when, opening the paper the minute it hit the doorstep at 7 A.M. one day, I saw an ad, "Small beach house, ideal for couple," and went right to the phone without stopping for my orange juice.

"Well, the first person to call was the man from the paper who set the type for the ad at eleven o'clock last night," the owner said, "but I told him that wasn't fair, and no one has been here yet."

"I'll be right there," I said, "name is Robinson," and, without breakfast, drove the couple of miles out to Willoughby Spit, a sandy point between Chesapeake Bay and Hampton Roads. The owner was waiting for me on the porch of his house, and as I came up to him, the phone started ringing inside.

"It hasn't stopped since you called," he said, "but you're the first one here."

Tucked into a corner of his yard, with the beach just the other side of the main house, was a tiny guest cottage, twenty by twelve feet, and as we came in, a distracted, inhospitable Navy wife in wrapper and curlers was packing to leave. I made sure it had a bed, a bathroom, a stove, and a refrigerator (and that was all it had!) and said, "I'll take it."

The owner and I were just shaking hands at the front door of the cottage when a trolley car stopped at the gate, and several people leaped off waving the classified page of the paper. The phone in the main house also began to ring again. I smiled smugly at the new arrivals as I walked past them on the way back to my car.

It was a great honeymoon cottage, although the ad had not said that the owner's teen-age son was a jazz drummer whose room was right above our roof and who practiced his art until all hours. When we

The honeymoon cottage, all 20 x 12 feet of it

Jane on the beach at Willoughby Spit

gave "dinner parties" for four, one person had to sit on the bed, but, as the weather warmed, we used the beach more and more and it was a very pleasant spot. Seaplanes from the Willoughby Bay base on the other side of the spit would take off right over us, still dripping water from their big hulls and pontoons, and their noise was even louder than Junior's drums.

Jane had one adventure at the cottage that still gives her the shakes every time she thinks of it. It was soon after we had moved in in late February, and the weather was still cold. After driving me to the base, she had come back to take a shower, and, as she pulled the door of the cubicle of a bathroom closed, there was a *klunk*, and she realized that the ironing board, which had been propped behind the door in the tiny hall or vestibule that connected the kitchen, bath, and bedroom, had fallen across the door and wedged itself, and she was effectively blocked in the bathroom. Since she had the car, I would be stranded at the base until she got out, and no one seemed to be within hailing distance, as almost everyone in the neighborhood worked during the day.

The only way out would be to climb out the window and go around the street side of the house to the front door, and she couldn't even wear a towel, as the towel rack was in the hall too. Clad only in a shower cap, she climbed out the window backwards and scooted through the frigid air around to the front door without causing a traffic jam on the street. In fact, no one saw her, and fortunately the front door was open.

Despite the great fun we were having, I was eager for sea duty, especially on some small craft like a YP, SC, or tug, where my small-boat background might be some help, but the only way to get it with a specialist commission was to go to the Ninety-Day-Wonder school in Chicago and qualify for a general deck officer rating. That was one of the more miserable episodes of my young life, where, after several months of the marital couch, I had to live nine in a room and go through nonsense like reporting to the "ground deck" and other such methods of familiarizing the would-be sea dogs with Navy lingo. As the course progressed, I was asked by my Navigation, Seamanship, and Gunnery instructors to stay on and be on the staff, which certainly held little appeal. If I was to stay on shore duty, why would I ever leave romantic Willoughby Spit and the honeymoon cottage?

I talked the Seamanship and Navigation men out of recommending me, but the Gunnery one said that personal considerations didn't matter and that a Gunnery instructor I would be. The only solution was to flunk the next Gunnery test, but then I flunked the one following by mistake, and I figured I just might be in trouble on an assignment. I happened to be the last of the nine in our room called for orders when the course finished, and the other eight went to cruisers or the newly formed Amphibs, tabbed as a sure suicide assignment and handed out to the less brilliant of the roommates. It was in some trepidation that I went for my orders when finally called, and my faith in the Navy was fully restored when the orders read to report to SCTC Miami. This had been hurriedly established on the old Clyde Mallory steamship piers to turn out officers for the hundreds of SCs and PCs that were popping out of yards all over the country at a steadily increasing rate, and the man in charge, Captain MacDaniel, "Captain Mac" to all hands, was a legend in the subchaser fleet.

He was a tall, lean, almost cadaverous damn-the-torpedoes type whose only concern was to get as many subchasers manned and operating as quickly as possible. Red tape meant nothing to him, and SCTC was one of the truly free-swinging, can-do establishments in the Navy, manned mostly by Ivy Leaguers and experienced yachtsmen. A new group of about thirty officers reported each week for four weeks of the most intense kind of training, and each group was greeted personally by Captain Mac with a fire-and-brimstone speech delivered in his heavy Southern accent, that has remained a classic to all who heard it.

Near the end of my group's course, I was sitting in a classroom struggling over a Gunnery exam (my weakest subject), and each time I raised my head to ponder a question, I could see an SC—No. 640—right outside the classroom with her crew making preparations for sea. My mind wandered to thoughts of the kind of duty I might draw, and I looked at the 640's slender young skipper with envy as he walked around his deck giving orders. If I flunked this test after my far from convincing performance in the man-overboard drill (when my "man overboard" ended up "drowned"), Lord knows what miserable assignment I'd draw: shipped out to the Amphibs, maybe.

This reverie was interrupted by the instructor suddenly calling "Mr. Robinson," and I started up guiltily. A messenger was standing next to him with a slip of paper. "Report to the personnel office immediately." I looked down at my half-finished test in confusion, and he said, "Never mind that. Hand it in now."

Worried and confused, I followed the messenger to the office, where, without any preamble, I was directed to report at once to SC 640 for duty as her Executive Officer. While the rest of my group were still sucking their pencils and huddled over the Gunnery exam, I was shaking hands with Ensign Bill Ludlington, my new skipper and the man I had been watching out the classroom window, and in five minutes we were casting off her lines and heading out Government Cut for her last day of shakedown. It seems her Exec (there were only two officers on SCs in the early days) had been qualified for command and transferred, and a new Exec was needed immediately. I don't know yet whether it was a compliment or an insult to be pulled out of class and assigned so precipitately, but I figured they knew I wasn't ready for command, and it was worth it to me just to get out of the Gunnery exam and some other final ones coming up. And it was also worth it to catch the eye of some of my friends in the classroom and see their amazement as SC 640 backed out of the slip with me aboard.

At last I had my sea duty.

Worth It All?

SC 640 had been assigned to Key West for convoy duty in the Gulf of Mexico, and we were off for there the next morning after our last shakedown session. This consisted mostly of familiarizing me with all her workings.

Jane was uprooted from our apartment on Miami Beach, a performance she was to become very used to, and took off by bus for Key West, where she found us a furnished room over a restaurant by the time the ship got there. We settled in for a couple of very pleasant months, considering that there was a war on and ships were being sunk all along the coast. Our run was to New Orleans and it was virtually a *Captain's Paradise* situation, with Jane in Key West and the fleshpots of the Vieux Carré at the other end. I didn't find any nightclub girl there like the setup Alec Guinness had worked out in that classic movie, but the partying was good at both ends.

It was particularly good in New Orleans for the crew, and sailing day often found us at the local police station or Shore Patrol headquarters trying to round up our wandering crew. One of the classic carousers was the quartermaster, an intense, bearded fellow who was one of the world's better self-dramatizers. Each minute on watch was a brush with imminent death, and he was always finding "targets" on our sonar and radar—a primitive set that specialized in reverse echoes on reciprocal bearings, so that there always seemed to be a contact in the opposite direction from the ship we were convoying. Porpoises were torpedoes, sea gulls were dive-bombers, and life was one continuous menace, due to end at any minute.

On our first New Orleans convoy he had been a police station recruit, brought back aboard in sheepish, hung-over humiliation, so he was restricted to the ship for our second visit, a punishment which brought great wailing and gnashing of teeth.

"Take away my rating, Captain; put me on bread and water at sea, but don't take away my liberty. Who knows how much time I have left to enjoy life? I may never get to a place like New Orleans again!"

Despite this heart-tugging appeal, Lud stuck to his guns on the restriction, and the quartermaster was a sad, glowering gangway watch as the liberty section tripped ashore, hooting and hollering at thoughts of Bourbon Street.

Late that night, Lud and I heard a disturbance topside and went to check, and there was the quartermaster, drunk and fighting mad, being wrestled aboard by his watchmates after obviously having been over the hill. His shipmates were between laughter and exasperation in trying to keep him quiet, and he was cursing and muttering threats of murder at all in sight. When we appeared in all our officerly dignity, the group subsided into a shambles of muttering and suppressed giggles and the center of it all was hustled off to his sack, still muttering and swinging fists at empty air, by one of the chiefs.

Eventually the story came out. He had told his watchmates on the liberty section that he was going to go over the hill no matter what the consequences as soon as we were out of the way, and this he did by climbing over a barbed-wire fence, since he had no pass to show at the gate of the Section Base where we were berthed. His friends had told him that they would be at a certain night club and would have things set up for him, and he managed to make his way there and join them.

It was a club with a sexy, off-color floor show, and after it ended some of the entertainers joined the sailors at their table.

The quartermaster had been rubbing his hands in glee at the sight of the member of the floor show that had been promised to him by his friends, chortling, "I don't care if I'm on restriction the rest of the war. This is it! This is living!"

There was much cuddling and fondling, running of hands up and down knees and thighs, both Navy white and satin, lewd suggestions, breast grabbing, and general buildup to a rare experience, and finally plans were made to go on "to my place," since the last show was over. The quartermaster's friend gave him a big kiss before leaving the table, breathing huskily and saying, "Wait here, baby, I'll be right back."

The quartermaster could hardly contain himself, mumbling things like "Oh, God, am I horny. I can't wait. What a build. This is all worth it," and was hard at it when two delicate-looking young men in sports jackets, still with eye shadow and makeup on, flounced up to the table. One of them put an arm around the quartermaster's shoulders and said, "Well, come on, honey. What are you waiting for?" Puzzlement changed to consternation and then to fury as the quartermaster realized that this was his "date." His shipmates had been in on the whole thing, luring him to a female impersonator club.

Fortunately, he didn't murder anyone, and he did not end up restricted for the whole war—just one rate knocked off and restriction after one more convoy, when he remained docilely aboard.

De Lawd Was Kind

Our *Captain's Paradise* was too good to last. The convoys were relatively uneventful, as the U-boats generally refused to come in where there were escorts, and, except for some heavy rolling in the short, steep Gulf of Mexico seas, it was good duty. Life in Key West was very pleasant, with almost the flavor of a foreign country because of the strong Cuban influence, and New Orleans never failed to offer excitement.

However, after a couple of months, I was transferred. It seems that my assignment to SC 640 had been so precipitate that no one had checked my date of rank against Lud's. When the next Alnav, the

Navy's blanket promotion system by date of rank, came out, I made j.g. and he didn't. I hadn't had enough sea duty to qualify for command, so I was ordered off to Philadelphia as Exec of a new ship, SC 699.

Lud and I had hit it off famously. We had mutual interests and mutual friends and the same civilian approach to life in the Navy, and he ran a good, relaxed ship with the proper combination of firmness and understanding, since the role of skipper of an SC wasn't too far removed from that of counselor at a boy's camp.

My new skipper, whom Jane and I came to call Poppa with no hint of affection, was very different. Everyone in the Navy had his own Queeg at some time, and he was mine, though there was no conflict quite so dramatic as the mutiny on the *Caine*. Actually, Poppa was very unsure of himself in trying to act like a proper naval officer, and took it out in screaming and invective that was a rather poor imitation of Charles Laughton in *Mutiny on the Bounty*. He was also prim and fussy, leaving me little notes in the head like, "If you must urinate on the deck please wipe it up."

It was a good lesson in adjustment for me after the easy camaraderie with Lud, and it was also an example of that easiest of pitfalls for junior officers—sympathizing with the crew against the skipper. I was thrown into the middle of this time and again as he mishandled various key men, screaming like a bad racing skipper on a sailboat. It was a difficult tightrope to walk between showing the men that I understood and not undermining or bad-mouthing the skipper, but it never got serious enough to come to an open break or excessive friction. Only Jane knew my real feelings, and she had her own gripe, because he would never tell me until 1700 whether he was going ashore or I could have the night off.

The 699's trip down the coast to Miami for shakedown was an easy one in pleasant weather, and there was only one odd incident. We were convoying a Liberty ship off the South Carolina coast on a dark night, with two YP boats, converted trawlers, as the other escorts. Our station was on the seaward beam of the ship with the YPs ahead and astern of her. I had the midwatch and noticed, as the time went by, that the YP astern was drifting far out to sea from her assigned station. She could just be seen as a dark blob against the faint trace of horizon, and I made it my business to keep track of her.

Eventually she had moved out on our port quarter, and suddenly she turned on a set of recognition lights. These were in certain color combinations for the day and hour and were for use in answering a challenge, which was always in the form of a letter for the given period, flashed by Aldis lamp.

I could only assume that she was so far off station that she felt it necessary to identify herself, as the lights were never used as a challenge, but I thought it an odd act and was just saying so to the man next to me on the bridge when a burst of 20-mm. tracer fire came across the water at us from the YP. When aimed right at you, they look as slow as flares arcing in lazy patterns, but they were high, and they whizzed past fast enough when above us. The steward's mate, who was on lookout duty aft with earphones and mike on his head, screamed through the intercom, "Red balls of fire overhead, red balls of fire overhead!" in his thick Alabama accent.

They were indeed overhead and continuing toward the Liberty, which had a cargo of ammunition, but a few came lower and there was a *thunk, thunk* and a loud *pop* as a couple of them hit the hull near the stern. Frantically, I flicked on our recognition lights, and the firing stopped.

In Charleston the next day, we faced the young YP skipper with a "What the hell did you think you were doing?" accusation, and his answer was that he thought we were a sub and challenged us, being a bit confused over the difference between the challenge and answer in the recognition procedure.

We had two splintered holes just below the deck aft, right underneath the steward's mate's lookout station, and when I showed them to him, his eyes widened whitely and he shook his head in amazement.

"De Lawd done took me by de hand," he said, "but he let me go again."

What's in a Name?

Finished with shakedown in Miami, the 699 went on to Key West for Sonar School, and Jane traipsed faithfully along, seting up in a one-room apartment we shared with another SC couple. It had two double beds, and we separated them with a bedspread hung up like the famous "Walls of Jericho" Clark Gable and Claudette Colbert rigged in *It Happened One Night*. We pretended it was very private and got along fine.

When sonar training was finished, 699 was ordered to escort the tug *Kevin Moran* to Guantánamo Bay on the southeastern coast of Cuba, the big U.S. Navy base that was to be our home port. Jane and

I had a sad farewell as she headed for the bus and an eventual return to New Jersey, and I went off to the ship.

As we steamed out of Key West, *Kevin Moran*, trailing in our wake, started to fall behind and then came to a full stop. We circled back to her and found that she had engine trouble and would have to return to port for repairs. She inched her way back to her berth, and we were ordered to return to base and wait for further orders.

As we hit the wharf, I jumped ashore and made a mad dash for the bus station. I knew when Jane's bus was due out, and I literally pulled her out of her seat just before the door closed. We had two more nights in port, and I was able to get ashore, since we now had a third officer. Eventually we were told to proceed to Gitmo independently, as *Kevin Moran* was waiting for spare parts, and this time the bus left with Jane on it, and 699 left too. When Jane got back to New Jersey, she thought, for a few days, that we had managed to start a family in our extra time at Key West, and we had a big gag going in our letters that the firstborn would, if male, be named Kevin Moran Robinson.

After all that, it turned out to be a change-of-climate false alarm. When we did start a family several months later, tugboats had nothing to do with it, and, inevitably in wartime with Daddy overseas, the baby was a Junior.

A Tour of a Red-Light District

From Gitmo, our first assignment was to go to nearby Santiago and escort a tug to Jamaica, and this meant a day and night of liberty in that ancient city, whose cathedral on the central square dated from 1522. Santiago was colorful to see, and the crew, most of them barely out of high school, made a colorful liberty of it. As contraceptive officer, I was the busiest man in the Caribbean for a while, dispensing sixty-six condoms to eighteen men in half a day (the other six men in the crew either didn't indulge or were careless).

Poppa and I had an introduction to two young ladies of good family (they had a "de" in front of their name) who were allowed to go out with Americans without the presence of a duenna under the somewhat dubious logic that their cousin had gone to Princeton. Our rendezvous was in the tiled, dark-paneled lobby of the hotel across the square from the cathedral, with fans on the high ceiling thunking lazily, stirring the potted palms. The meeting was easy to accomplish, since we were the only U.S. naval officers in sight, and the introduction was delightful. The older, taller, less good-looking of the sisters had better command of English, and she made the opening speech.

"We are Carmen and Rosita. This is my sister Carmen, who is beautiful. I am Rosita. I am ugly, but I am charming." Which just about covered everything succinctly.

We had a pleasant and completely polite day with them seeing the sights of the city and visiting their parents' *casa*, an ancient edifice with plain white walls along the street and lovely cool rooms around a courtyard on the inside. I'm no antiques expert, but the furniture seemed old, beautiful, and probably priceless.

In contrast to our genteel day, the crew roistered through a monumental orgy. Most of them had never been out of the country, nor had they carried on sex (if ever) in a foreign language, and they were in high glee over the whole episode. As sailing time approached, though, there was one problem. "Pappy" was missing (Pappy, not Poppa, who was only called that by Jane and me in private). Pappy was the oldest member of the crew, a white-haired, distinguished-looking Machinist's Mate who always kept himself scrupulously well-groomed and neat, and, though friendly, was a bit aloof from the juvenile high jinks of most of the crew, as he must have been all of forty-five.

He had not been seen by anyone else in their forays through the numerous brothels of Santiago, but the possibilities were endless there, and, with an hour to go to our 0630 departure, the Chief Motor Mac and I set out on a search expedition, giving me the chance to admit publicly that I have visited the red-light district of Santiago.

Dawn was just starting to cast a pearly half-light over the wet, fetid streets of the old city as we stepped around yesterday's garbage in the gutters and tried to ignore the rich mixture of odors. Cocks crowed, but there was little else stirring. The Chief knew his way around all right, taking us to a succession of street-front doors, where we would rap on the panel and wait until a sleepy, puffy-eyed Madam, shapeless in nightclothes, would open up a crack and say, "Closed! *Cerrado*. Go 'way." With foot in door, we managed to explain our problem, and she would shrug and usher us in grudgingly, taking us to whatever cubicles still had American customers. Everyone was asleep amid an overpowering, mixed stench of urine, sweat, beer, rum, and cheap perfume, and we would check each gently snoring male customer to see if it was Pappy. Sometimes the girl would come half awake and curse us until the Madam shushed her.

Similar repeats of this scene in several stops failed to turn up a lead, and the next resort was the police station, brightly lighted and noisy after the torpor of the whorehouses. When we explained our mission, the desk man put his pen down with a flourish, smiled in great satisfaction, and pronounced, enunciating carefully for dramatic effect, "Americano say-lore ees een beeg howss."

"Big house? Oh, jail. What for?"

"For trying to murder Cuban soldier."

This didn't sound much like Pappy, but we took a look anyway, and the unfortunate man behind bars proved to be a dead-drunk merchant seaman.

Forced to admit failure and with sailing time approaching, we went back to the ship, and there was Pappy, chipper as could be, strutting up the gangway all smiles.

"Where the hell have you been?" I asked, and he smiled condescendingly.

"I wasn't going to mess around in those dirty cathouses," he said. "I went out to the country to a quiet hotel, and I found me a nice cooperative schoolteacher. Boy did I have a time!"

"Well, you almost missed the ship."

"Yeah. I had a little trouble finding a taxi to bring me back."

Amid admiring glances from the crew already gathering for special sea detail, he went below to change out of his whites, saying, "No sir. No goddam cathouses for me."

And ten days later, who but Pappy out of the entire ship's company was the only one to come down with the good old "clap."

Big Blue Ones

The Gulf Stream off Fowey Rocks rated No. 1 as the nastiest sea condition in two years of SC sea duty, but the highest waves were on the Santiago–Kingston, Jamaica, run the morning after the crew's big orgy (with an understandable effect on a good number of stomachs).

The sky was a clear, hard azure and the temperature was in the seventies, but the inky blue of the Caribbean was lumped into monstrous seas by a norther blowing through the Windward Passage between Cuba and Haiti. This only happens a couple of times a winter when a particularly virulent cold front sweeps that far out from the North American continent. It was not hitting much over 30, and we were going with it when we pulled out of the narrow, dogleg entrance to Santiago, scene of the big naval battle of the Spanish-American War, so we weren't too worried about taking a beating.

However, as the mountains of the Sierra Maestra slowly faded from green to a dim purple astern, and we moved farther out of the lee of Cuba, the seas began to build on our port quarter into great rolling heaps that crested and broke in long cascades of foam, majestic in their sweep. We corkscrewed along, having the usual SC steering difficulties in a following sea, fanning across the tug's course and watching her lurch and lunge along her way as the wind continued to blow, and it seemed forever before the mountains faded below the clear horizon.

There was certainly a kinship among the tugs escorted by 699, because midway through the afternoon, this one came to a stop and blinked the message that she had to make engine repairs. This meant that we had to circle her while she lay dead in the water, and then we really came to realize the full size and sweep of the seas. When we turned back into them, we crashed and smashed, burying our bow up to the pilothouse even at dead slow speed, and the turn across the seas to continue our circle produced near capsizes well past 45 degrees as every man had to hold tight to something solid. When the waves were approaching, they loomed high above us on the flying bridge, which had a height of eye of nineteen feet for taking sights. There's a special thrill in an eyeball confrontation from that height with a roaring wave crest as it avalanches toward you.

Our gyrations were mere wiggles, though, compared to the incredible heaving and wallowing of the tug. Without way on, she was literally rolling her keel out, and two big questions were: Would she capsize? and How could anyone work in an engine room in motion like that? Somehow somebody did manage something, because we finally got a welcome blinker that she was ready to proceed, and we were at last able to steady away on a more civilized course, Jamaica bound.

By nightfall the wind and sea had moderated, and at midnight, as we rounded Morant Point at the eastern end of Jamaica under a brilliant moon, the sea was calm and the rich mix of wood smoke, vegetation, and flowers so typical of an island in the tropics wafted out to us on a gentle land breeze.

It was a strange place to be on Christmas Eve.

The Empire at Play

The British naval personnel in Jamaica couldn't have been more hospitable. Even though it was Christmas, the operations officer took us to his house for supper, and the next night we were invited to a Boxing Day ball at the St. Andrews Tennis Club, a rambling building of wide porches set high in the hills above Kingston. From these cool heights, the humid sprawl of the city was a panorama of lights twinkling out of the blackness far below, and the ball was a spectacle of the Empire doing its ceremonial best at play. If C. Aubrey Smith had been standing in the receiving line, I wouldn't have been surprised.

We were introduced to pretty girls, plied with fine Scotch, and greeted with jolly camaraderie by more Empire types than I had ever seen outside Noel Coward's *Cavalcade*. In fact, I had a continuous feeling of being on a Gaumont-British movie set.

From all the colorful characters we met, two anecdotes about them stand out in memory. Prominent on the dance floor were two tall, handsome Scots, impressive in formal kilted uniforms, twin brothers named MacGregor, or something equally Scottish, and, with great glee, we were told the story of their birth notice that had been placed in the local paper by their father some twenty-five years before and had tabbed them with a nickname forever after.

The notice read, "Born to Mr. and Mrs. Angus MacGregor, twin sons Angus and Ian." Being a true Scot and not wanting to pay for two notices because of the twin birth, Mr. MacGregor had added the instruction to the ad-taker: "Single insertion only," and in one of those happy accidents of typesetting, this phrase had appeared in the paper at the end of the notice. And so, in full adulthood, Angus and Ian were still known as the single insertion twins.

The man who chortled through this story for us was a perfect personification of Colonel Blimp, stout, red-faced, with a walrus moustache, poppy eyes, and a brush cut of red hair, who spluttered and hemmed and hawed beautifully as he talked. He was a retired major who was now in charge of a POW camp in Jamaica, and he lived in a room at the all-male Jamaica Club, as nearly classic a bastion of Empire as the major himself.

Someone else told us a tale about him. He was playing cards with other members in his room at the club on, as usual, a very hot night, and, as usual under the circumstances, he had no clothes on. The short-wave radio was on in the background, and suddenly there was a blare of martial music and the cultured voice of the BBC announcer proclaimed, "We interrupt this program for a special address by the Prime Minister, the Honorable Sir Winston Churchill."

As the Churchillian oratory began to flow forth in a message to British fighting forces around the globe, the major hopped up from his chair in great distress, crying, "Oh, my God, my God! This is awful—awful!" and fled to the bathroom. A moment later, in complete composure, he returned with a bath towel draped decorously around his midriff and sat down to listen to the speech.

A Passable Speaker

Churchillian oratory recalls an earlier incident when I was on the code board in Norfolk. It was a few days after Pearl Harbor, and Churchill had come to Washington to address a joint session of Congress, a truly historic event. It was announced on the base that the speech would be carried over the loudspeaker at the Officers' Club at lunchtime, and many of us from the office went over to listen to it.

Since it was Norfolk, most of the officers on the code board were Southerners, and one in particular from North Carolina had one of the most mealy-mouthed, nasal, consonant-swallowing accents, so broad as to almost seem a parody, I have ever had to suffer hearing, and day after day at that.

Churchill's speech was filling the room with its rolling phrases as we were held enthralled by the drama of the occasion, when there was a slight pause, and the model of mal-diction turned to me and said, "Y'know, he ayn a bad speekuh fo a Engishmun."

First Impressions

After a few more convoys, 699 was ordered back to Miami for re-assignment, and, upon arrival, Poppa and I parted company with no reluctance whatsoever. I had enough sea duty to qualify for command, and, no doubt eager to be rid of my unmilitary ways, he recommended that I be given a ship. From the balmy tropics I flew north in January to snowbound, ice-girt Nyack, New York, on the Hudson River's Tappan Zee, upriver from New York City.

I was assigned to SC 743 as skipper and reported to the Julius Peter-sen yard in Nyack, builder of many famous yachts, for the last month of construction to work with a nucleus of the key men in the crew assembling her gear and organizing her for shakedown. She had already been launched and sat in the basin at the yard. Although she was a jumble of half-finished work and almost invisible under an army of yard workers installing her machinery, armament, and electronics, my first command was still a stirring sight to me.

About eight or ten of her complement of twenty-five had been assigned to the yard even before I got there, and the initial meeting between skipper and crew was naturally fraught with nervous anticipation. Everyone was trying desperately to make a favorable first impression on both sides as we held our first meeting in a small conference room at the yard. I knew how important this could be to a good relationship, and, happy with what I saw in the men, I hoped fervently that I was their perfect image of a captain as we went through introductions and began to check over the status of supplies and equipment.

After a while, the time came to go down to the ship for a firsthand inspection of some of the items, and, since there was more than a foot of snow on the ground, we all put on overcoats, galoshes, boots, and whatnot to trudge through the stuff. As a captain certainly should, I led the way, slogging through the snow, and was soon disconcerted to hear suppressed giggles behind me. I turned my head to see what this was all about, trying to look severe, since I wasn't too happy at the thought of a bunch of giggly kids as crew. What the hell had I inherited anyway?

Most of them clammed up and tried to look serious, but the quarter-master, Nelson, a fresh-faced former milkman from South Dakota

SC 743 in silhouette

with curly blond hair and a ready grin (and who saw the ocean for the first time in his life the first day 743 poked her bow out of New York Harbor), couldn't contain himself.

"What the hell's so funny?" I asked in the most dignified, captainly manner I could muster up.

"Your galoshes," Nelson chortled and burst into loud laughter, pointing to the trail of footprints I'd left in the snow.

It seems I had put my galoshes on the wrong feet, and, with the toes curving into the middle, they certainly made a weird pattern, like the spoor of some pigeon-toed idiot.

Close Neighbors

My footwear became a local joke from then on, with much good-natured joshing, and we gradually made some order out of what was really only the normal chaos of the rush commissioning job all SCs went through. I remembered Ludington's story about his first command when she was in about the same stage at the Boston Navy Yard. He was standing on the deck surrounded by crates and boxes, with gear strewn around, trying to sort some sense out of it, when a man in civilian clothes walked aboard and said, "How do you do, my name's Knox."

"Hello, my name's Ludington," Lud said, giving a perfunctory handshake to what he thought was one more yard technician, and went back to his work. The man didn't go away and began to ask a few questions, and when an aide appeared and said something to "Mr. Secretary," Lud suddenly woke up to the fact that this was Frank Knox, Secretary of the Navy, who had never seen an SC before and had come aboard out of curiosity.

We had plenty of visitors, but none so distinguished, and the yard people were helpful to a man and woman. The townspeople of Nyack, a pleasant, small city, turned themselves inside out with hospitality—in fact almost literally in at least one case. The crew boarded with various families, and the three men from the engine gang, older and wiser than the rest, found their landlady extremely accommodating in taking care of all their needs. Evidently she had needs of her own, as she kept telling them in great sadness, as they took their turn with her at almost any hour of morning, noon, or night, how tired her poor husband was all the time from working in a defense plant.

Jane and I found a place to live in a makeshift apartment in a big old Victorian house that had been split up into small units. Our first night in bed, which was right next to a thin plywood partition that separated us from the next apartment, we learned that its bed was only separated from us by the plywood, which was far from soundproof.

The husband, it turned out later, was a bulldozer operator working on construction at an Army camp, who never came home sober and treated his wife somewhat the same way he must have operated his bulldozer, only more noisily, as we cowered silently in our bed inches away from them. When Jane and the wife became acquainted, they soon got to the stage where the poor woman wanted someone to tell her troubles to, and she confessed, in hushed confidence, and the understatement of the year, that "Ed and I don't get along very well."

It was all Jane could do to keep from saying, "Yes. I know all about it."

More First Impressions

The first crew contingent was introduced to their august captain through his ass-backward galoshes, and the rest of the crew, reporting aboard when 743 arrived at Brooklyn Navy Yard for commissioning, had an even more unsettling impression of the man who was to lead them into battle.

Before she could be turned over to the Navy, the ship had to be taken on builder's trials, and the day she started down the Hudson for Long Island Sound to run through them, there was so much floe ice charging seaward on the tide that her propellers and shafts were knocked out of alignment. She had to be hauled at the Nevins yard in City Island for inspection and repairs, since the ice was too heavy to go back to Nyack, and while she was out of the water the temperature went down to 10 degrees below zero, freezing the Sound solid and stranding her on the ways, blocked from her element for more than a week.

To sweat it out, Jane and I found a room in a sleazy theatrical boardinghouse in midtown Manhattan and had a few days of fun gallivanting around the city awaiting a thaw. Eventually it came, and 743 was refloated and taken to Brooklyn.

I wasn't there, though. For a couple of days my eyes had been hurting whenever I looked at lights, and one morning I woke up with a rosy red rash all over my body. When the rest of the crew, starry-eyed and expectant, arrived aboard for the commissioning, which by coincidence was to take place on our first wedding anniversary, they found the new Exec, Worthy Adams, but they were informed that their leader, Lieutenant j.g. Robinson, was unfortunately unable to be present, since he was sick in bed with the German measles.

Worthy's First Landing

The measles didn't last long, and I was soon aboard the ship and undergoing preliminary shakedown at the Small Craft Section Base in Tompkinsville, Staten Island. We were to be checked out for a period of several days by a warrant boatswain, a cheerful, stout man with a jauntily trim moustache, who was friendly and pleasant as he put us through our paces, always helpful in making sure things were going right without any fake military put-on.

When we did depth-charge tests off Ambrose Channel and brought a good supply of fish belly-up to the surface, we followed with "man overboard" drill picking up the fish, which he took home to dinner each night, a major ploy in the days of meat rationing.

On our return to Tompkinsville one afternoon, he suggested that Worthy Adams, the Exec, a boyish-looking, self-effacing, but engaging ensign right out of Yale and Ninety-Day-Wonder School, take over the conn to make the landing, his first since coming aboard, and I stepped aside to let Worthy have the voice tube from the flying bridge to the wheel and controls below us in the pilothouse. We all knew the crew was watching his first landing with interest.

"All ahead 400," Worthy called down the tube, giving the usual order to slow the twin diesel GM 268-A engines to their idling speed of 400 rpm's as we entered the long slip between two of the old steamship piers that served as the Section Base.

"All stop," was his next order.

This was the correct order, but things didn't feel right, and the warrant and I both looked aft. The propellers were still churning slow whorls of wake, and we had not slowed down. I didn't want to break into Worthy's act so quickly, but I thought that perhaps his order hadn't been heard.

"Better stop your engines, Worthy," I said, as we drew nearer to the end of the slip.

"They are," was his answer.

"Well, put 'em in reverse, then."

"All back 400," Worthy called down the tube, his voice edgy, but still we surged toward the dead end of the slip, where a damaged, half-sunk lifeboat was lying in the corner against a concrete bulkhead.

"All back 800!" he cried anxiously, and we felt the ship jump ahead faster.

"Jesus, she's still in gear!" the warrant cried.

"I'd better take over," I said quickly to Worthy and called down the tube, "You're still going ahead. We want the engines in reverse."

"The controls ARE in reverse, Captain," came back from Smitty, the motor mac working them, in an injured tone, as though we were accusing him of gross stupidity.

"Well, put them on stop," I cried, looking anxiously back at the churning wake and then forward to the fast approaching bulkhead. Obviously, we were still going ahead. "They must be stuck in forward. Get the engine room to put them on manual or something." I wasn't too sure whether this made any sense, but I couldn't think of anything else to say. The controls were operated from the pilothouse by levers working solenoid switches, but the thought filtered through my vast ignorance of things mechanical that there was some other way to work them from down below. Meanwhile, I had to do something about the imminent crash. There were sailors and workmen standing along the pier watching our approach in openmouthed amazement, and I could see people scattering away in panic from the spot our bow was aimed at.

Boats, sensing the situation, alertly had his men grab fenders and stand by forward, and I gave quick helm orders intended to spin the ship and put her alongside the sunken lifeboat, which, I hoped, would buffer her some; better that than a bow-on crash into a concrete bulkhead. We slammed sideways into the lifeboat, and there was a great sound of splintering wood as its planks caved in and its thwarts buckled. Our bow was scraping sideways along the concrete, with fenders rigged, and I called to Boats to try and get a line ashore somehow, but there were no bollards nearby.

Suddenly our surge stopped before there was any real damage to the bow, and I was just breathing a big sigh of relief when the ship started in reverse, doing another good job on the hapless lifeboat, with our square, boxy stern aimed right at the hefty pilings of the pier. I called for hard over rudder to try to spin her away, but there was not enough room for a full turn, and we began to bounce along the pier. By now the workers on shore realized that something was wrong, and would-be line handlers were chasing us back and forth in our yo-yo moves from bulkhead to piling.

"Kill the engines," I called down to Smitty, realizing that no power at all would be better than these unreliable spasms, and I remember muttering "goddam motorboat" repeatedly. Eventually we got lines on the pier and settled alongside with dignity highly ruffled but no real damage to the ship. It seems the solenoids were sticking unpredictably, a problem which was solved by installing new ones, and we never had this unnerving experience again.

Ever afterward, however, whenever we would see another SC making a crash landing or otherwise in trouble around piers, one of the crew would say to Worthy with exaggerated innocence, "Remember your first landing, Mr. Adams?"

In Expert Hands

Our next shakedown assignment was to make speed trials in Long Island Sound, and we set out on a gloomy, raw Saturday through the East River. The trials were conducted in the western end of the Sound, and all during them the weather deteriorated until a shroud of wet, blinding snow enveloped us just as we started back through the tortuous, tide-roiled East River to return to Tompkinsville in midafternoon.

Visibility was so bad that I decided that the only prudent thing to do was to anchor off Fort Schuyler until the weather cleared, since we could barely see the bow of the ship. This meant that our arrival at Tompkinsville would be delayed, and everyone in the crew rating Saturday-night liberty began to fidget a bit. Jane and I had a dinner date we wanted to make, and I had no desire to spend the evening at anchor off Fort Schuyler, either. I said something about this, but discretion still held sway.

After a while, our friend the warrant, who had been looking disconsolately out into the blinding white stuff, muttered quietly to me that he had a heavy date that night too.

"I've got a pilot's license, Skipper," he said. "I think I can get us through all right if you'd like me to try."

"Well, if you really think you can," I answered, with a sigh of relief, impressed at these qualifications, "it's o.k. with me. See what you can do."

Up came the anchor, with the crew, especially the liberty section, turning to more willingly than usual, and we started nosing through the murk. A nun buoy appeared close aboard to starboard and the warrant gave a little grunt of satisfaction.

"Here we go," he said, and soon another nun showed up. I was watching the compass with some skepticism as to how this course was going to get us through the East River, but he was so delighted each time we came to a nun buoy that I didn't want to spoil his fun. It was spoiled, however, when can buoys began to show up close aboard to port and I mentioned that our heading was now north. Since there is no place in the East River where a consistent heading of north will get you through, and no place where nun and can buoys are a couple of hundred feet apart across a channel, it was obvious that we weren't going to make Tompkinsville this way. I didn't say anything directly, just reported the buoys and the heading and looked at the warrant with what I hoped was a challenging stare, and it worked.

"This ain't right," he admitted dolefully.

"I think we're in the Bronx River," I said, "and I think we'd better turn around before we can't."

By now the shoreline could be dimly seen on each side, as the river was only a couple of hundred feet wide, and we began a backing and filling turn, since there wasn't room for a single full turn to reverse course. At one point we nudged the edge of the channel with our rudders and props, and a muddy swirl eddied forward along our starboard side, but we weren't hard aground, and eventually we got her headed in the other direction.

The warrant's optimism soon returned as he found another system of nuns, and we edged slowly along picking them up until we lost contact and, heading south, had no reference points left. The warrant put his face out the pilothouse door and stared up into the thickly falling snow for a while, blew the stuff out of his moustache, and turned a doleful gaze on me.

"Christ, Captain, I'm lost," he admitted.

I shrugged, and down went the anchor again in not very deep water. Fortunately, the snow cleared on by in a few minutes, and landmarks began to appear. We were right in the middle of Flushing Bay, and we had managed to go quite a distance north and then south without getting any closer to the East River.

With improved visibility, we quickly got under way, and the only other incident on the way back through the East River was a loud alarm bell ringing on the starboard engine, followed by a report to the bridge that they had had to stop it. The filters, they said, were full of mud (obviously from the Bronx River) and the engine wasn't getting water. This happened to be at the trickiest turn of Hell Gate, where the current is about 4.5 knots, and several big tug-and-barge combinations were sweeping by us close aboard and looming up ahead, but the port engine purred along faithfully, and we made it to Tompkinsville in time for all dates and liberty hours.

As we passed the Statue of Liberty and headed for home, the warrant muttered an apology to me.

"Well, we're making it o.k., Skipper, but I'm sorry I couldn't find the way for you sooner."

"It was a good try anyway," I said. "And you must know the harbor pretty well with a pilot's license. What was your job when you had it?"

"Oh, I ran the ferryboat between Sixty-ninth Street, Brooklyn, and Staten Island."

The Garbage Admiral

With shakedown complete, we were ordered to proceed to Miami for the official SCTC shakedown that would clear us for duty in a combat area, and our first stop was to be Norfolk, Virginia. Everything went well until we approached the channel through the minefields off Cape Henry at the entrance to Chesapeake Bay. Except for the channel, the rest of the mouth of the Chesapeake was mined, and you had to stay precisely in the channel to make it through without having your bow blown off. Zero fog rolled in as we passed the first buoy for the channel, and it was a tense time of careful course plotting and steering as we edged our way from buoy to buoy into Lynnhaven Roads, just beyond Cape Henry, where we anchored until the fog lifted. It was good to gain confidence in the accuracy of our compass this way.

At the Naval Operating Base in Norfolk, we were a tiny frog in a very big puddle, with carriers, battleships, tankers, supply ships, and all the other vessels of the Atlantic Fleet looming over us like skyscrapers next to a dog kennel. We were awed and impressed as we nosed into our assigned berth, and we had to crane necks back so far to look up at the ships we passed on the way to it that you couldn't keep a hat on.

I spent the afternoon ashore chasing supplies and picking up orders for our next leg down the coast, and I came back to 743 in late afternoon to find Worthy frothing at the mouth in anger and frustration. It seems that a lieutenant had come aboard just before I got back, an admiral's aide resplendent in all the specialties of his position—"chicken guts" (aiguillettes on his shoulder), gloves, and a supercilious manner.

"Who is the garbage disposal officer on this vessel?" he demanded.

"Well, I guess I am," Worthy said in the SC Navy's usual informal manner of communicating.

"Stand at attention and say 'sir' when you're addressing an officer senior to you," the aide barked.

"Yes, sir," Worthy gulped.

"Have you read Lantfleet Bulletin 43 slant 582?"

"No—sir. I haven't. I don't believe we have it aboard."

"Well, it's your duty to have all bulletins. Who is your communications officer? He should have it."

"I am—sir."

"You are derelict in your duty in two ways. You don't have the bulletin and you are not complying with it. I would like to speak to your executive officer about this oversight."

"I am the Exec, sir."

This stopped the aide for a moment. "Well, where is your commanding officer?"

"He's ashore—sir."

"This is most unfortunate. Do you realize that I could have you court-martialed for something like this and you would lose your commission and be an enlisted man for the rest of your career?"

Worthy had no answer to this threat, but he was beginning to wonder about this all-important bulletin and what it must contain, and, as a former Yale lacrosse player, he was seriously contemplating body-checking the aide overboard and taking the consequences for the rest of the war for the sheer joy of the act. Instead, he swallowed his pride and tried to sound polite.

"What should we be doing in compliance with the bulletin, sir?" imagining something to do with gunnery procedures or special communications at the very least.

"You should be separating your wet garbage from your dry garbage, but you have sent all your garbage ashore mixed in the same containers!"

Some of the crew who had been watching the confrontation in awe and amazement had to duck quickly out of sight after this ringing pronouncement before they further enraged the aide by hooting with laughter, and all Worthy could do was stand there with his mouth open.

"See that it is done properly from now on," the aide said as he stalked ashore.

It took a bit of soothing to cool Worthy down, and I tried to calm him by saying that the aide was probably some very inbred Annapolis type who resented all the reservists who had moved into the holy precincts of his profession. Worthy couldn't buy anyone being that stuffy no matter what his background or his excuse, but he gradually simmered down to coherency and began to laugh it off, although every so often he would shake his head and utter a string of four-letter words in memory of the encounter.

It was pretty well forgotten when we went ashore to join Jane at dinner at the Officers' Club that night, leaving the duty to a temporary officer who had come with us from New York to gain experience. Jane and Worthy and I were standing in the lobby of the club checking our coats, when Jane spied someone across the room just as he saw her, and they let out mutual cries of recognition and met in the middle with a big clinch. It was a lieutenant with "chicken guts"—no one I'd ever met before—but as soon as Worthy saw him hugging Jane, he broke up in uncontrolled laughter.

"Is that your friend?" I asked, knowing that it must be.

Worthy was laughing so hard he could only nod yes.

"Come on," I said, winking at Worthy. "Let's meet him socially."

We moved up and stood behind Jane just as she broke out of the hug and turned her head to look for me. "Oh, this is my husband, Bill Robinson. Bill, this is Mike Blake."

"Hello," I said, stepping forward to shake hands. "And this is my Exec, Worthy Adams."

Blake gave me a hearty handshake and a big smile and then turned as I introduced Worthy and did the most wonderful double take I've ever seen outside of the movies. His face fell a mile, and he was very subdued as he shook hands.

"Oh, yes. We've met," he said lamely. Worthy just nodded.

Jane had heard the tale of Worthy's "garbage admiral" and had been suitably shocked and outraged, and she sensed what the situation was. Worthy moved off, and she and Blake made awkward small talk for a moment, while I stood silently by. We started to turn away, but he touched my arm and spoke in an abashed voice.

"Had to talk to your Exec this afternoon," he mumbled. "Might have seemed a little severe, I guess, but it was just line of duty of course. You know what this job is." He made a small gesture toward his aiguillettes, shrugged apologetically, and faded away.

Worthy could hardly contain himself as we started toward the dining room.

"Some friends you have, Jane," he kidded.

"I didn't know you knew any Trade School boys," I said to Jane. "How did you know Blake?"

"He's not from Annapolis," she said scornfully. "He used to date a roommate of mine at Smith when he was at Amherst."

Another Friend of Jane's

From Norfolk south to shakedown at SCTC we had the usual things like a tug that broke down off Hatteras while we were convoying it, and some of the crew got into a fight in Key West, but most of these could be considered routine. Shakedown produced some of the Gulf Stream adventures already chronicled, and then we were off to parts unknown via the Panama Canal. Jane went home when we left Key West in early May, and this time it was no false alarm that a family was started, although I didn't know it for months.

We now had a third officer, Bill Pitcairn, who had roomed with my cousin at Princeton three classes behind me and was an old Star sailor from Great South Bay. I found out that he was in a group at SCTC when we were finishing shakedown and were told that we rated another officer, so I requested him. He was pulled out of class just the way I had been for the 640 and was on duty aboard while his group was still listening to a lecture. Short, stocky, with a big nose, large brown innocent eyes, and a ready laugh, he was the world's greatest bird dog in locating hard-to-find supplies, whether we needed them or not.

His first assignment was as supply officer for the ship, and, always in a lather of sweat, he would come back with extra fans, cases of chipped beef, even radar, and, his greatest triumph, a rescue breather. We didn't have the slightest use for one, but he was so proud to have found it

With Pit (left) and Worthy (center) on the bridge of the 743

that he wouldn't give it up. I told him, jokingly, that the only way we could keep it was if he stowed it in his own bunk, and there it stayed for several months. He ended up with something of a last laugh, as parts of it eventually were used in some homemade diving equipment the engine gang fashioned. He was excitable and impressionable and easy to kid, and, typically, once reported that there was a ship on fire on the horizon when the moon was rising. The crew looked on him as a character and loved him, and Worthy and I, good friends by now, both enjoyed him tremendously.

Panama was to the crew what Santiago had been to the 699, and post-liberty hilarity was unrestrained. Songer, it seems, was well known in Panama from peacetime duty there years before. He led the boys to a favorite house, promising to fix them up like they'd never been fixed before, and lived up to every word of it. When he walked in, the Madam exploded in shrieks of delight.

"Professor!" she cried, hugging and kissing him, "you've come back!" Beaming like a scoutmaster at a cookout, Songer led his troops in, and "Professor" he was from then on to everyone aboard. Seems he'd been able to educate even such well-versed young ladies as the ones of the house.

Meanwhile, a visit to the Operations officer revealed that we were assigned to the Seventh Fleet in the Southwest Pacific, and our first stop in heading there would be Bora Bora.

"Bora who?" I asked.

He took me to a large wall chart of the Pacific and showed me, 4,800 miles away, a little dot in the Society Islands by that name.

"Since we have a range of less than 1,500 miles, that's going to be an interesting passage," I said.

"Don't worry, you'll be going in a convoy of LSTs, APCs, and another SC, and you will be fueled at sea. I suggest you get together with the other SC and compare notes before you leave."

We had come through the Canal with one other SC and several APCs, 100-foot wooden coastal transports built on trawler hulls and intended to serve as auxiliary support vessels to the Amphibs. We had the only Canal pilot aboard for a group of about ten small ships, and he chuckled at the assignment, since his previous trip had been as one of five pilots on the carrier *Essex*—one master pilot on the bridge and one on each corner of the flight deck.

The other SC was berthed next to us in Balboa, so I made a point of getting together with the officers to see how they were facing up to the great adventure. We compared notes on how our ships were organized and what our routines were, and I soon realized that we had slightly different ideas.

"How do you handle the serving of wardroom meals?" the earnest skipper of the SC asked me. "We don't have a steward's mate and I find it difficult to work out officers' mess duty in the regular crew."

I had to admit that we didn't eat in the wardroom, a fancy name for the single cabin under the pilothouse that had three bunks and a couple of desks, since it was too much trouble to bring the meals there. We ate with the crew at their mess table in the after quarters, where the galley was located.

"Oh, but we find it very valuable to have our meals in the wardroom," the SC skipper said, obviously shocked. "We always discuss one day's operations and plan for the next."

Worthy and Pit happened to overhear this, and I could see them smirk and turn away, as I don't think we had ever once "discussed operations" at a meal since we'd been aboard. From then on, though, that phrase was a quote, and we still use it in the family whenever someone is uptight about not enough communication.

The Exec of our sister SC, a slender, vapid sort of poseur, had a guitar and used to bring it on deck after supper and start to strum it, waiting for the crew to gather around for a jolly sing-along, and we were always tickled to watch the performance when he appeared. One by one the crew members would duck around the pilothouse or slip down the hatches, and he would be left singing to a couple of embarrassed types who hadn't been quick enough to get away.

He visited with us and started to play "do-you-know," which was always one way to break the ice when trying to get acquainted in the Navy. Crew members used to say "Anyone aboard from Jersey?"—or Texas—or whatever, when ships came alongside each other in port, but the officers were a bit less direct, going into home towns, colleges, prep schools, and the like.

When our Exec friend found that I was from Elizabeth, New Jersey, he brightened immediately and ran through several college types that he knew from there, and I nodded and said yes or no as he mentioned them.

"Oh, and then there was that gorgeous, sexy blonde at Smith," he went on. "Jane Dimock. Do you know her?"

"Yes," I said very pleasantly as Worthy and Pit all but exploded. "I do know her. I married her."

Ready?

The transit of the Canal, with the endless expanse of the Pacific there before us just outside the harbor at Balboa, marked a psychological end to training, and to "playing war," which everything had seemed in the Atlantic. We had seen no gunfire in anger and the sub menace had been a remote and almost mythical one to us, even when I was momentarily waiting for the one off Fowey Rocks to crash into us during the night.

I felt that we knew the ship and knew how to handle her, I had confidence in almost everyone in the crew, and I had even managed to develop confidence in myself. I found that I really liked the role of skipper. There was something special about being lord of all you surveyed, even if it was only 110 feet of wooden motorboat, and to have your word as law for all the people around you. I'd read about the mystical relationship of captains and their ships, never really believing it, but I now understood it. With the lives of more than two dozen men confined to the little world of the ship and intensified by this very confinement, the inanimate case of frames and planks became more than so much wood, a force that we dwelt with daily in an emotional involvement more often reserved for living things.

Uncle Billy had intensified my pride in command when he came aboard the ship in Tompkinsville one bright January day. Although he was over seventy-five and using a cane, he seemed to grow younger and stronger as he stepped aboard and walked around the decks. He had been skipper of a converted yacht on anti-sub patrol in World

SC 743 heading to sea

War I, his last formal sea duty, and he was fascinated and very knowledgeable in learning about everything on board.

"Well, Bill," he said, as we shook hands goodbye, "you're the youngest member of the family ever to have command of a ship, younger than your grandfather or Uncle Sam. I'm very proud of you, and I know you are of yourself. Good luck with her." Even though my circumstances were vastly different from theirs, I was really touched by his remark.

It was the last time I saw him, as he died while I was overseas, dropping dead quietly one evening at Nantucket of a heart attack after a full day of golf and playing with his grandchildren.

My pride in command and confidence in myself extended to most of the crew. In general, we had a bunch of cheerful, well-adapted youngsters who knew their jobs and made little fuss about the unnatural condition of their lives beyond the usual service gripes and bitches. The only cloud was in the "black gang." They were older, tougher, and more worldly than the rest of the crew, and we had a couple of troublemakers. It was becoming obvious that Capshaw, the chief, was not a diesel man and was having his troubles, and the lack of leadership hurt.

The main problem was O'Hegan, a fast-talking former union organizer who seemed to have the idea he could "bargain" with me over the crew's rights. He bitched more than the others, argued more, and did less work, and there was a big blowup in Key West when he, Smitty, who was his chief pal and supporter, and Songer came back to the ship roaring drunk after a fight in a mud puddle. They were covered with blood and slime and were making a terrific row, and when Worthy, who had the duty, tried to calm them and get them below without more fuss, they threatened to get physical with him.

It was close to a really serious situation, but Worthy, with the help of a few of the crew on duty, got them stowed away below without violence. The threat of it was always there with O'Hegan and Smitty. Songer had just been along for laughs, and his Navy training was deep enough to keep him from stepping over the line, but the other two were tough physical specimens and they had a habit of staring at an officer with an expression that said "If you didn't have that uniform on, I could beat the shit out of you" (which was very true).

I had a system of a reprimand and a warning the first time someone stepped out of line and then throwing the book doubly if he ignored this. It was a second offense for Smitty and O'Hegan, and they both lost a rate at captain's mast. Songer got a warning and that was all he ever needed.

The Key West thing hung over us still, though they had been behaving themselves pretty well, and there was that little tension there, that look in the eye, as we faced the Pacific and the long months ahead.

PART V

~~~~~~~~~~~~~~~

The Navy—Pacific

The transit of the Panama Canal on a day of torrential downpour was a "watershed" in more than one way in the career of SC 743. We knew we had been heading for the Pacific for a long time, and now it came home to us that we were really there. It seemed a srtange, exotic, alien area, remote from anything we had ever known, and a cutting off from all our pasts.

A Simple Message

On June 7, 1943, our convoy of the two SCs, four APCs, and a few LSTs, the boxy, awkwardly lumbering craft that were the largest types in the Amphibs, nosed out of Balboa onto a flat, shining Pacific Ocean headed west and a bit south for Bora Bora, an estimated three weeks-plus away.

Trying not to sound like Noel Coward in *In Which We Serve*, I made a pre-departure speech to the crew, saying that we would no longer have unannounced drills or routine General Quarters. If the buzzer went off, it meant business. I also said that we would probably have many long, boring hours of watch standing and that everyone, therefore, would have one day per week off the watch bill to sack out, relax on deck, and do whatever he wanted to amuse himself, wondering all the time what Admiral Ernest King would say at such a proposition, delivered to a crew clad only in cut-offs and sandals, from a skipper in the same sort of costume.

After working out of the calms and rain showers of the Gulf of Panama, we picked up the southeast trades, and for day after day we chugged along at a stately 8.5 knots with the breeze at 16–20 knots on our port quarter, an endless procession of fleecy white clouds marching westward overhead, and the waves a perpetual-motion machine of whitecaps over bright blue water. Each evening the most spectacular sunsets I have ever seen anywhere in the world flared up to fill the sky ahead in a briefly brilliant show that mixed the most delicate and violent colors in quickly changing patterns, a breathtaking display that seemed to grow more vivid night by night.

Life aboard was relaxed and quiet, and I even managed to read all of *Moby Dick*, which seemed appropriate reading matter for these waters, until the tenth day or so out of Panama, which marked the end of the incubation period for social diseases. I was hoping that everyone had been careful, but there's always at least one overconfident type, and this time it was the signalman who had to come to me with the sheepish confession and a request for medical assistance.

The dandy little handbook all SC skippers had that covered everything from just such emergencies to burial at sea recommended absolutely unbroken bed rest, lots of fluids, and a certain dosage of sulfadiazine, which was then the newest miracle drug, so I went through the recommended steps and ordered Flags to his sack and to stay there except for absolutely necessary trips to the head. He grumbled and groaned at this, and things went well for a day or two, when he started complaining that things weren't any better.

The treatment was supposed to take a few days, but, to set his mind at ease, I said I would signal the LST that had a pharmacist's mate aboard to check on what I was doing. The problem with this was that I didn't think Flags should leave his sack to do the blinker work, leaving Nelson, the quartermaster, as the only other man who was qualified in blinker. I could read it, but I couldn't send it.

I wrote the message out for Nelson, starting "Signalman has gonorrhea; am dosing with sulfadiazine—" then gave the dosage plus information on bed rest and fluids, ending with a request for confirmation that this was the correct procedure. Nelson took one look at it and started to giggle, scratching his head.

"Cheez, Captain. All those big words," he groaned.

"Yeah, I know it's a tough one, but see what you can do."

He went nervously to the light, raised the LST we wanted, and then began to send the message. The shutter would start out at a confident rate, but time and again there would be a break in the rhythm and he would have to start over. By now he was sweating and he was getting so upset that his hands were shaking, which was no help at all to his performance. A couple of times he got through "gonorrhea" without stopping, though Lord knows how it was spelled, but he never could get past "sulfa—" and he was getting repeated requests to start over from the LST. Finally he just stepped back in frustration and said "Aw gee, Captain. I can't send all those big words."

"Well, let me see," I said. "Take it easy for a few minutes."

I went to work rephrasing the message in basic English and gave it back to him.

It started out "Flags has clap," and "sulfadiazine" was reduced to "sulfa d," and finally we got it across, with a message back that we were doing the right thing. Two days later Flags was cured, and when we got to Bora Bora, practically everybody in the convoy came over to ask with great glee about his health.

Sinking in Mid-Pacific?

Another problem to disturb the even tenor of our days as we wheeled westward across the blue and white treadmill of the southeast trades was the prospect of having to fuel at sea from an LST. We had been assigned a specific one as our fueling ship before we left Panama, and I had tried to consult with the skipper, a weathered Coast Guard "mustang" (enlisted man promoted to officer), on how we would do it, but he brushed me off with a wave of the hand as he and his fellow skippers were drinking beer at the Officers' Club.

"Don't worry about it, son," he said. "I've done it all my life. Just come alongside, and we'll handle things."

When fueling time came, we did just that, and his orders were to put a spring line and breast line out while the fueling hose was passed across, put our engines in neutral, and he would tow us along, with the spring line keeping us clear of his high, steel side.

I wasn't happy with the arrangement, but he went ahead with great confidence. We had barely taken the hose when we surged over a swell much faster than the wallowing LST, fetched up on the spring line when it went taut, and slammed in out of control against the side of the LST. There was a crash and a crack, but it didn't look as though we had done any damage. When the same thing happened very soon again, I'd had enough, and I gave the orders to cast off the lines and put our engines in gear.

By megaphone we worked it out that we would handle our ship independent of the LST and all they would pass us would be the fueling hose. We would maneuver by engine adjustments and wheel orders. It took some tricky doing, but Nelson, who had developed into a fine quartermaster despite his difficulty with medical messages on the blinker and his non-nautical background, had a good feel for the wheel, and there were no more smashes and crashes.

A day later, however, Capshaw reported that we seemed to be taking water in the bilges more quickly than we should, in rather an uneven pattern. It had come up so fast in the past hour or so that the bilge pump had burned out trying to keep up with it, and we were now on an auxiliary pump. This was disturbing news, especially in view of the fact that I had just figured out in the past day or two that we were in that spot on earth which is farthest from any land of any description, even a rock or a sandbar, when we were halfway between the Galápagos and Marquesas.

We surmised that the smash against the LST while fueling must have started a plank somewhere that was working loose unevenly. I swam over the side and under the hull as far as I could, feeling for a crack or loose section, but found nothing, and then decided I had better inspect the bilge from inside. Putting on my oldest, rattiest clothes, I lowered myself reluctantly into the greasy slosh of water and started crawling around the maze of pipes under the engines, feeling the planks as I slithered around.

Since the convoy was so slow, we had been running on one engine at a time, alternating them in four-hour periods, as an easy way to hold station and as a fuel conservation measure. The port engine had been running, but while I was in the bilge they switched to the starboard one, and the thought crossed my mind that the uneven rate of flooding might have some connection to the engine alternation. I was completely stumped otherwise, as I could find no hull damage that could cause a leak.

I was sitting under the recently stopped port engine, up to my armpits in a foul slosh of bilge, thoroughly disgusted and completely baffled, when, through the network of pipes between me and the starboard engine, I saw a steady stream of water pouring out of a hole in its seawater intake pipe. A small drain plug had worked loose, or perhaps been jarred loose when we bounced off the LST, and the starboard engine had been doing its level best to pump the whole Pacific Ocean into us.

The Man for the Job

Our other problem was generators. We had two Hill diesel generators and they had been a maintenance headache ever since the ship had been commissioned. Shortly after we left Panama, one of them dropped a rod with a *thunk* heard all over the ship, and the black gang went to work on tearing it down and rebuilding it, while the other one stood solo duty. We had been alternating them, but now the lone survivor was it, and even to my untutored ear it didn't sound too healthy as it rattled along for twenty-four hours a day.

Capshaw was a Regular Navy veteran who had done all his previous duty in steam on big ships, and it was as much a mystery to him as it was to me why he had been assigned to a small diesel ship. His normal method of working on something was to take bigger and bigger wrenches until something broke, and then he would report in disgust, in his twangy Tennessee drawl, that the "damned thing weren't no good nohow."

We had trained diesel mechanics in the black gang who had to work under Cappy but let it be known, in devious ways, that he didn't seem to know much about diesels, and meanwhile the repair job went on and on and on, while the operational generator became noisier and less reliable-sounding in alarming progression.

Finally, coming into Samoa at the end of the leg after leaving Bora Bora, Cappy announced that repairs were complete, and the sick generator was about to be restarted. I suppose I should have taken it as a sign of something that he remained on the bridge after making this report instead of returning to the engine room. He sat there with an inscrutable look on his long, lean face as the generator started to cough and chug in start-up action. This was followed by a great blast of black smoke out of the generator exhaust, a crescendo of clattering and banging, and then a loud and very final *clunk*. This time it had thrown a rod through the side of the block. Without a word, Capshaw sighed deeply and walked off the bridge.

Pitcairn, as engineering officer, suggested that I should talk to Patterson, a laconic, no-nonsense oil field mechanic from Illinois, who had spent his life working with diesel pumps. He had kept a low profile in the black gang, but he had convinced Pit that he knew plenty about diesels. We all agreed that Cappy had had it. He just didn't have the background.

After a talk with Patterson, I too was convinced that he knew his stuff, and we decided that the best thing to do was to put Cappy ashore at the Naval Base in Samoa and put Patterson in charge of the engine room. When we got to Pago Pago, I talked to the personnel officer at the base and convinced him that Cappy should be transferred.

"He's a great worker," I said, "and I have nothing against him, but he belongs in steam. That's where his knowledge is."

Patterson took over the engine room and we had an absolute minimum of trouble from then on. A few days later, just as we were preparing to take off on the next leg to Fiji, Cappy, who had had no hard feelings about being transferred, came aboard all smiles.

"Gee, Mr. Robinson. I want to thank you for setting me up here. This is great duty."

"That's fine, Cappy," I said. "I'm glad it's working out. What have they got you doing?"

"I'm in charge of the diesel repair shop," he answered.

"The Captain's Lost"

Navigation was a challenge, and I enjoyed doing it. I had a very easy break-in, since most of our passages were in convoys, and the convoy commodore would be responsible for all the ships. I worked every day, checking my figures against the convoy's, and it was reassuring to have them work out in reasonable relationship.

Our convoy, which had been going on so long it seemed to be the only life I had ever known, was due to disband in Noumea, New Caledonia, after the leg from Fiji, and we were approaching the south end of the island, a big one over two hundred miles long, some eight hundred miles east of Australia, at night. Reefs and small islands extend far out from the main one, and, as far as I could see, we were headed right for a large, unmarked reef. We were too far north and should be turning to the south before rounding the bottom of the reef and turning north up the west coast of the island to Noumea.

I checked and rechecked my figures and was really getting concerned, wondering whether I should break radio or visual silence to question our position. We had about half an hour more of safety on this course at most, and things were getting tense. Had I finally made an error in disagreeing with the flagship, or was he leading us into trouble?

Just before something definite had to be done, we got an emergency radio signal for a 90-degree course turn to port, and we got the hell out of there. Later, in Noumea, checking with other skippers, I learned they had all been facing the same dilemma when the course change came.

This gave me a boost in confidence, and I needed it the next time I had to navigate, since I was on my own. When we left Noumea after a long stay for repairs and resupply, we were assigned to escort

Liberty ship halfway to New Zealand to a point that was considered out of the danger zone. She was then to proceed independently, and we were to break off and head for Brisbane, Australia, to report to the Seventh Fleet.

My point of departure for this solo passage across the Tasman Sea therefore had to be taken from the Liberty's navigation. We were zig-zagging across her bow on a sonar search pattern and had to accept her navigator's word for basic course and speed and position of splitting off. I kept a careful dead reckoning and celestial plot, and everything was falling together nicely until the evening star sights the night before we were to arrive in Brisbane. They made a fine, tight triangle, but it put us over thirty miles away from the position that everything else I had been doing indicated.

Nelson, who usually started the stopwatch at the chronometer for me, had been off duty, and the Yeoman, a precise and careful workman who had little seagoing experience, had done it this time. I figured it must be an error in time to have such a good fix be so far off, and I put the Yeoman through a careful catechism on the steps he had taken. He resented the implication that he had made a mistake, and he went off duty spreading the word "the Captain's lost."

As I checked back on all my figures, the date, the star identification, and every other factor in the sight, I noticed crew members who rarely paid any attention to my navigation work surreptitiously looking over my shoulder and then talking to each other in whispers. I tried not to show any concern, but there definitely was tension building as I continued to work. A subchaser is so small that everything that goes on is common knowledge, like the gossip in a family.

Fortunately, the night was clear and there was a moon, so I took some shots of that body, usually considered unreliable because it moves so fast and because it is hard to get a precise horizon, and they checked with all my other figures. The only thing to do was to make a firm decision and throw out the evening star sights. By now it was almost the end of the midwatch, and I came on deck with a great show of confidence and said, "Cape Moreton Light will be on our port bow within the next ten minutes."

I sat down in what I hoped was a relaxed manner, and just as I did, Oats, who had been qualified as a watch officer and had the deck, said, "There it is."

To my intense joy, the light's beam flashed over the horizon, but instead of jumping up and shouting the way I wanted to, I just accepted the report in routine manner and went below to my sack, leaving orders to be called when we were off the entrance to Moreton Bay. I don't

think it was my imagination that saw a few broad smiles on the faces
of the watch on deck when I went down the ladder to the wardroom.

Enchanted Evening

The stop at Noumea had been helpful, because we had managed to
wangle two new generators out of the supply depot there. It wasn't
hard to convince anyone that we needed them. One look at the hole
in the block of the defunct one and one minute of listening to the
asthmatic wheezings of the one that had been running steadily since
a few days out of Panama were enough to clinch the situation, and
fortunately, there were two new GM 2–71s available.

Our convoy had disbanded, putting us on our own as a Seventh Fleet
vessel, and we were rid of the other SC none too soon. If the Exec
referred to Jane once more as "La Dimock" when we rafted in the
various harbors of our transpacific hegira, I would have puked,
punched him, or thrown him overboard, and Worthy and Pit were
really giving me the business about him.

"We like Jane; she's a geat girl," the routine would go, "but between the 'Garbage Admiral' and this character on the other SC, she
sure has some pretty weird friends."

It wasn't until we got mail after a three-month lapse that she ex-
onerated herself by saying she was "amused to hear you found him a bit
trying, because I certainly did too," and Worthy and Pit had to let up.
The mail also brought news that an addition to the Robinson family
was on the way.

In our enforced stay in Noumea, I made so many visits to the
Operations Office on business that I became quite friendly with the staff
there, and one of them from a shipping family that was also very active
in yachting, and whose piers SCTC used in Miami, Cliff Mallory, and
I had a lot of mutual friends. To break the monotony for me of life on
a ship out of commission in a repair yard, he began including me in
some parties at the Officers' Club.

One day he invited me to join a group of officers at a dinner party that night at an inn out in the country, away from the shambles that had overwhelmed the sleepy little tropical city of Noumea while the American Navy was ensconced en masse. We were to drive some twenty miles out of town in a couple of weapons carriers and eat at a place that was really just a plantation house with one dining room that could be booked for dinner parties by advance reservation.

The hilltop house was a three-sided one, with wings enclosing a courtyard, and the architecture was French provincial, with the dining room in the main section of the house across the end of the courtyard. As we drove in, several little children, who looked like Asians but were dressed in European clothes, scampered out of our way and stood and watched us with big black eyes as we climbed out of the vehicles.

The dining room was plain and spotless with heavy furniture and whitewashed walls, giving onto a balcony that looked down on a stream with a waterwheel churning away, and then a longer vista over the meandering course of the stream through a valley lush in tropical growth. While we had a few drinks, the dinner was cooked on a wood fire in an outdoor kitchen in the courtyard by an Asian woman who looked to be at least eight and three-quarters months pregnant. The food, which she also served, was exotic, delicious, and largely un-dentifiable, and halfway through dinner the proprietor, a handsome, mature Frenchman of imposing stature, came in to greet us with warmth and dignity. The officers based in Noumea all knew him, and we had a pleasant chat with him for a while before he wished us *bon appétit* and went back to his own part of the house.

As the evening wore on, the moon rose over the hill on the other side of the valley, making the stream a silver ribbon and the valley a misty Eden, and the war seemed an impossibility, as far away as the life we'd left behind in the States on the other side of the globe.

It was such a contrast to the rest of my Pacific experiences that it remained strongly in memory, and years later, on meeting Cliff Mallory again in New York, I mentioned what a great evening it had been and how much I had appreciated it.

"Well, you know whose house that was, don't you?" he asked. I had to plead ignorance.

"The planter who owned it was Michener's model for Emile de Becque in *Tales of the South Pacific.*

"—and the kids—"

"—were the ones who bothered Nellie Forbush—"

"—and 'Bloody Mary' cooked the dinner?"

"Right."

Drinking Problems

Brisbane, a city of some 300,000, was like a wonder world after ou months at sea and in the islands, and Worthy, Pit, and I, leaving Boat as officer of the deck, repaired to a restaurant to celebrate the new that had finally filtered through from Jane that, as she put it, a "littl monster" was on the way.

"Let's have a martini," I bravely suggested, looking for the mos civilized symbol I could think of. When they came, they tasted lik poor, weak vermouth, and we politely suggested that we had ordere martinis, not wine. The waitress looked confused, and the proprietress Mrs. Kelly, came bustling over to see what was the matter. I explaine that we were a little disappointed in the martinis.

"And well you should be," she said. "We don't know much abou making drinks like that. What I suggest, love, if you want to have good belt, is to order one of my 'Body Lifters.' Just tell the girl yo want Mrs. Kelly's Body Lifters, and I think you'll be all right."

And we were.

But the crew was having its troubles. I had read in the Brisban paper that an American soldier had gone blind from drinking black market booze he'd bought on the street from someone, and the watc returning from liberty the first night reported that prices were murder ously high and that all they could get most places was beer. As th clincher on how they had been taken, one of them sheepishly showe a bottle of "booze" he'd paid twenty dollars to an Aussie soldier for some alley. It was nothing but brake fluid, and a shot or two of whisk had been floated on top of it so that the first swig tasted all right.

Imagining my crew poisoned and blinded, not to mention swindle if turned loose on their own in a strange city, I worked out a solutic to the problem in a way that Navy Regs hadn't allowed for since befor Josephus Daniels was Secretary of the Navy and banned all liquor c naval vessels. As officers, Worthy, Pit, and I were allowed to go to tl Red Cross headquarters and draw an allotment of so much gin ar brandy per man per month. The fact that we had nowhere legal keep it didn't seem to make any difference.

This we did at a price of about $1.50 a bottle, and we stashed tl boxes, which were hurriedly carried aboard from a Red Cross station wagon, in the shower in the wardroom, which we seldom used at any time and didn't use at all in port, since showers were available at the base.

The drill then was that any man going on liberty could see the captain and, at cost, buy a bottle to take with him. Again, visions of Admiral King's stern face floated by me as I did it, and the crew made a strange sight with their bulky blouses as they hid the stuff under their arms on the way off the base, but they were pathetically grateful and seemed to do well on liberty without getting into trouble, and, since I was never caught, I did not spend the rest of my career at the Naval Prison in Portsmouth, New Hampshire. My conscience was clear.

I had only one complaint. Loomis brought his bottle back with one sip gone from the neck and asked for his money back very apologetically. "It don't taste so good," he said.

The Forward Area

Brisbane was a brief respite before we were off to the islands again. We were ordered north to join the Seventh Fleet Amphibs in New Guinea, and the passage up the inside of the Great Barrier Reef was a tantalizer for someone with dreams of cruising there under sail. From Townsville we took off for romantically named China Strait at the southeast tip of New Guinea and learned quickly about Coral Sea monsoons.

There are two seasons in the Coral Sea, the Northwest Monsoon and the Southeast Monsoon. In either one, the wind blows very hard directly across the course from northern Australian ports to Port Moresby or China Strait, and the deep blue seas are of a size and period that are fiendishly adapted to making an SC roll her guts out.

We made an early-morning landfall on New Guinea, with great blue mountains looming out of the morning mist and waves dashing a fringe of white against the reefs along the bright green vegetation of the foreshore. Seen under different auspices, New Guinea would have had immense impact in its scenic grandeur, and even under the tensions and deprivations of operating in a forward area, its beauty would sometimes strike home with breathtaking effect. Now, however, its major impact was in the fact that this was where the fighting was. Not far up its northeast coast, the Japs were in control, but, over the past year, this was where they had been stopped in their southward advance. A few minor gains had been made in turning them back, but it looked like a long road ahead up its mountainous, mysterious shores.

Amid its reefs and harbors, its palms, dust, mud, and torrential rains, the thought of turning the tide around and actually ending the war seemed the most distant of dreams. Here we were concerned with the immediacy of the next convoy into a combat area, the difficulty of navigating with rudimentary charts through an incredible maze of reefs and islands, the problems of maintenance and supplies, of food, and, most of all, of water. We couldn't make any, there were very few places to take it on until we found supply ships, and we were twenty-eight sweaty men living in very close company.

In hot, blinding sun, the whole crew lined the rail to gaze at the shores of China Strait, narrow between lush green jungle hills. We had an Aussie coast watcher returning to duty from leave as a passenger, and he showed us the sights as we steamed through. In among the palm trees on an island on the east side of the Strait was a straggly collection of low, red-roofed houses, and our friend identified it as Samarai, which he called the "Miami (pronounced Me-ah-me) of New Guinea," bringing a laugh from the SCTC veterans in the crew.

Scrawny, angular, and tough, he had regaled us with tales of the coast watching service and of prewar plantation days in New Guinea, and had been a delight to have aboard, with only one awkward moment. He came on deck one morning indicating that he had bare feet tucked into his shoes.

"It's the strangest thing," he said. "I can't find my socks anywhere." He had been "hot bunking" in the wardroom. "I know I took them off when I turned in, and I just can't seem to locate them."

Pit started to laugh and disappeared below, coming back with socks in his hands in a moment.

"These yours?"

"They certainly are. Where on earth were they?"

It seems Worthy, the champion heavy sleeper of the ship, in staggering out of his sack to take the midwatch, had put on the Aussie's socks and Pit had found them still on Worthy's feet, removing them without so much as a murmur from Worthy, who had once slept through a fire that filled the wardroom with smoke, caused by his hanging his shirt over a desk lamp that was still lit, when he executed one of his better and quicker tumbles into the sack.

It wasn't long before we knew firsthand that this was a combat area. Milne Bay, a deep, almost fjord-like indentation in the southeast

The crew of the 743 in New Guinea

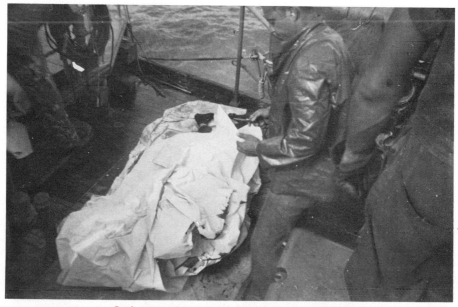

Smitty works over the dead Japanese pilot

tip of New Guinea, just inside China Strait, was the base for our mother ship, but we were not allowed to linger long. The Lae landings on the Huon Peninsula, halfway up the north coast of New Guinea, had recently taken place, and we were needed on resupply convoys from Buna, halfway between Milne Bay and Lae, and the Huon Gulf.

The trip north was an exercise in navigation, as the charts were ancient ones that were obviously inaccurate, and most of the navigating had to be done from specially prepared sailing instructions. One spot, the Tufi leads, was so tricky in its safe course through reefs that there had actually been a range light established on shore. The scenery, again, was magnificent, with the mountainous islands of Normanby, Fergusson, and Goodenough to starboard and the soaring peaks of the big island well inland from green coastal hills on the port hand, but there were certain distractions that kept us from much contemplation of nature.

We had barely arrived at Buna and reported to the senior officer present when we were ordered, with two other SCs, to head north to the Huon Gulf, where the destroyer *Henley* had been torpedoed, and search for survivors. Our passage was in blinding, driving rain that cut visibility more effectively than fog as we charged through the night at flank speed in a tight column, keeping station on a tiny stern light on the vessel ahead. The *Henley* was the only ship lost to a submarine in New Guinea waters, as the Japs used them mostly for resupply of isolated and bypassed bases, seldom attacking shipping. We found an oil slick and a great deal of wreckage, but all her survivors had been picked up by the time we arrived.

Back at Buna a day later, we had an extraordinary panoramic view of a Japanese air raid on landing craft loading for Lae resupply on the beaches at Buna and Oro Bay. Out of a bright sky, clumsy, fixed-wheel dive-bombers known by the code word of Vals swooped in on the beaches, with Zeros hovering overhead as cover. We got under way at General Quarters, but the planes were not after us, and the whole horizon around us was a multi-ring show of planes diving, the black splash of bombs, and the uneven patterns of anti-aircraft puffs.

Suddenly, a new element changed the picture, as swift, twin-tailed Lightnings, P-38s, from nearby Dobodura Airport, buzzed onto the scene in a fury of diving, swooping attacks. The Zeros did not come in to mix it, and the P-38s had repeated clear shots at the Vals that had dropped their bombs and were trying to make a low-level escape back to home airports on New Britain. One by one they were picked off, falling into the sea, as pillars of smoke rose all across the seaward horizon. This was the day that Major Richard Bong, who became one of the country's top aces, had his single biggest score.

Watching this distant drama had been almost like a newsreel, al though the orange disks on the wings of the planes were shockingly real, but now we and our sister ship, SC 742, received radio orders to proceed to downed planes and bring back any survivors or wreckage we could handle to turn over to Intelligence.

We headed at flank speed for the nearest pillar of smoke and, as it died down, came on the body of a pilot floating face down in the water with a few bits of debris around him in the slick made by the plane's crash. Farmer, our Pharmacist's Mate, was the newest man aboard, having just joined in Milne Bay, a lanky, pleasant Texan who had been a dental student, and whose most serious case on board was a hangnail, and I called down to him from the bridge.

"There's a dead body coming alongside. Will you take charge of it, please."

"Who? ME? A dead body?" He looked up incredulously and went hesitatingly to the rail.

At the words "dead body," one crewman went to the opposite rail and was sick, most of the crew hung back fearfully, and about three men, led by Smitty and Songer, with the pharmacist lending a tremulous hand, wrestled the body onto the deck. The top of his head had been shot off.

We picked up a chart with courses marked on it from Rabaul, the big Jap base on New Britain, and lots of Japanese writing on the sides, one "pants leg" cover for a Val wheel, and a couple of other small pieces of wreckage. Radioing this report in, we were told to deliver the body to an LST that was serving as a floating hospital ship for the port and to hold the rest of the material until an Intelligence Officer came for it. The tougher hands in the crew had started to strip the body of personal effects for souvenirs, but I made them leave everything as it was, amid a storm of grumbling.

Later, it turned out that 742 had come upon a pilot in the water who was still alive and who leveled a pistol at the bridge and tried to fire it when they stopped next to him. As he raised it, the Exec had killed him with a burst of machine-gun fire. His body was brought aboard, along with material similar to ours, and the crew was allowed to split it up for souvenirs.

When my crew heard this, they grumbled even harder and complained bitterly about being robbed of their souvenirs, and I felt like a mean parent who makes his kids come home earlier at night than all his friends, but we had turned everything over to Intelligence as instructed.

Eventually, though, the tables were turned when we received a letter of thanks and commendation from Intelligence telling us that valuable information had been gathered from the material we had picked up. First of all, the condition of the pilot, the kind of nutrition he had been receiving, anti-malaria measures, and his clothes and personal effects, were important indications of the general state of things at Rabaul.

In addition, the chart and a small tag of radio frequencies that had been attached to his life jacket gave valuable information that had not been known before. With the help of the new information, a later air raid had been intercepted and dispersed with heavy Japanese plane losses.

After all this, when we rafted with 742 the next time, our crew really went to town on them about their thoughtlessness in keeping souvenirs. When 742 men pooh-poohed the bragging, they were invited aboard and shown the letter posted on our bulletin board.

"You guys have been hindering the war effort," Songer, who had bitched the loudest of all our crew, told them solemnly.

A Fair Bargain

SC 742 and my old SC 699 operated with us frequently, and when we were back in Austrialia on a rest and recreation leave while our ships were being overhauled some months later, I had an odd brush with several SC 742 crew members in the little Queensland town of Innisfail. It was a couple of hours' ride inland from Cairns, the Naval Base where the ships were, by a toonerville trolley–like vehicle called a rail-bus, a regular autobus body with railroad wheels that ran on a track and stopped at every farm gate.

Innisfail was not much of a metropolis, but it was away from the military mess at Cairns and Townsville. It had one hotel and a few pubs, so attractions were at a minimum for sailors on leave, unless they wanted a real rest. I had been getting a few days of that, and was walking down the main—and practically only—street in town one morning, when three men from the 742, spying me from across the street, came over and started walking with me in a great show of friendliness, asking about 743 men and chattering away.

Ordinarily, enlisted men on liberty would quietly stay out of the way of officers whenever they had the chance, and, although I knew these men well, it was highly unusual to have them pay so much attention to me. Then, noticing they were looking nervously over their shoulders, I got a clue when I saw four or five husky-looking "diggers," Aussie soldiers in their distinctive lopsided hats, following us menacingly and purposefully. One had his belt in his hand.

The Aussie military, especially at enlisted level, was not too happy about the American "occupation" of their country. They resented the higher pay, better food, and display of chest ribbons Americans had (Aussies didn't get a ribbon until they were dead and couldn't understand how Americans got one simply by crossing the ocean to get there), and they were particularly unhappy at how Americans had moved in on their women while they were off at the siege of Tobruk, or some such drawn-out ordeal. It looked as though we had a good example of it right here.

Although I was scared stiff, I didn't see how we could keep running from them, so we stopped on a corner until they caught up, and the 742 men huddled behind me.

"What's the matter, Yanks? Have to hide behind an officer's skirts?" the man with the belt sneered.

"What seems to be the trouble, fellows?" I said as pleasantly as I could manage, trying to keep my voice from quaking.

"Tell 'em to come out on their own, sir. It's nothing to you. We just have a little something to discuss with them."

"Well, let's cool it a little, shall we? This is no place to have trouble."

"But they've insulted Australian womanhood, they have," the belt-wielder thundered.

"I'm sure they didn't mean to. Let's call it off, eh? You're sorry, aren't you, fellows?" I said, turning to the trio behind me.

"Yeah, sure, sure. We are."

"Well—all right, but don't let us catch you again—" and amid mutters and grumbles, the Aussie put his belt back on and they walked resentfully away.

"What the hell was that all about?" I laughed at the men in relief.

"We didn't do nothing," they said, wide-eyed and innocent. "We just asked them where we could get a piece of tail for a carton of cigarettes."

Arawe and the "Ghost Ship"

With Lae and the Huon Peninsula secure on the New Guinea side of the Vitiaz Strait that led northward to Dutch New Guinea and the Philippines, the New Britain side also had to be controlled so that American convoys could pass safey through, and so that Rabaul, on the east end of New Britain, and its big concentration of Japanese forces, would be bypassed.

The first part of the operation to take over the western end of New Britain was a landing at Arawe, a small harbor with off-lying islands on the southwest coast of New Britain across from the Huon Peninsula. It had a small airstrip and about five hundred Jap troops defending the harbor, which was an important staging point in the coastal barge traffic that kept bases like Rabaul supplied.

The landing took place December 15, 1943, and our troops got ashore safely on three of the four beaches, with 742 as the control vessel for the landing. A fourth beach, where a pre-dawn assault in rubber boats was to be the first move of the landing, turned into a disaster, as Jap machine-gun emplacements at both ends of the beach were alerted to the approach of the boats by the noise of landing craft moving about offshore, caught the rubber boats in the path of the late moon, and sank them all in a brutal crossfire.

Most of the troops who survived the gunfire would have drowned or been shot in the water, but my old ship, SC 699, with the man who had been third officer when I left her, Jim Forristel, now skipper, moved in close to shore and picked them out of the water despite more machine-gun fire from the beach.

We were assigned to bring the first resupply echelon across from Finschhafen on the Huon Peninsula, arriving in midday the day after the landings. Our convoy consisted of several LCTs, the clumsy 105-foot landing craft that were the workhorses (and stepchildren) of the Amphibs. They needed us as navigational guide and anti-aircraft protection, such as it was. There were also two APCs, the 100-foot wooden transports we'd crossed the Pacific with, and one YMS, a 135-foot minesweeper that was assigned to escort duty like ours, since there were no mines to play with in the area. Ours was the senior vessel of this little armada.

On a bright, warm day of gentle breeze and a cloudless sky, we arrived off the green lumps of the Arawe Islands in the glare of midday and were met by an Army Engineers landing craft at the entrance to the harbor with instructions for bringing the LCTs in. He told them which beaches to head for and asked us to report to the beachmaster who was in a small boat in the inner harbor, to arrange for the return schedule after the LCTs were unloaded. The APCs also came into the harbor to unload, and the YMS was left on patrol outside the harbor mouth.

We were at General Quarters and had been for the last hour of approach, but there had been no sign of enemy activity, and the beachmaster told us that the harbor area was virtually secure and free of any pockets of resistance, but we were told to be alert for sniper fire

There had been no air raids, he said. There was a bustle of action along
the beach and a few small craft were moving around, but there was
almost a feeling of pastoral peace in the bright green of the vegetation
on shore and the glint of midday sun off the water.

I was leaning over the side windscreen of the bridge talking to the
beachmaster when my eye caught a row of splashes zipping toward
us across the water, aimed just forward of the pilothouse. For a weird,
frozen instant, there was no noise with them, and they seemed dis-
embodied and impersonal. Then came the realization "They're shooting
at us!" along with the rush and roar of plane engines and the chatter
of gunfire. After all the months and months of preparation and of
having this moment in the back of your mind as a vague possibility,
here, suddenly, in an instant's perception in noonday sun, was the
shock of reality.

Looking up, I saw orange meatballs flashing by, and then we were
enveloped in deafening sound, as guns went off on board and all over
the harbor, and sharp, nasty bomb blasts cracked alongside. The smoke
of gunfire and its smell followed the noise, adding to the sense of wild
confusion, and there was nothing I could do but watch helplessly.
There was no way to give voice orders to wheel and engine controls,
and I just had to stand and hope the crew would leap to the duties they
had performed so many times in drills.

I did collect my wits enough to look over the ship for damage, and
as far as I could tell she was intact, but my eye caught a large pool
of blood on the midships deck, and, looking forward over the
windscreen, I saw two men down. Kilgore was lying on his back with
not a mark on him, and Gentry was face down, with the middle of
his back completely ripped away. Next to me, Burklow, firing a
.30-caliber on the wing of the bridge, had blood on his hands, and
Wiser, on the other one, had some on his arm. Kilgore and Gentry
were loaders on the 40-mm. gun on the foredeck, but Worthy was
pitching in to work with the gun crew in their place.

It lasted a very few minutes. The planes, Zeros, had come in un-
detected at sea level behind the hills around the harbor, barely
skimming them as they hopped over the trees, strafed the harbor, and
dropped anti-personnel bombs. I had watched one of them absorb fire
from our 20-mm. and .50-caliber guns aft as it swept by close aboard
to port. Then it started leaving a trail of smoke and crashed into the
island across the harbor. At least one other plane went down while I
was watching, and when American P-47s came over a short while
later, there were bursts of fire on them, but fortunately no hits.

The post-gunfire quiet, as the acrid smoke swirled slowly away in
the sunlight on light eddies of breeze, was almost as unnerving as the
attack, and every action carried on as we collected ourselves and sized

The 20-mm. guns and the twin .50-calibers we traded gin for

up the situation was done with a nervous eye and ear cocked to the bright blue menace of the sky.

Kilgore was dead from one tiny bullet hole in his chest, and shrapnel from a daisy-cutter anti-personnel bomb that landed close aboard had killed Gentry. Kittelsen, who had been on a midships 20-mm., had been hit on both inner thighs with a large piece of shrapnel, and it was his blood I had seen on the deck. He was the tallest man on the ship, and anyone of average height standing where he was would have been killed by the hit. Farmer was working on him in the pilothouse to stop the flow of blood. Burklow and Wiser had minor shrapnel ticks that were easily treated, but we were able to transfer Kittelsen and the two bodies to a medical unit on shore. Kilgore, Gentry, and Kittelsen were all under twenty years old.

The ship had minor bullet and shrapnel holes, but the only damage was to a dial in the engine room that was hit by a piece of shrapnel that came through the hull.

From what I could see, the crew had done a magnificent job, with lookouts filling in for the casualties when they were knocked away from their stations. Only one man had folded. O'Hegan, stationed at a machine gun, left it and ran around the deck in a panic, shouting that his gun was jammed, which someone else quickly freed, and ended up actively sick at his stomach, hiding behind a locker. When this was reported to me, I asked him what the matter was, and he

Keeping an anxious sky watch

just groaned and said he was sick. I ordered him to his bunk and told him to stay there until further word, and he wasn't seen for the rest of the trip.

The harbor was no place to stay, and I told the beachmaster, as we passed our casualties over, that we would patrol outside the entrance until the LCTs were unloaded, which they hoped would be sometime that night. Kittelsen, smiling wanly from his stretcher as he was lifted off to the small boat, raised a hand and called, "See you in Finsch." (He eventually rejoined us.)

It was a subdued, shocked crew that turned from unloading the casualties and took up General Quarters stations again while we threaded our way out the harbor entrance to go on patrol offshore where the YMS had been all the time. The night was a long, tense one of standing at Quarters, with turns at sleeping on station, while we waited and waited for the LCTs to appear. Several single planes made bombing runs on the harbor, and one dropped a bomb near us, but we held fire, as it was more likely to reveal our position than to hit a plane at good altitude.

When the late half-moon rose after midnight, anxiety increased in the brighter light, and there was one more bombing run. I would have liked to get the LCTs away before daylight, but they still hadn't appeared when the sky began to brighten in the east, paling the brilliance of the moon. The crew had been almost totally quiet through the night watches, and I was sure that everyone was thinking his own thoughts, as I was, about having been in action for the first time, and about the haphazard fate that lay a foot or two either way in the scattering of shrapnel fragments and the path of machine-gun fire, known in wartime for centuries, but new and real to us on our own deck.

Realizing how useless I had been with all our guns firing, I worked out a system for giving orders to the wheel and controls while we were firing and verbal orders could not be heard through the voice tube. It was so simple that other officers later kidded me about it when I advised them to try it, but it worked. We put a white flag on a swab handle and I would lower the flag over the windscreen to the ports in front of the helmsman when we started firing. If it pointed straight down, he was to hold course. If I moved it over to starboard, he was to put on right standard rudder until I put the flag back amidships, with the same system for a turn to port. The engines were to be kept at standard speed ahead, with the inboard engine slowed on turns according to the control operator's discretion to reduce load on it. If I wanted engines stopped for any reason, I would hang the flag straight down in front of him.

We worked this out during the night watch, and it wasn't long after dawn before we had to use it. The LCTs still hadn't appeared out of the harbor mouth, though if watching eyes had been magnets they would have long since been pulled through, and we viewed the wide, light sky of the new day with a measure of loathing. Never had a bright, clear morning looked so menacing, and soon, low over the water from the direction of Rabaul, we saw them coming, Zeros in several flights of three each. Some veered in over the harbor as we watched tensely, and then one flight banked the other way, wings flashing in the low sunlight, and zoomed right at us. At the same time, lookouts reported Vals overhead, easily identifiable by their fixed wheels.

I put the ship in a fast turn away from the planes to present our biggest volume of firepower. Not satisfied with the capability of our standard complement of three 20-mm.s aft and the 40 forward, I had traded bottles of Aussie gin to flyboys at Dobodura for two twin .50s, now mounted amidships, and the .30s on the wing of the bridge to add volume, and all of them opened up with a great spewing of smoke, lead, and tracers as the planes kept coming in.

One of the most welcome sights I have ever seen in my life was the underside of the wings of those Zeros as they banked away without pressing in. One of them was making smoke and some of the crew swore it crashed near the beach, but we couldn't be sure. Anyway, they left us alone. The Vals were working over the harbor, where a great cloud of smoke from AA fire enveloped the whole area, and in the midst of it we saw an APC, headed out the entrance, take a direct hit.

When the smoke of it cleared, she was already low in the water and she went down rapidly. Small boats were near her to pick up the crew, and we heard later that all had been saved, with some wounded.

Finally, in midmorning, the LCTs lumbered out of the cut and we began the long, slow trip across to New Guinea, relieved to be away from the lethal atmosphere of Arawe and its islands. Never had the crew been so alert at lookout duty, and the wide, clear arc of tropical sky was scanned incessantly all the way across. One man came down with a case of sun blindness so painful that he cried in agony as it hit him, but two days in the crew's quarters in semi-darkness eventually cured it. I had had three hours' sleep on the deck of the bridge in fifty-four hours, and ever since those two days at Arawe I have been constitutionally unable to hear an airplane in the sky without trying to locate it.

O'Hegan, quiet and almost whimpering in manner, had stayed to himself for the crossing, and as soon as we got back to Finschhafen, I called him in and told him I was transferring him to the hospital for observation and that he would not be back aboard. He shrugged and said very little, and absolutely no fuss was made over his departure. He simply packed his gear and left with no goodbyes.

Soon after he had gone, I had a curious visit. Smitty, who had manned his 20-mm. with obvious relish during the air attacks, putting out the greatest volume of fire possible and shouting encouragement to the rest of the crew in the lulls, came to see me, subdued and serious, and asked if we could have a private chat. He had been the most challenging of the bully boys in the crew in his implied opinion of Ivy League–type officers and in his general manner and demeanor, although he had let O'Hegan do the "organizing" and "bargaining" and had not been especially vocal in his disruptions. He was a burly, black-haired ex–football player, hairy, swarthy, and rough-voiced, with dark eyes that could flash in anger or humor, and a smile that was all the more surprising because it was so infrequent.

"Captain, I just want to say something to you," he began quietly. "I know I've been trouble for you, and I know my attitude hasn't been so good. I don't like all this military horseshit, and that's what officers mean to me, but I sort of got the message at Arawe. I want you to know I'm with you 100 percent. This is the best SC in the fleet, and I'm proud to be on her. We know what we're doing, and I'm here to help you in every way I know how."

I don't know whether my surprise or gratitude was greater, and I thanked him as sincerely as I knew how and told him what a great job he had done on his gun. Not a word had been said about O'Hegan, but the knowledge of him was there. We shook hands solemnly, and he gave me a wink as he turned to leave. From then on he stuck to his word, and he was practically a superman in doing all he could to keep the ship going at top level.

After the shock of the deaths had been better absorbed, the crew began to display a quiet pride and a confidence they had never had before, and there was a new sense of unspoken understanding among all of us. Not that there weren't rough moments after that, but a bunch of boys had done some growing up.

None of this made it any more appetizing to get orders on Christmas Eve to take another resupply convoy to Arawe. A convoy in between had been attacked by aircraft, and there were still bombing raids on Arawe almost every night. No one was exactly in a holiday mood as we finished a turkey dinner that sat too heavily in the New Guinea heat (our temperatures were continuously in the eighties and nineties and much hotter in the direct sun), and I couldn't help thinking that this was an even stranger place to be than Jamaica the year before.

It had been amusing to listen to Tokyo Rose's broadcasts during the Arawe campaign. The night after our first visit, she reported the sinking of a large transport (the APC) and severe damage to a cruiser— presumably us, since we were the only other non-Amphib vessel attacked—and we wondered what she would do to make this convoy of an SC, two APCs, and several LCTs sound like the second battle of Midway.

We had reason to be optimistic that we wouldn't get as much attention this time, however, because the major landing of the campaign to control Vitiaz Strait was taking place the next morning, December 26, at Cape Gloucester at the western tip of New Britain. We figured that the Japs would forget Arawe when they saw the large transports, LSTs, destroyers, and support vessels converging on Cape Gloucester, and we knew they knew the movement was on. All night long as we plodded across to Arawe, the horizon to the west of us was pocked with the fitful glare of green flares dropped by search planes tailing the main Gloucester attack force.

"Pretty green Christmas lights! Huh!" one of our crew muttered as he watched them slowly dip toward the sea.

At first light we approached the all too familiar profile of the entrance to Arawe, and the LCTs and APCs went on through the narrow entrance to unload while we began the old patrol routine outside of the islands. We had hardly started when I became aware of a distant drone in the east, and, looking up there, saw a big flight, high in the sky, catching the first rays of a sun that was not yet over the horizon.

All of us scanned the sky anxiously as the drone grew louder, and I began to count planes, intending to make a contact report to Cape Gloucester so that they would be ready. I had passed thirty when the lead one wiggled his wings and began to dive, followed by the flights behind him.

"No! No!" I yelled idiotically. "You don't want us! They're over that way!" meaning the Gloucester force.

They didn't get the message.

Evidently they had thought that the ship movement they had seen during the night was a larger resupply of Arawe and had not yet got the word that Gloucester was the target.

I got out my swab handle and flag, everyone manned guns tensely, and we began eccentric course changes. There was nervous silence except for Smitty, who was certainly alone in his thought, but probably really meant it when he started yelling, "Come on, you bastards! Come on down here! We're ready—"

He didn't have long to wait. Vals started coming at us from two directions, in the most determined dive-bombing attack we had ever been under. I remember looking at the one on our stern as it hurtled closer, its markings and colors becoming ever more distinct, and then looking down at the water and thinking that I didn't really want to be swimming in it a few minutes from now, followed by the reaction that at least I hoped I could swim. The next fleeting thought was that I probably would never get to see my firstborn, and then the Val dropped its bomb and veered away while still off our stern. The bomb made a great splash about a hundred and fifty feet away, and the plane crashed as it neared Pilelo Island off the harbor.

The next threat was on the bow in a gliding approach from another Val with only the slow-firing 40-mm. and the little 30s on the bridge to shoot at it. I switched the flag for a turn in the opposite direction, and this plane turned away too, dropping its bomb too far away. If we hadn't turned, it would have been closer, but they weren't pressing home with real determination.

No more came after us, and, as we anxiously kept a watch for new attacks, we could see that the harbor was under a really heavy one. Plane after plane was diving down through the pall of smoke and dust, probably frustrated at finding so few targets after a big buildup. It was by far the heaviest raid on this minor, ten-day-old operation that had virtually mopped up the situation on land, and it was an awesome sight to see the bombs raining down on the tight little harbor.

Out of the murk of the harbor smoke, an APC, No. 15, could be seen heading for open sea after unloading her troops, and, while we watched, she disappeared completely in a great upheaval of spray and smoke as Vals completing their dive on her flared up and banked away. We thought she'd been hit like the one on the first convoy, and it was a surprise to see her stubby, dark green bow emerge from the mess, headed our way. I put the glasses on her to see if she had been damaged and could see no evidence. It was puzzling, though, to see heads in the water near her. I hadn't seen any smaller landing craft near her when the bombs landed, but I thought there must have been some there that had been sunk, leaving their crews in the water. If this was the case, I couldn't understand why APC 15 was continuing to move away from them.

Her blinker light suddenly stabbed out at us with two words.

"Pick up—" and that was all.

We could now see a great many heads in the water, and APC 15 was almost out to us. I studied her intently and could see no signs of damage, and not one vestige of life on her bridge or decks. Her unmanned guns were swinging idly to her slight roll.

"Do you see anyone?" I asked Nelson, who also had glasses.

"No, sir. I sure don't. Looks like a ghost ship."

The nearest people in the water were not too far ahead of us, and we continued on to them as the APC steamed out to sea on a course that curved slowly to the westward. The first man we came to was the APC's skipper, a j.g. I knew, and we slowed down to pull him aboard while anxious lookouts continued to watch for more planes.

He was pale, shaken, and distraught as he struggled up to the bridge, and right with him in the water and next aboard was a man with a badly damaged eye.

"Can you pick up my men, please, Bill?" the captain gasped. "That's my whole crew in the water ahead of you."

We moved slowly down on the men, who were in small clusters over a stretch of perhaps half a mile in the wake of the APC, and eventually we got them all aboard. About half a dozen were badly injured, and several others were in shock or had smaller wounds. I was too busy conning the ship and trying to keep the propellers away from the men in the water, all the while turning a nervous eye skyward, to ask any questions yet, but it was one of the strangest set of circumstances I'd ever seen. The APC's men were quiet and controlled during the rescue operation, waiting their turn without scrambling, whether wounded or not, except for one obviously uninjured Ensign who kept crying, "Save me, save me." I waved to him reassuringly and left him till last.

Farmer had set up emergency first aid and was tending to the men as they lay on the deck, moving about briskly and efficiently, and suddenly I noticed that Herriott, a radioman who was one of the quietest, most unassuming and low-profile men in the crew, was pitching in with Farmer, applying tourniquets, giving morphine shots, and working with brisk competence. It turned out later that he had been taking pre-med in college when he joined the Navy but had never mentioned it for the record until this emergency came up.

"We have all but three," the skipper reported to me after taking a census of his men and returning to the bridge. "I'm afraid they must be dead on board, because there's nobody else in the water and we all had life jackets on."

"What happened?" I finally had the chance to ask.

"We had bombs straddle us close aboard," he said. "They weren't direct hits, but the one to starboard was close, and their splash washed a big wave across the afterdeck, knocking several of my men over the side. The others saw them go, and I guess they thought we were sinking, because one by one the others jumped in after them. Only Flags and I"—indicating the man with the eye injury— "were on deck, and I couldn't raise the engine room on the voice tube to stop the engine. I guess no one was down there. With the rest of the crew in the water, Flags and I couldn't handle her, so we said 'Abandon ship' to each other and jumped. He sent you a message to pick us up. Did you see it?"

"Yes."

By now, APC 15 had circled back and was not far away, headed inshore, and we could see her starboard side. While her port side had shown no damage, on the other side the whole cabin and many parts of the hull were smashed, with gaping holes, twisted stanchions and gun mounts, and shattered ports. Her circling was tighter now, and she had made another turn and was headed off to the northwest toward uncontrolled territory on the New Britain shore. If she grounded there, her codes and documents could easily fall into Japanese hands.

"I think we'd better get your ship under control before she gets too far away and grounds somewhere where we can't get to her," I said to the captain. "There'd be plenty of trouble if some Japs got hold of her. Do you have enough men who could go with you?"

"I think we can manage with half a dozen or so who aren't injured. How do you think we should do it?"

I wasn't too eager to try to "rope" the runaway, and was just contemplating launching our rubber boat, when a solution appeared in the form of an Army LCVP, a small landing craft that had been sent out to find out what had happened to APC 15. Her coxswain agreed to take the APC's men over to her before taking her injured ashore, and they went aboard quickly. Soon she came to a halt and sat quietly at rest, rolling slightly.

When we eventually came alongside and took her in tow for the return passage—our last, thank God, from Arawe—we learned the rest of her story.

When her crew reboarded, they found two men on deck dead of bomb injuries. The third, very much alive in the engine room, never knew that he had been aboard alone with two corpses for several hours. The bomb damage had severed the voice tube, so he had not heard the captain's orders, and he sat there patiently awaiting relief or some word of what had been happening on deck.

"I knew something must be going on when I heard all that noise up there," he said, "but I figured that somebody would let me know if we were really in trouble. It sure did seem like a long watch."

Tensions

After Arawe and Cape Gloucester, there was a lull in activity and we were sent back to Milne Bay for much needed repairs and maintenance. Leave in Sydney, Australia, was authorized for two-thirds of the crew, and the more sobersided married members stayed aboard, leaving the bachelor party boys free to sample the delights of the Aussie metropolis. As an expectant father, I thought it prudent to stay in New Guinea awaiting word, but there was none while we languished in Milne Bay, and two weeks later we were off to the wars again with the crew full of hilarious tales of Sydney action.

An old school friend, Clayton Jones, was shore-based at Milne Bay, and we had arranged for Jane to send him word of the birth as soon as possible, since he got mail and messages much more quickly than we did while wandering around in a ship. About a week after we'd gone back north, I received a radio message from Clayt that read, "Jane's relief William arrived safely January 29," neatly circumventing the regulations about personal messages on official channels.

The rest and recreation had been important, as the constant confinement to the little world of a small ship in the forward area, with nowhere to go off the ship and the threat of enemy action as an added strain, had obviously been creating tensions in the SC fleet. In the four months we had been there, four SC skippers had breakdowns of varying degrees of seriousness. One man had confined his two junior officers to their quarters, with armed guards on them, while he made the crew dress in whites, unheard-of in New Guinea, and stand repeated inspections. When he began to tell them that he was doing this because President Roosevelt was coming aboard for an official inspection, someone in the crew finally was able to get word to a doctor on a base ship.

Another skipper jumped overboard at night when his ship was on a solo passage from Milne Bay to Buna, intending to commit suicide, but the shock of hitting the water and swallowing some, which made him sick at his stomach, brought him around to a different outlook. He made water wings out of his pants by knotting the bottoms and filling them with air, a method that had been taught to us for possible survival use, and floated on them for several hours. Eventually he was missed on the ship, and she was turned around on her course and reversed it until he was found and picked up, glad to be alive.

I was personally involved in another bizarre case. One of the other SC skippers was having a running battle with his pharmacist's mate, who insisted on his rights under Navy Regs, which provided that pharmacist's mates did not have to stand watch or perform any other duties. He said he wanted to be a surgeon, and doing deck work would damage his hands, and he made a great fuss over standing watch. Most pharmacist's mates, including Farmer on 743, begged to be given something to do to keep them busy, as there were very few medical problems for them to deal with. An occasional Band-Aid was about the most serious treatment they had to hand out, and they all wanted to be a part of the regular ship's routine.

The recalcitrant PhM had been found asleep on sonar watch, and his captain ordered a Deck Court Martial, which could be administered by the skipper unless the accused objected, in which case another officer would have to hear it. Evidently, I had a reputation as an easygoing skipper, and the PhM requested that I be the Deck Court officer. I had never conducted one and had no desire to get mixed up in this one, but I had no way to get out of it, so I studied up on procedures and prepared to run as careful and conscientious a trial as I possibly could. Sleeping on watch in wartime is a serious offense and could even receive the death penalty, so I was going to make sure that the accusation was proved without a doubt, on very strong evidence, divorcing myself from the background of the case and sticking strictly to the specific offense.

After all this, it was something of a shock and letdown to have the PhM plead guilty right off the bat. All I could do then was ask the skipper what punishment he wanted, and we knocked the man down a rate, which could have been accomplished without all the rigmarole of asking me to handle the trial as long as he was going to plead guilty anyway. Evidently, it was just a move in his continuing war of nerves with his skipper, and he ended up the victor in it in the most gruesome sort of denouement.

A week after the trial, the skipper, without saying a word in advance or writing a note or message, got up in the morning, stood in front of the mirror in the wardroom head, put his .45 in his mouth, and pulled the trigger.

A Big Buoy

The post–New Britain lull lasted a couple of months, and then it became obvious that things were stirring again in late March, as rumors began to fly about the next move. We were back in good shape and doing routine convoys up and down the New Guinea coast, and one day at Buna we were commandeered for a special assignment to take Admiral Dan Barbey, head of the Seventh Amphibs, to nearby Oro Bay to inspect a new floating drydock that had just arrived. He came aboard with a couple of aides, and, since it was a calm, pleasant day, we set up chairs on the foredeck for him, with a pitcher of cold lemonade at hand, while we made the run of about ten miles. An aide came up on the bridge, and I inquired if everything was o.k.

"Everything's fine," he said. "This is very nice. There's just one thing. For Christ's sake don't run aground."

As usual, the charts were sketchy, but the route was pretty clear of dangers except for one big unmarked coral head that was not far off our course, and I kept careful bearings to make sure I knew where we were at every instant. As we neared the location of the reef, I noticed a Liberty ship ahead of us with her prop turning, and I said to myself that it was good to have her on our course under the circumstances.

Before long, I realized that we were closing on her much faster than we should have if she were under way, and, sure enough, as we came abeam of her, it was obvious that she wasn't moving at all. She had found the head for me, the biggest "aid to navigation" I'd ever had the benefit of. Admiral Barbey raised his eyebrows and shrugged as we passed the ship.

"Someone's in trouble," was all he said.

The Big Time with Captain Bernie

Rumors changed to definite indications as there was a buildup of landing craft in all New Guinea harbors, and bigger ships, destroyers,
attack transports, and supply ships began to appear in good numbers.
Eventually, we received an operation order, and I was called to a
meeting of ship captains on Admiral Barbey's flagship with one other
SC skipper to go over plans for what turned out to be the Hollandia
landing. It was to be a giant leapfrog up the coast to Dutch New
Guinea, bypassing a big Jap base at Wewak, where 40,000 troops were
stationed—the biggest move yet on the way back to the Philippines.

The other SC skipper and I tried to hide in the back corner of the
flagship wardroom, two j.g.s surrounded by three- and four-stripers, but
there came a moment in the admiral's rundown of the operation order
when he asked, "Where are the SC skippers?"

We meekly put up our hands, and he went on. "I've heard that SCs
don't keep station very well, so I've put your two ships one each on
my bows, five hundred feet away. I don't want you wandering off and
getting lost, so I'm keeping an eye on you, and I want you to be right
there."

We gulped inaudible "yessirs" as the rest of the august gathering
looked around at us and laughed condescendingly. Before the meeting
ended, I was introduced to a four-striper, whom we always referred
to thereafter as Captain Bernie, who was to be the landing control
officer at Hollandia. He was to be with us for a practice landing at
Lae and, for the two to three weeks the operation would take, living
aboard, since SC 743 had been assigned as the control vessel for the
landing waves, marking their line of departure for the beach. Captain
Bernie was a mild, almost Milquetoasty man, small, worried-looking,
and a soft-spoken moustache-chewer. He was not exactly overjoyed
at the prospect of living aboard an SC, but he did his best to adapt and
didn't ask for the impossible. We heard tales of other SCs with four-
stripers living aboard under similar circumstances in which, in one
case, the visitor ousted all the officers from the wardroom and took it
over for himself, and in another the visitor never once went below-

decks for the weeks he was aboard and was never once detected going
to the head in all that time.

Pit slept in an empty bunk in the crew's quarters when we were in
port and hot-bunked with Worthy while we were at sea to make room
for Captain Bernie, and we also did have to arrange for him to have his
meals in the wardroom. The crew was completely in awe of someone
with that many stripes, and they acted as though they were walking on
eggshells for the first few days until they realized that the captain was
not going to eat them alive.

There was a nervousness in dealing with him, and Nelson, who
always had had trouble controlling the giggles, starting with the moment he saw me in my galoshes, was on the bridge with Captain Bernie
and me on watch one night, when, while leaning over the windscreen,
I heard a noise behind me and thought that the captain had said something to me in his usual soft voice. I turned around and cupped an ear
and said something like "Eh?"

Nelson immediately fled the bridge, and I could hear his familiar
cackling giggle down in the pilothouse as he practically went out of
control. When he calmed down and came back a while later, I asked
him what had hit him so funny this time, and he just about died
laughing all over again, with Captain Bernie having gone below unaware
of the furor, before he could tell me the reason. It seems that the noise
the captain had made when I turned around and cupped my ear had
been a good solid fart.

With Captain Bernie aboard, we happened to be the senior vessel
of the convoy that took us on the first stage of the Hollandia operation.
Task groups of landing craft and escorts were staging in from all
New Guinea ports to a rendezvous in the recently captured Admiralty
Islands, northwest of New Britain. From here the main task force
would be formed from all these separate groups for the advance on the
Hollandia area, where it would then split into three separate landing
forces.

We were with some destroyers, LCIs, LSTs, and a couple of large
attack transports, and, though we were very much the smallest ship,
Captain Bernie was senior officer, and Flags and Nelson had the time of
their lives sending orders to all these large ships as we got under way and
formed up off Finschhafen.

The next day, crossing the Bismarck Sea between New Guinea and
the Admiralties, we ran into the roughest weather we had seen in all
our months in New Guinea, where calm seas were the usual rule. We
had a real blow right on the nose, and we all began to make heavy
weather of it as short, steep seas built up, just the wrong size and
period for a stubby-bowed, 110-footer. As we pounded ahead, spray
was flying over the bridge, and every so often green water would

come over the bow as it disappeared into an especially big one.

Captain Bernie had not been on a vessel this small in years, and he stood tensely in the pilothouse, visibly worried about conditions. The seaman on mess duty brought him lunch on one of those indented trays the Navy inflicted on its personnel, and offered to hold it for the captain so that he could hold on with one hand, but the offer was gruffly refused.

"I can handle it, son, don't worry."

He had barely taken hold of the tray when the bow rose on a whopper of a sea and pounded down with a tremendous crash, and tons of solid water burst across the foredeck to break against the pilothouse with a loud crack. To someone not used to head seas in an SC, it sounded as though the house was splitting off. Captain Bernie's tray flew out of his hands and splattered against the overhead, sending his lunch in all directions, some of it back down on him, and he gasped out, "Jesus, Skipper! She won't take it. You better slow her down before she breaks up."

"Yes, sir," I said. "What speed shall we signal to the convoy?"

"Oh—" Light dawned on the captain. The convoy speed was established in the operation order. If we slowed down, everyone else would have to as well. Senior officers were not usually on the smallest vessel. "Well—do you think she can take it, Skipper?"

"She always has before, sir," I answered.

"Well, let's hope she does. We shouldn't make the convoy late."

The storm was a fast-moving one, and we were soon out of it and back in the normal calm conditions. When we arrived in Seeadler Harbor in the Admiralties, one of the largest and best harbors in the world and ideal for collecting this great array of ships, we came alongside a supply ship for our usual refueling and resupplying, and, as we were making fast, a four-striper high on the bridge of the big ship looked down from his perch and spied Captain Bernie on our bridge.

"Hey, Bernie! For God's sake!" he yelled down. "What the hell are you doing on that thing?"

"I've been submerged for twenty-four hours," Bernie yelled back, blowing at his moustache, "that's what I've been doing on this thing."

The Admiralties had been secured except for a few snipers, as the Japs had not staffed the islands heavily despite the capacity of the harbor. It had been a hideout for Count von Luckner in the raider *Seeadler* during World War I and was named for his ship. If it had been in a commercially important area, it would have been one of the world's great harbors. Here it was just another jungle-girt body of water.

We were not bothered by snipers, but there was one incident that had happened shortly before we were there. The son of a nationally famous radio newscaster was on a PT boat that was based there, and one night much of the father's broadcast back in the States, always delivered in highly emotional tones, was a real tearjerker about receiving a message from the Navy Department that his son had been injured. That was true, but the manner in which the injury occurred was not fodder for father on his broadcast. While taking a leak over the side of his PT, the young man had been hit by sniper fire in the hand that was directing the operation. Better that—

After all the elements of the Hollandia operation had gathered in Seeadler, the task force formed up for the final staging, constituting the largest collection of vessels the U.S. Navy had ever assembled in one place up to that time. The basic formation was a giant circle, with Admiral Barbey's destroyer flagship right in the center (and our two SCs five hundred feet off her bows), and the force was so big that we could just see vessels on each perimeter from the center, but the ships on one edge of the circle could not see those on the other one. In addition, out of sight over the horizon astern, but very obviously with us from the evidence of their planes, was a special force of carriers on loan from the Third Fleet. It was the first time since we had come to the Southwest Pacific that we had seen U.S. Navy planes over us. We used our stadimeter constantly and never wavered more than ten feet in our station-keeping.

It so happened that I had been reading an article in the *Atlantic Monthly* by naval historian Fletcher Pratt about the desperate plight of an old four-piper destroyer caught in the Philippines at the time of Pearl Harbor, and the incredible makeshifts that had been used in her lonely flight from the advancing might of the Japanese fleet. To sit on our bridge two years later with that article on my lap and look out across the impressive array of ships spreading from horizon to horizon in every direction was a dramatic tribute to the Navy and to the whole country. This mighty fleet was the best answer possible to all the bitching and griping, and to the obvious minor inefficiencies we'd all had to suffer through. For the first time, I began to feel that the war would be over in the foreseeable future and that we wouldn't be condemned to operate forever in heat, humidity, and dust against the bright green background of New Guinea's hills.

In the midwatch darkness of the next night, the task force split into three landing forces, and we remained with the center one, headed for Humboldt Bay, the main harbor of Hollandia. Admiral Fechtler, later to become Chief of Naval Operations after the war, was in charge of this landing, and it was our job to proceed with the fleet until it reached the fire support and staging areas, and then to continue on by ourselves to take up the control position for the landing waves inside the entrance to the bay, the first vessel to enter the harbor.

Landing craft headed in

We had had continuous trouble with our radar ever since Pit had scrounged it from the supply depot in Key West, until we were given the job of setting up this line of departure. Then, miraculously, we had received the undivided attention of the best radar mechanic in the Southwest Pacific, a civilian attached to the admiral's staff, and we now had the brightest, most accurate screen any SC had ever boasted.

As we left the big ships behind and proceeded on our own, I read it steadily to keep a continuous reading on the range to the beach, and, looking at it, I couldn't help but notice the two big points that jutted out on each side of the entrance to Humboldt Bay. They were high and prominent, and the legend "gun emplacements" was clearly on the charts that came with the operation order. They looked awfully close on the radar screen, and they looked even closer, higher, and more forbidding when I checked them visually on deck. It felt very lonely poking between them by ourselves in the quiet pre-dawn blackness.

We reached our assigned station right on schedule, and, even though I knew the timing and knew it was going to happen, the first barrage of shore fire from the cruiser *Brooklyn* offshore from us in the fire support area almost sent me over the rail as it shattered the stillness. The shells winging shoreward over our heads sounded like runaway subway trains charging down an echoing tunnel, and they also dropped little bits of shrapnel on our decks. A few crew members who had yet to put helmets on, ignoring orders, jammed them on their heads in a panic when the gentle rain of steel splinters began to fall on us.

Our job was to dispatch the waves of landing craft in a carefully timed program. When the first wave was about a hundred yards off the beach, Navy dive-bombers were to drop a row of bombs at the water's edge, and the landing boat coxswains were to head for the middle of the splash in front of them. Presumably any defensive land mines along the beach would be detonated by this countermining, and it would be safe to make a landing through the circle left by the bomb splash. If the boats were too early, they would be hit by the bombs. If they were too late, the splash area would no longer be visible. Each following wave had to be timed at a certain interval so that there would not be a jam-up on the beach. We were to control the waves by hoisting battleship-sized signal flags, either "Afirm" or "Negat," plus the numeral pennant for the wave number.

Everything was going so smoothly that the first wave arrived at the line of departure well ahead of schedule. They charged down on us with their bows in an even line, their troops all crouched low in tense attitudes, rifles poised, and their set, determined faces pale green in jungle camouflage (or was it just the ghostly pre-dawn light combined with the way they felt?). It was indeed a stirring sight, and Captain Bernie was completely carried away by it.

"Look at that!" he cried. "Look at that formation. It's beautiful, beautiful. Hoist Afirm. Hoist Afirm."

"Sir," I said to him as unobtrusively as possible as he continued to exult, "they're five minutes early."

"So what!" he cried happily. "They're in beautiful shape. Send 'em in. We don't want to break up that formation. Hoist Afirm."

"If they're early, they'll run right into the countermining planes," I reminded him. "They could be hit by the bombs."

"Oh, Jesus Christ! Hoist Negat! Hoist Negat!" the captain cried, and the assault boats screamed to a halt opposite us, with the occupants glaring at us with so much hostility we might have been the enemy ourselves. The faces of men who think they may die within the next few minutes are not a study in tranquillity.

From then on, the landing went smoothly, with practically no opposition, as wave after wave of assault boats with combat troops charged by us, followed by more prosaic support craft like LSTs, and then, in midmorning, a cruiser came over the horizon from seaward and dispatched a small boat that paused by us to check on the situation on shore. There, in his familiar floppy cap, was General MacArthur on his way to the obligatory news photo of him wading ashore in knee-deep water. Hollandia was secure.

When the landing wave schedule was complete, we were relieved from our station at the line of departure and told to seek out targets of opportunity along the shore in the western end of the bay. We poked carefully into a cove, not knowing exactly what to look for since no American troops had landed here as yet, and we discovered

The 40-mm. gun crew did its training and pointing manually

some Jap barges camouflaged in trees at the head of the cove. I pointed them out to the 40-mm. crew and told them to commence firing at them when ready. The 40 was manually operated by a pointer and trainer, and it was up to them to sight their target and fire when they were all set, but Captain Bernie touched me on the elbow as they began moving the gun and said, "They're much too low. They'll hit the bow or be in the water at that elevation."

From the bridge it did look as though the gun was pointed at our own deck, an optical illusion we were used to, but I thought it best to let him have his say.

"Elevate," I called to the gun. I got a quizzical look from Connors, the pointer, but the barrel lifted a bit.

"More, more," Captain Bernie kept calling to them. Finally he was satisfied. "That's more like it, Skipper."

"Fire," I said, and the shot arced high in the sky and disappeared over the hill far above the barges.

From then on the crew did its own fire control, and we watched our tracers blast into the barges, kicking up a lot of dust and debris. What good we did we have no idea, but after a while an Army small craft came into the cove and ranged along the shore, and we ceased firing. Soon we had a voice radio message from the boat.

"We have some men on the shore with their hands up. They say they're Sikhs."

"What's the matter with them?" our radioman asked. "What are they sick with?"

"No. Not sick—Sikh. S-I-K-H. Some kind of Indian. They have turbans on. They want to surrender."

I sent the order for them to be brought out under guard, and they turned out to be British Army Sikhs who had been captured near Singapore in the early days of the war and had been used as slave labor ever since. Our shore fire had flushed them out, and they were delighted at being liberated. We sent them on to Army headquarters in the small boat.

Our next orders were to report alongside Admiral Barbey's destroyer, which had come in from checking the other two landing operations that morning at Aitape to the east and Tanahmerah Bay to the west to see how the main landing at Hollandia was doing. Admiral Barbey, Admiral Fechtler, their aides, and several Army officers came aboard 743 for a trip ashore to inspect the main town of Hollandia, which had been declared secure and free of enemy troops an hour or two before, and we nosed into the town cove in the southwest corner of Humboldt Bay.

What had been the town pier showed considerable damage, and wrecked barges and small coastal craft littered the way in. Remembering Admiral Barbey's aversion to running aground, I had the ship at idle ahead on one engine as we threaded through the wrecks toward the pier. If we hit something, we should be able to reverse quickly and avoid damage, but Captain Bernie was fidgeting next to me on the bridge urging me *sotto voce* to speed her up. I pointed out the dangers and he finally subsided, moving down to talk to the admirals.

We nosed in alongside, and the admirals and entourage piled ashore like a bunch of boots on liberty. The town was a shambles of wrecked buildings, hot and dusty and abuzz with flies, and the smell of death filled the still, humid air. A few natives peeked at us cautiously out of the wreckage, and American soldiers could be seen poking casually through the rubble as the inspection party disappeared into the maze of buildings.

They were a while in returning, and when they did, they were in high spirits, lugging packages and bundles and a couple of suitcases. Somewhere they had come across the local bank and found a cache of Japanese occupation money, Dutch guilders printed in Japanese and Dutch, and they were absolutely loaded with stack after stack of it. Someone had also discovered a supply of *sake*, and there were many bottles of that in evidence. Both admirals were laughing and kidding each other about who had more souvenirs, like kids on Halloween trick or treat, and they began to play "last of the big spenders" with the money, passing it out in great fistfuls to everyone in sight. Our crew lined up and made off with a good haul for every man, and the atmosphere was more like a gold rush than an official military inspection as we landed them back on the destroyer.

From there we proceeded to a nighttime patrol station off the entrance to the bay in the area we had been slipping through with such fearful caution less than twenty-four hours before. I went below for some welcome sleep as we resumed a watch-and-watch system with half the crew at skeleton General Quarters, and I was fast asleep in my bunk below when a great *whoomph* of an explosion woke me up. I rushed topsides, calling for General Quarters, to find that the whole landing area that had been receiving a stream of LSTs all day was on fire.

One plane had come over at good altitude and, obviously knowing exactly where it was, had dropped bombs on a Jap ammunition dump located right where all the material had been landed all day. Everything that came ashore had to be taken along the beach for some distance, since there was a swamp directly inshore from the landing area and only one road on firm ground leading inland. This caused a mammoth traffic jam along the beach, and most of the stuff was still piled up there when the ammunition dump exploded (and woke me up five miles away) and started fires in the massed equipment, vehicles, and ammunition. For the rest of the night there was a chain reaction of fires and explosions all along the beach, with sudden bursts of shells winging up like the Fourth of July when American ammunition would be caught in the flames. It was a nightmare of danger and helplessness for the men trapped there, and an uneasy one of listening to explosions and looking for more planes as we continued our patrol. There were no more enemy air attacks, but that one plane had accomplished about as much with one bomb run as several squadrons of bombers could normally hope to do.

In the morning, the beach was a graveyard of charred wreckage, with fires still smoldering, and a whole new convoy of resupply LSTs had arrived at the harbor mouth ready to unload. We had been directed to guide them in, but when they came between those two big capes (that didn't look half as sinister in the sunlight as they had in the darkness before H-hour), it was obvious that they couldn't unload on the original landing beach, and some new area would have to be found.

As we lay idly with no way on, we noticed a small personnel boat charging around among the LSTs with a hatless, gray-haired man shouting at the big, lumbering craft and waving his arms like a crazy man. As the boat came closer, we recognized Admiral Fechtler, and, spying us, he came charging alongside and started to climb aboard. Captain Bernie rushed to the main deck to greet him, and the Admiral shook hands briefly and brushed on by him, headed up the ladder to the bridge with Bernie puffing along in his wake.

As the Admiral stepped up, Captain Bernie, following proper protocol, started to introduce us. I had grabbed a helmet liner as the only head covering, and Worthy and Flags stood stiffly beside me.

"Admiral Fechtler, I think you met Lieutenant Robinson, the skipper, and his Exec, Mr. Adams," Captain Bernie announced.

The Admiral, all business and anxious to get on our radio as a better way to direct traffic than riding around in an open boat, grabbed my hand briskly, and then gave Worthy's the quickest kind of shake. Not really looking at Flags, he put his hand out as he went down the line, but Flags was frozen at attention, not knowing whether to shake, salute, or drop over the side, so the Admiral took his hand away just as Flags came to and put his out. They went through a wonderful Alphonse and Gaston pantomime of this a couple of more times before the Admiral finally reached over, grabbed Flags' limp hand, and practically shook it off. (Later Flags wrote home, "The Admirals are very friendly here. I shook hands with one the other day.")

This little act over with, the Admiral went to work at our voice tube giving orders to our radio to direct the LSTs to a substitute beach, and we charged around the convoy under his orders like a sheep dog herding a flock. The senior officer of the LSTs was on the first one to land, and the Admiral wanted to go alongside her stern and have a conference with him, so we poked slowly in toward the beach with Captain Bernie urging me, as usual, to go faster, and the admiral standing by impatiently. When we were still about fifty feet off the LST's stern, I felt us slide onto the sand and come to a gentle halt, just as the Admiral said, "Closer, Skipper, closer. Bring her alongside."

The temptation was almost too much to say, "We're aground now, sir. How much further aground would you like us to go?" but the Admiral was obviously in no mood for levity from a wise-ass j.g., so I simply reported, "Sorry, sir. We've gone aground."

A small boat took him over to the LST, and we were no longer the senior vessel in the harbor, but we soon had another brass-ferrying assignment. There was a back bay off the main harbor, reached by a narrow channel between two sandspits. We had no charts of this channel or the back bay, only color aerial photos that showed the channel to be quite shallow, perhaps six feet, which was our draft, with good deep water inside and a landing stage at a road that led directly inland to the airport. The Army and Seabees wanted to survey this area for bringing in smaller landing craft, and we were elected to take the party on the trip.

Once again, I had us proceeding at idle ahead on one engine to minimize damage and trouble if we should run aground or hit a sunken barge, and we poked slowly through the pale green of the channel with Boats heaving the lead off our bow. With each throw, the depth came closer and closer to the one-fathom mark, and on one throw the line seemed to stop almost before it had left the bow. Boats looked up at me with wide eyes and reported just over a fathom, so I stopped the engine and let her glide ahead. Captain Bernie was jumping up and down in impatience but not saying anything yet, and the next throw showed deeper water, so we slid across the hump and into the dark blue of the inner bay.

"O.K., Skipper. Open her up," Bernie said. "These officers are in a hurry."

"Sir, I'd rather keep her at idle. If we hit a submerged wreck at speed, we could suffer enough damage to strand us in here, and we'd have a lot of trouble." Captain Bernie and I had had uniformly polite dealings, as he wasn't the blustery type and was actually a very pleasant guy, but it always took some persuading for him to let me do things my way. This time he was pretty insistent.

"Oh, come on, Skipper. It's clear in here. You can see how deep the water is. Let's go. Put her up to standard speed."

Instead of arguing further about lack of charts and unknown obstructions, I decided to hand it to him. "Sir, I will put her up to standard speed if you will allow me to log the fact that it is at your specific orders. I can't take the responsibility on my own." I was as polite as I knew how to be, and all this had been carried on in very gentlemanly fashion.

"Oh, well, Skipper," he chuckled, backing away and waving a hand, 'she's your ship. She's your ship."

The only other excitement before we left Hollandia was the establishment of an Officers' Club in a hastily thrown up shack on some pilings in the bay that had once held some native huts. There wasn't one legal bottle of booze in Hollandia outside of the sick bays of the ships, but somehow, as each small boat disgorged officers at the club, which opened on about D-day-plus-three, the officers, from admirals to ensigns, all had "package goods" tucked under their arm including me, with some of what was left of the Red Cross gin) and the club was in full swing.

Captain Bernie was ordered back to the headquarters ship and left us with obvious relief, but no hard feelings, and a couple of days later we were ordered to take a convoy of empty LSTs back to Finschhafen. The senior vessel was a brand-new destroyer that had just arrived in the area from the builder's yard, captained by a former Annapolis football hero. The convoy was routine and went smoothly, as we ran back down the coast past bypassed Wewak and the string of little volcanic islands whose names have always intrigued me, since they ran like a verse of Jabberwocky nonsense: Blupblup, Bagabag, Karkar, Bam; Vokeo, Kairiru, Mushu, Manam.

Our only problem was with the convoy commander in his bright new tin can. Never before or afterward had we seen such a volume of instructions come over the blinker light. His shutter never stopped, citing conditions of readiness under fleet bulletins we didn't have (shades of the Garbage Admiral), course and speed information every few moments, communications procedures, and just about everything but the Apostles' Creed. Flags and Nelson were physical wrecks from their hours on the light, and the final irony flashed across to us as we disbanded off Finsch. Flags faked active nausea as he read it to me.

"Thank you for your cooperation, my little fellow escort. Well done for keeping up with the big boys!"

PART VI

~~~~~~~~~~

Back Home—
and a Family

Hollandia was in April 1944, and my orders home came in August, with Worthy promoted to skipper. I was to go back to SCTC for a refresher course and reassignment, presumably to a bigger ship, but I was fortunate to be picked for the staff of SCTC, now dignified by the name of Naval Training Center, and the last year of the war was like a premature return to civilian life. We had a house in Miami Beach, and we bought a little seventeen-foot cabin sloop. Before returning to Miami, however, I had some leave coming, and my cousin, Marie Parks, Uncle Billy's daughter, offered us the use of Jetsam at Nantucket.

Headed for the south shore on our bikes

Jane and the peaceful, deserted beach

Peaceful Nantucket

Jane had never been to Nantucket, but she had listened long to my tales of it, and, with Robby parked with grandparents, she was dying to go. It was shortly after the September 1944 hurricane, and the entire island was seared brown as we made the familiar approach through the jetties and around Brant Point in the steamer, but it looked great to me. Jetsam was loaded with nostalgia, and Uncle Billy's absence wasn't as marked as it would normally have been, because Ittldo was closed.

We rented a Baby Rainbow, the first time Jane had ever been in a sailboat (fortunately, it took), went on lobster picnics to Coatue, and wandered around town looking at landmarks. We called on Mag, and Suggie was there too, married to a naval aviator who was an instructor at a training field on Cape Cod, and we had a pleasant reunion reminiscing about the cruise of *Bona*, with a good laugh about Mag's plans for effective chaperonage.

The highlight of Nantucket, though, I kept telling Jane, would be to hire bikes and pedal out to the ocean beach on the deserted south shore somewhere between Surfside and Tom Nevers Head. "We can take a picnic and spread a blanket behind a dune, and there won't be anyone in sight on the beach for as far as we can see in either direction. There's no better way to get away from it all," I said, building up the plans with great anticipation, and everything started out perfectly.

It was a warm, hazy day, with a light southwester riffling over the sun-splashed ocean and a gentle surf curling its patterns onto the sand. The air had the clean, sharp smell of salt as we found a perfect, sheltered spot between two dunes and spread our blanket.

We had barely stretched out in the sun with a great sighs of delight when the peace was shattered by the all too familiar whine of a descending dive-bomber very close to us. As the screeching *wheeee* increased in frenzy, I instinctively covered my head with my hands and rolled for the nearest patch of beach grass.

There was, as we found out later from Suggie's husband, a dive-bombing training range on Tom Nevers Head, just to the east of our cozy spot in the dunes. We had our picnic, but, as the planes kept coming in, the peaceful day at the beach was not too great a success.

Hurricane to Hurricane

After the leave, we drove to Miami in Jane's good old Hudson, arriving in the middle of a hurricane at the house we had arranged to rent through friends, and, a year later, with VJ-day history and my separation papers in hand, another hurricane threatened to louse up our departure.

We had bought the seventeen-foot Bahamian-type sloop as soon as my assignment to teach at NTC was official, assuring us of a good stay in Miami, and we had a great time with her, exploring Biscayne Bay and the uninhabited islands of Virginia Key and Key Biscayne. The boat had a low-aspect Bahamian rig, a little cabin where Robby could be put down for a nap if he ever flagged (which was seldom), and a one-lung Palmer inboard engine that was so simple even I could understand it.

We named her by a complicated process. While we were based in Milne Bay, a bunch of SC skippers used to take beer or booze, which we could buy on shore but could not drink legally aboard, over to a little island, meeting by dinghy in the late afternoon at what we had dubbed the Officers' Club, a fallen log on the beach. Someone told me that it was a tradition in New Guinea to plant a tree for each new child, so we found a sprouting coconut and buried it with due ceremony, drenching it with beer and placing a rough-carved sign reading "The Monster" over it in honor of Jane's news.

I wanted to name our boat for this island, but I couldn't find a name for it on the chart of Milne Bay I'd brought home. Near it, however, the Maiwara River, whose thickly jungled banks we had explored several times by dinghy, entered Milne Bay, and I figured the "Monster" coconut might have come down it before beaching on the island, so we named her *Maiwara*, and of course everyone thought it was because Jane's name was Mae and mine was Warren.

Now, with return to civilian life at hand, I wanted to hold on to her very much, but there was no way to bring her north. Jane was

Maiwara in Biscayne Bay

pregnant again (with Martha), and the only sensible thing to do was sell *Maiwara*. I advertised her and quickly developed a buyer. He was to take delivery on a Saturday, but, on Friday night, a hurricane was howling its way up the Gulf Stream, headed right for us.

"She's all yours," the buyer informed me cheerfully when I checked with him Friday night. "I'll see you next weekend." That meant we would have about a day to close the deal before we had to head for New Jersey.

Maiwara was berthed in the Collins Canal, a narrow waterway that leads into Miami Beach from Biscayne Bay alongside the Venetian Causeway, and it did seem like a good protected spot. In a frantic evening of activity, as the wind and rain grew steadily stronger, with that peculiar, heavily ominous feeling of foreboding that precedes a hurricane, I moored her to trees on both sides of the canal in a cat's cradle of lines that would have held the *Missouri*. She was not insured, and this web of ropes was the only insurance I could provide at this hour.

With everything as secure as possible, I repaired to the house to ride it out by making milk punch out of all the milk in the refrigerator, since the electricity was already off. There wasn't anything we could do any more, and it was a painless way of making the hours pass as the wet wind howled and the palm trees bent to the ground, lashing furiously.

The next morning, in the calm, moist aftermath, threading through the downed trees and fallen wires, I made my nervous way to the Collins Canal, and there was the wonderful sight of *Maiwara*, riding jauntily to her burden of lines, covered in blown palm fronds and odd bits of debris, but completely unharmed.

The buyer was good to his word and took her over the following weekend for fifty dollars more than the five hundred and fifty dollars I had paid for her (probably one of the first evidences of the inflation that hasn't stopped since), a happy ending to a happy episode. It was fun to own a boat, and I didn't want to be without one for very long.

A Sad Lesson

It took a few years to get another *Maiwara*. Moving to Rumson, on the North Jersey coast, settling into a small house for two years and then a larger waterfront one on the Shrewsbury River, and attending to the needs of a growing family—Robby, Martha, and then Alice as a new baby—we weren't able to swing anything more than a little sailing pram until 1948. Then I found a far from new clinker-built day sailer, eighteen feet, with a cuddy cabin and a small air-cooled auxiliary in the cockpit. She looked ideal for our type of family.

Noises were made by some friends about taking such young children sailing, but it had never crossed my mind that there would be any problem. Then, very soon after we got the boat, a friend and I were in her at the Atlantic Highlands Municipal Marina. We had just tied up and were phoning home for a ride. The booth was just across the street from the marina slips, and I noticed, as I came out of the booth, that people were running out on the pier and pointing to a certain spot, and we could hear shouts for help.

We ran out too, and saw a middle-aged woman treading water in the slip and crying out.

"He's right down here," she said. "A boy fell in."

We both stripped quickly to our shorts and dived in, and the next few minutes were about as desperately unpleasant as any I have ever spent. We gathered from the breathless woman that she had seen a young boy ride off the pier on a bike and disappear under the water, and she had tried to do something about it but wasn't a strong enough swimmer. When we arrived, he had been under for four or five minutes.

We surface-dived down in about ten feet of water that was dim and murky, with almost no visibility, groping along the bottom trying to find him and filled with the mixed emotions of wanting so much to rescue him clashing with the instinctive revulsion against suddenly touching a limp body. We kept at it for perhaps ten minutes, with no success, until the first-aid squad arrived with professional rescue equipment, and the body was eventually found wedged under the hull of a boat, where he had come up after belatedly freeing himself from the bike.

This terrifying experience was the most forceful kind of reminder about the problem of the safety of children in boating, and I went home in a funk of depression determined to have ours take swimming lessons right away, along with a new respect for the necessity for life jackets and a careful routine. Whenever I hear of children drowning, the memory of groping along the murky bottom comes back to haunt me.

Who Threw the Overalls —

This *Maiwara* was great for family outings, as the cockpit was large, and the kids could also play house in the cuddy cabin when they became bored with things on deck. We never sailed for any length of time without stopping at an island to roast marshmallows or dig sand castles, since attention spans were short.

It was a problem for Jane to bring everything aboard that was needed to keep three children happy, and by the time she had organized all the life jackets, sand pails, picnic supplies, marshmallow forks, fishlines, crab nets, picture books, sweaters, swimming trunks, sneakers, diapers for Alice, ice chest, beers, Kool-Aid, and Lord knows what else, a day could be half shot before we were able to leave home.

The air-cooled inboard was a great addition, meaning that we were not dependent on vagaries of wind and/or tide for getting home when everyone was tired and had had enough, but it had not been installed very artfully, as we were to learn all too well. It had been open in the cockpit, with just a canvas cover, when I bought the boat, and I had

The first family yacht after the war—an
eight-foot pram

made an engine box that served as a table to cover it, but of course the
forward end had to be open to allow air to get to the engine, leaving
the hot metal exposed there to the poking of small fingers. There were,
unhappily, a few contacts.

The shaft was also uncovered, running through the cockpit to a
bearing aft, and we always put the kids in the cuddy or made them sit
still on the seats when the engine was running. I had plans for a cover
for the shaft, but they had not yet been implemented when we started
out one day on an outing that seemed more disorganized than ever in
the collection of kids, gear, and clothing, plus our dachshund, who
hated the boat but hated more to be left behind.

Impatiently, I had started the motor, which was direct drive, with
no gear, so I had to hold the boat alongside the bulkhead to keep her
from moving while the shaft turned. Jane kept having to go back to
the house for something she'd forgotten, and the last item was a pair
of blue jeans for Robby. She came dashing out with them, as I kept
telling her to hurry, and threw them into the cockpit before jumping
aboard herself.

Our New Jersey *Maiwara* (with temporarily borrowed Comet sail)

The open propeller shaft in the cockpit was a hazard

The younger generation takes over

As can be imagined, they fell right on the turning shaft and immediately wrapped around it in a grinding tangle. By the time we had worked what was left of the jeans loose, it was too late to go out, but it did give me the impetus to put a box over the open shaft.

Happy Fourth of July

July 4, 1949, was hot. The wind was in the west, blowing off a sun-baked continent like a blast from a furnace, as Robby and I sailed *Maiwara* over to the Shrewsbury Sailing and Yacht Club on the south shore of the shallow, two-by-three-mile tidal flat that was our home body of water. There was to be the dedication of the new SSYC clubhouse that afternoon, and I was invited as a friend of some of the members and also as the boating columnist of the *Newark Evening News*, which I had been for two years.

My first job out of the Navy was public relations manager of the Elco Yacht Division of Electric Boat Company in Bayonne, New Jersey, but it soon became obvious that Elco, which had turned out hundreds of PT boats in World War II, wasn't going to make it in peacetime cabin cruiser construction, and I was lucky to find a spot at the *News*, eventually becoming a full-fledged sportswriter from an entree as a boat columnist.

The SSYC dedication took place on the open porch of the new clubhouse, and a crowd of members and special guests gathered in the stifling blaze of the sun to listen to an oration by the local congressman. He was an old warhorse of many years' service, who took the opportunity to invoke every cliché on motherhood, the flag, apple pie, and the glorious heritage of American seafaring, while we sat and sweltered.

Those of us who had come by boat began to cast an eye on a bank of purple-black clouds building in the northwest, as the speech droned on. In later years, when we came to know the river well, we learned that this was the "danger bearing" for squalls. When clouds pile up over Tower Hill in Red Bank, we are sure to catch it on the Shrewsbury.

The black buildup rose higher, while rumbles of thunder muttered behind it, until it finally covered the sun. The speaker, still in full flower, paused for effect and tried for a laugh by saying "Now there's a nice Republican cloud to cool us off," but he didn't get the message the clouds were sending to the rest of us and kept right on in praise of motherhood. By the time he finished, we could see a line of foam advancing across the river from the north ahead of dark wind streaks, which would make the club waterfront a lee shore, and the boat-owners didn't even pause to applaud. We leaped from our chairs and dashed madly for the pier to get the boats out of there and to some better protected spot before the squall hit. They were all jumbled together in a rather small area and would be bashing into each other if caught there.

We didn't make it.

The line squall walloped us hard, and the wind switched from a moderate westerly to a 60-knot-plus screamer from the north in fifteen seconds. I was just casting *Maiwara* off from the pier when it hit, and I didn't even get a chance to start the motor before she was blown against a muddy sedge bank to leeward, with waves breaking sheets of spray over her as the short expanse of open water in front of the club kicked up a vicious chop in no time at all. Fortunately, Jane, who had driven over, had the children inside the clubhouse.

I was still trying to start the engine, hoping to slug my way out of there and not feeling as though I was in too much trouble, when two large teen-agers clumped aboard with all the grace of Newfoundland puppies, bent on trying to help me. One landed on the engine box and smashed it, and the other did the same to my new shaft cover, effectively jamming the shaft. Somehow they also managed to let the halyards go up the mast before I could convince them I didn't need help and to please go look for someone else who did.

The waves were really slapping the boat around now, and, since my "helpers" had deprived her of all her forms of locomotion, I decided the best move was to tow her by hand to a little cove behind a bulkhead a few hundred feet to the west. Putting the painter over my shoulder like a lead rein to a horse, I started slogging my way through the chest-deep water, with waves breaking in my face, and finally made it to the lee of the bulkhead, where I tied her up.

The storm, the same one that capsized hundreds of boats in one swoop in western Long Island Sound that day, had been a vicious one of blinding torrents of rain and a wild display of lightning, but now it had moved on by, leaving persistent rain and a lessening breeze. I sat in *Maiwara*'s cockpit contemplating the wreckage of my engine box and shaft cover, and figured the only way I could get her out of there was to sail, so the halyard ends would have to be retrieved from up the mast.

I was never much for climbing things like tree trunks or ropes, but the halyards were dangling there, tantalizingly close to retrieval, and I made the optimistic decision to shinny up the mast to grab them.

I took a good grip and heaved myself up about half a length with the first effort, but I was wet, my feet were wet, and the mast was wet, and I simply slid back down like someone on a greased pole. Unfortunately, my foot slid right onto the upper prong of the mainsheet cleat on the side of the mast and was impaled there almost an inch deep.

When Jane and friends found me after the storm had cleared, I was sitting there like a wounded puppy with my foot in my lap, and a month on a cane was a good reminder that I wasn't built to shinny up masts.

Hurricane Alley

We thought we had left hurricanes behind in Florida, but no sooner did we buy a waterfront house in New Jersey than the Jersey coast seemed to become the center of a new Hurricane Alley. All during the 1950s hurricanes slashed up the coast and battered our area, bypassing Florida, and we began to take it personally.

Actually, the hurricanes with girls' names, while they frightened us and gave us some fairly good goings over, were never as bad as some unnamed storms that developed near the Carolinas and pounced on us overnight. The tropical storms would be tracked for days on end as they curved out of the Caribbean and started northward, and we knew all about Carol, Hazel, Edna, Donna, and the rest by the time they arrived. We had boats all secure, cars moved to high ground, and the house battened down and ready.

It was those sneaky coastal storms that would catch us unawares. The first was the Saturday of Thanksgiving weekend in 1950, when we had been in our house two years. The house had been built before 1910, and, since it was on low ground, we asked some of the old-timers in the neighborhood if it had ever been flooded.

Old Mr. Harvey, who was in his nineties, said that he thought the only time was the 1914 storm, the worst that ever hit Sea Bright, the beach resort right across from our spot on the Rumson side of the

Shrewsbury. "That's the one that took the Octagon Hotel, biggest one on the oceanfront, and washed it clean away," he said. "That was bad over here, and I think all the houses were flooded, but there's never been another one like it since. The '38 and '44 hurricanes weren't anything like that one."

This was encouraging, but I sure didn't like the look of things when I got up that Saturday morning. There had been no prediction, but the wind had been shaking the house with violent gusts during the night, and the flood tide outside our front door was shouldering in like a millrace. With hours to go to high tide, the water was already seeping into the yard. I was supposed to cover the Rutgers-Colgate football game that day, and it was a relief to get word from the paper that the game had been canceled because of high water flooding the bridges over the Raritan River between New Brunswick and the stadium. Soon after that, our phone went out.

I moved our car up the street to higher ground and then came back to tend to our dinghy and sailing pram, floating them into the yard and tying them to trees. *Maiwara* was on her mooring in front of the house, and the rest of the day was spent in anxiously, and helplessly, watching the water fill our yard and gradually creep up the porch steps toward the floor level, and also watching *Maiwara's* gyrations in amazement.

She was balanced between wind and tide, and first one, then the other, force would be dominant as she sashayed back and forth. Time and again she would fetch up at the end of her chain and hang there as a heavy gust would hit her, and she would almost capsize from the weight of wind against her slender mast, but she fought it out for hours. She was also filling with rain as well, however, and finally she became sluggish, and one big gust that hit her forced her leeward rail under and she kept on going in a slow-motion capsize until there was nothing left but a few feet of the side of her hull above water. Then that disappeared, and I thought she had sunk or broken loose.

Meanwhile, we watched the water's rise with bated breath, gauging it against the time for the tide to turn. It was almost to the top of the top step when we noticed the nun buoy in front of the house straighten up, then begin to bend the other way, as the ebb began. In the yard, leaves, twigs, and bits of driftwood that had been flowing in, slowly took a reverse course out toward the river. The water was actually lapping at the bottom of the boards of the living-room floor when this change became noticeable, and a few minutes later it was apparent that it was beginning to go down. The wind was more around to the northwest now, and the storm was definitely going by.

I put on waders and went out to check the car. I had moved it far enough, I thought, and, a block away, it had been just beyond the tide

Our yard taken over by a high tide

line. I turned on the radio for news of the storm, and, twiddling the dial, was amazed to hear the end of the Princeton-Dartmouth game, which had been played despite the storm. Princeton, finishing an unbeaten season, had managed to beat Dartmouth even though punts blew back over kickers' heads and water was inches deep on the field.

I sloshed down to the riverfront for signs of *Maiwara* and found her just awash fetched up against a big bulkhead at the end of the cross street just north of us. When she sank, the force of the ebb tide had moved her, mooring and all, downstream until she hit the bulkhead. She was amazingly undamaged, but the air-cooled engine had definitely had it. As the tide went out, I was able to get aboard and pump her out, and eventually got her back safely to our beach. From then on we had outboards on a bracket for power.

Everyone in the neighborhood was sure that this was the worst we'd ever see. Some houses had been flooded farther down the street, but Mr. Harvey and his cohorts all said that we would be safe forever if the flood had missed us.

This gave us a sense of security for three years. Then, on November 7, 1953, I was in New York for a sports banquet and arrived home on the midnight train through a wild, blustery night of hurricane force winds and unseasonable snow, a thick, wet cloud of it slanting horizontally. As I drove the car, the first new one I'd ever owned and had had for four months, into the garage, I was relieved to see that the water was only ankle-deep in the yard. I took off my shoes and waded through the icy slush to the house and put on the waders to tend to the boats. I didn't take time to check the tide table, and I didn't realize that it was actually dead low tide at the time.

Maiwara was at the bulkhead, moored fore and aft, and I managed to float her through the gap in it and into the yard, tying her to a tree, then secured the small boats, and finally, shivering cold, collapsed into bed about 0300. Sleep was difficult, as the wind was the strongest I'd ever felt at any time. It buffeted the house with great shuddering blasts amid a deep, hollow roaring high above us that sounded like a tunnel full of subway trains. The house shook until I was sure it couldn't take it.

Huddled together in fright, Jane and I finally did drop off, and I woke with a sudden start to gray morning light and absolute stillness. The wind had stopped completely, and I hopped out of bed to check the situation. Looking out the window to the back yard, I could see that the water was extremely high, and my first reaction was that the car had to be moved. I dashed downstairs and stepped right into a foot of water over the dining-room floor at the foot of the stairs.

What a shock and what a mess! Looking in the living room, with the bottom shelf of the bookcases all awash, I could see that the front door out to the river yard was open, and I sloshed out to close it, in one of the more useless gestures of all time. There was a small "surf" on the water's surface, coming through the open door in little wavelets that broke against the inside wall. In an armchair, curled up and fast asleep with the water moving by a few inches below them, were our two cats.

Needless to say, the car was beyond moving, as the water was over the dashboard. We had it dried out and repaired eventually, but it never really recovered.

The calm that had awakened me was the eye of the storm, another unpredicted one that had formed over the Carolinas the day before, and the wind was soon howling just as heavily from the southwest, but our worst was over.

We set about moving furniture and doing what we could to rescue undamaged things, sloshing around in boots. I tried the phone in a vain hope that I might get through to Jane's aunt, who lived nearby on higher ground, to ask if we could bring the children over when we could get them out, but I couldn't get through. The phone was not dead. There was a lot of buzzing and static, but I couldn't place a call.

It was really a shock, then, as we continued wading around the rooms, to hear an odd gurgling sort of ringing noise and to realize that the phone box, which was underwater, was actually ringing. I dashed to it with a great feeling of drama that at last we had contact with the outside world.

"Hello. Hello!" I said, expecting a relative, or maybe the police asking if we needed help.

"Bill," a man's voice said. "This is Russ Garvin. There's some school-board business I'd like to discuss with you if you have a minute."

"School board!" I exploded. Russ and I were fellow members of the high school board. He lived about three miles inland from us.

"Yes. School board. What's the matter with that?"

"Well, Russ, I'm up to my ass in river water flooding my house, and I guess I have a few other things on my mind," I said.

"Gee. I had no idea, but I did think the wind was strong last night," he said. I said would check with him later, refused his offer of help, and hung up shaking my head.

It took a couple of months to clean up, dry out, and refurbish—all without insurance, of course—and we then developed an "abandon house" drill to move the car, roll up carpets, lift books and furniture, disconnect the furnace motor, and other emergency measures.

If the water rose higher than the middle step with the tide still on the rise, we pushed the "alarm" and went to work.

Jane became very good at it, fortunately, because I was away the only two times the drill was needed. In hurricane Donna, I was on a press junket at Lookout Mountain, Tennessee, but Jane and the kids got everything ready, and the water just seeped and sloshed at the boards of the ground floor without actually coming in.

In March 1962, I was in Australia checking up on their America's Cup preparations when the great Atlantic storm that created record high tides devastated the east coast, particularly the Jersey coast and Long Island. A storm circulation that covered the whole ocean between Europe and America pumped storm winds and tides for three days on top of the highest perigee moon tide of the year. Our house was flooded on two successive tides, but Jane and the girls had everything ready and the damage was slight.

I was staying at the Royal Sydney Yacht Squadron, and I came back from a day of sailing with the Aussie Twelves to find a message to call back on an overseas call. My imagination ran riot while waiting for the call to go through, but Jane's voice was cheerful when she finally came on the line.

"Why are you calling?" I asked.

"We didn't want you to worry about us," Jane said.

"Well, that's nice, but I haven't."

"I thought you might see that we were a disaster area and get worried, but we're o.k.," and she went on to tell what had happened. I didn't waste too much time explaining that Sydney papers weren't that concerned with Sea Bright, New Jersey, being a disaster area, and in fact had only had a one-paragraph mention of the storm, mostly as it affected shipping in the English Channel, but we had a pretty good phone bill anyway by the time I finished talking to both girls. It was 3 A.M. in Rumson and they were all three in bed together to keep warm.

We had no more floods before we sold the house in 1966. We had paid $13,500 for it and, after eighteen years, only got $18,500 for it because the area was known for floods. It has not been flooded since, and in 1976 it came on the market at $49,900, described as a "water-front bargain."

A Neat Crew

Robby really took to sailing, and by the time he was nine, I felt he was ready for his own boat. Sportswriters were not exactly in the fleet-owning league, but I scouted around and located a Wood Pussy, the kind of thirteen-and-a-half-foot catboat that was raced at SSYC, which we had since joined despite the dedication disaster. It was for sale for a hundred dollars, minus a boom and a sail, and the hull was old and dried out, but it was the best we could do.

One of our good friends, Bourne Ruthrauff, who was active in the fleet, had just bought a new sail, and he donated his old one to us. I scrounged an iceboat boom from a boatyard, and, after some caulking and painting, we were in business. Everyone in the fleet had been very helpful, as they were trying to build up the fleet, and we received all sorts of encouragement. It was Robby's boat, but the routine was that I would be the skipper in the club championship series, with him as crew, but he would sail her with an adult crew when I had to be away covering some other regatta, and he would also sail her in the junior series.

In our first race, we happened to get second place, and suddenly all our kind friends were coming by to tell us that we were illegal without black bands on mast and boom, that our boom didn't look regulation (very true), plus other bits of legal information. But they didn't throw us out.

One day when I had to be away, I asked a friend of mine, who had some sailing experience but was no expert, to crew for Robby, as I felt there should be an adult in the boat in the championship series. I came home to find that they had done respectably, with a third place in the race, and I asked Robby how my friend had been as crew.

"Oh, he was o.k.," Rob said, but I detected a certain lack of enthusiasm. I could see that there was that situation where an adult had been a problem, but he didn't want to say so.

The hundred-dollar Wood Pussy

"Did you have trouble with him?"

"Not too much."

"Well, what was it?"

"Oh, it wasn't much. It was just that the telltale was tangled around the shroud once when we rounded a mark, and I asked him to free it. He just stood up and tore it off and threw it away," Robby said, his voice cracking in incredulity.

"Why did he do that?" I asked, laughing.

"He said he thought that a telltale was like an Irish pennant and that I wanted him to get rid of it."

Advice to the Skipper

One of the traditions at SSYC was an annual Ladies' Day Race. It was a fine tradition, but it was also difficult to find enough ladies willing to brave the challenge. For example, Jane had adapted to sailing very happily as passenger and crew, and she loved it as a venue for family outings and cruises, but she had no confidence in her own ability at the helm. (Twenty years later, she gained a measure of fame as the first adult ever to capsize a Turnabout during a Ladies' Race.)

The first time she tried to bring *Maiwara* over to SSYC on her own with the kids aboard, she had managed to run down a rental rowboat anchored for crabbing, and her own mortification wasn't helped when a woman in the rowboat started to scream that they were sinking and that she couldn't swim. Fortunately, the former wasn't true, and Jane considerably shaken, continued on her way, leaving behind the words "If there's any damage, tell them Bill Robinson of the *Newark News* did it."

Somehow, we did manage to talk her into entering the Ladies' Day Race with Rob as crew, and he, at age nine, took it extremely seriously. He did his best to keep quiet and let his mother sail her own race, but the situation got too much for him as the race progressed, and he began to coach her around the course. She took this moderately well, but there was a conflict between her desire to figure it out for herself and her need to be helped.

They were on the last windward leg, still in contention for a good finish (the level of competition was not too proficient), and Robby realized she was sailing into a bad header.

"You better come about, Mom," he said.

Jane took a while to ponder this advice, but she wasn't sure why he had given it, so she didn't react.

"Mother," Robby said, his voice rising, "you should come about."

Still Jane didn't react, as she felt she should see where the other boats were and not do anything too hastily, and this was too much for Rob.

Bursting into tears, he screamed at her, "God dammit, Mother. COME ABOUT."

She finally did, but she didn't win.

My Wife, the Champion

Jane had more troubles with Ladies' Day. A few years later, I was in charge of the event, and again the entry list was a bit small, so, at the last minute, I persuaded Jane to enter. It was much against her will, but she did it to be a good sport and a helpful wife. She could no longer have Robby to talk her around the course, with or without tears, as a rule had been passed that no males were allowed in the boats, but, with another mother recruited off the club porch, she boarded a Wood Pussy and went out to the line.

Approaching the windward mark, she was actually in second place. This was before the rule that marks could be rerounded if you happened to hit one, and the lead boat, sailed by the club's top lady skipper, did just that and fouled out. Suddenly, Jane found herself in the lead, and she managed to survive the onslaught of panic ("There's no one to follow!") and stay ahead for the rest of the race.

The gun, so welcome a sound to most competitive sailors, just meant release rather than triumph to her, and she collapsed on the floorboards with a great sigh of relief. When the boats all gathered back at the club, everyone called out congratulations.

"Nice going, Jane," they said, "and good luck in the Adams Cup."

"Adams Cup!" she exploded. "What do you mean?"

I had neglected to mention that the race had been designated that year as the club's elimination to pick our representative in the North Jersey Yacht Racing Association championship, the first step toward the women's national championship, known as the Adams Cup. I had had enough trouble just getting her to enter and I hadn't wanted to muddy the waters with this extra bit of information, since I didn't think it would ever become an issue. There was usually a separate Adams Cup elimination, but it had not been held this year.

Again it took some persuading, but once more she was a good sport, however reluctant. It meant that she had to sail in Jet 14s, light, zippy little planing sloops, far different from the staid displacement Wood Pussies she was used to, on the wide open waters of Raritan Bay against such well-known competitors as June Methot, who often made it to the finals and won the Adams Cup one year, and Rose Booz, a veteran campaigner.

"They know the rules," Jane wailed, "and I sure don't," but Martha, who had been racing for several years and did know them, said she would crew, and off to Raritan Bay they went.

Jane didn't win, but she wasn't last.

"It was fun in a way," she admitted, "but every time I got near June or Rose, they'd yell something like 'buoy room' or 'overlap' at me, and I just got out of their way."

How to Goof

Jane was not the only Ladies' Day champion in the family. Martha and her friend Kitty Gross, young teen-agers at the time, succumbed to the same blandishments of Father–Race Committee Chairman, which seemed to have to pull every year, and said they would help swell the fleet by entering, with Martha as skipper. Jane had made her yearly sacrifice and was also sailing.

When the starting gun went off, however, with all the mothers on starboard tack, taking each other's wind, pinching, and ending up in stays in a barely moving gaggle of badly sailed Wood Pussies, Martha and Kitty were a hundred yards or more from the line, yakking with some boys in a Boston Whaler. Eventually they sailed over to the line giggling, and Martha called to me.

"We goofed, Daddy. Sorry."

"That's no excuse," I said sternly. "You promised to race, and you can't back out now. You have to go ahead and sail around the course. That will teach them a lesson, I thought, as they shrugged, still gig

Martha and Kitty "goofing" to victory

gling, and went across the line on port tack at the other end from the rest of the fleet.

And so—the lesson they learned was a bit different from the one I intended. While the rest of the ladies, clutching their tillers in intense concentration, fell into a hole and lay all but becalmed, Martha and Kitty, sailing as loose as a goose, picked up a fresh lift out beyond the port tack end and simply sailed away from the desperately wallowing rest of the fleet to win by a mile.

So much for the lessons learned through parental discipline.

Temper, Temper

By the time he was twelve, Robby wanted and needed more of a challenge than the staid, simple Wood Pussy offered. The hot class in the club was the sixteen-foot Comet, a planing boat. It was an adult fleet with a roster of experienced skippers that did well nationally in the class, and there was a question of how a sub-teen would fit in, but we went ahead and bought him a boat, No. 3090, which had twice won the class nationals. He was up to the competition on ability, and I would be crewing for him as a "stabilizing" influence—and driver when we trailed to regattas.

I wasn't the greatest crew, as I couldn't hike the way he wanted me to for any length of time. The old midriff muscles would start to quiver when I stretched out over the rail for too long, I would have to sit up, and we would wallow down out of a plane as Robby groaned. I was definitely not a tillerless skipper talking him around a course. I was strictly crew, and he made the decisions. I made suggestions and offered opinions only when asked. Except for my quivering midriff, we got along well in the boat, and I was occasionally able to help him with navigation in some of the strange waters, picking out buoys and landmarks and keeping him oriented. Once or twice we made significant gains by not following other boats blindly on a bad course.

In addition to close and exciting racing at SSYC, the Comet Class had a circuit of regattas everyone trailed to. The competition was top-notch, and it was a great experience for Robby to sail in different bodies of water against sailors from many clubs, and I wanted him to see how major regattas were handled. At twelve he had a lot to learn, but he was in adult competition, and I wanted him to act and be treated as one. Sailing by the rules, and the proper handling of protests, always a difficult element in sailing, was one facet I was particularly anxious to have him familiar with.

At one of the major regattas, we were doing well—somewhere in the top five starting the last of a three-race series—when we ended up in a protest situation nearing the first windward mark. The fleet was closely bunched, and we were approaching the mark on starboard tack for a port rounding in good fleet position, when two boats came at us on port tack too close to be able to cross us, and we hailed "starboard."

The nearest boat was from SSYC, and he started to respond to our hail by trying to flip, but the boat to windward of him, from the host club, refused to react to hails from both boats and carried on on port tack. To avoid a collision and a jam-up that would let other boats by, we luffed up head to wind. As we did, the local boat finally tacked and the other SSYC boat tacked with him. We bore off again on starboard, but we had lost speed and position by luffing, and we immediately put up our red flag, protesting the local boat.

At the time, we of course had no idea how a protest would affect the final outcome. We just knew that we had been fouled and had lost by it.

When we came back to the club after the race, in which we finished

Robby's Comet

fourth, which would put us in fourth for the series, we figured, I told Robby I would clean the boat and unrig her for trailing while he went to the protest hearing. I especially wanted him to have the experience of being involved in a "big time" formal hearing, which I assumed this would be, and I was definitely determined to act as a normal crew, not an interfering Daddy, staying strictly out of it unless called as a witness. Also, I was reporting the regatta for the *Newark News* and was therefore in a rather special position in that regard. I did think, though, that I might be called as a witness.

I had the boat all clean and snug on her trailer as time went on, but I had not been called as a witness, and Rob hadn't come back yet. I thought this was odd, and I was really surprised when the P.A. system announced that the prizes would now be awarded in the clubhouse, and still no Robby.

A few minutes later, he did show up, walking in a dejected slump, with his face down around his knees, completely subdued and glum.

"What happened?" I asked.

"I withdrew the protest," he mumbled, head down, his voice almost breaking.

"WITHDREW!" I exploded. "Why did you withdraw it?"

With this he dissolved in tears, and, his voice breaking, and seething through the sobs, he told me that the local boat had been third in the standings. If we protested her out, we would move up to third, the last place to be awarded a prize.

"They asked me if I wanted to win a prize by protesting, so I said I didn't and withdrew it."

I seldom lose my temper completely, and I don't like public displays of emotion, but the thought of a twelve-year-old boy facing a room full of grown men and being fed something like that was too much.

My top blew in a red flash of anger, and I dashed for the protest room and burst in just as the committee was gathering up its papers to go to the award ceremony. I was so hot I was practically incoherent with a string of obscenities, but I think the most elegant term of greeting I used was something like "chicken-shit bastards."

"What's this about our protest?" I shouted. "Why didn't you hear it?"

"Gee, Bill, we just thought we were doing the kid a favor with his friends. We thought he'd be embarrassed if he moved up to a prize by protesting."

"How did he know anything about prizes when we put up the flag? And what about your guy who's winning a trophy by getting away with a foul? How about him being embarrassed?"

"Well—" they looked at each other in confusion as I ranted on.

"How the hell do you expect a twelve-year-old kid to learn the rules, or how protests are handled, if you feed him horseshit like that? Some favor that is! I thought this was a big-time club that did things right, not some stinking little home-town trick like this."

"Gee, Bill, if you feel that way, we'll open up the meeting again and hear the protest. We'll hold up the prize awards."

"Never mind. It's too late, but if that's the way you run things, you'll never see us back here again," I said, storming out.

Every year after that, the head of the regatta committee would call up to ask me to sail and to cover the regatta, but my answer was always a polite refusal, saying I had made arrangements for someone else to get the results for the paper, with the reminder, "I think you know why I'm not coming."

I've never been proud of blowing my stack that way; it leaves a bad aftertaste. But every time I think of that committee I get mad all over again.

Keeping Up with Youth

In our first year, we managed to qualify for the Comet nationals at Port Clinton, Ohio. Robby was the youngest skipper ever to sail in the nationals, and it was a thrill for him to be there, especially since the trip was to such a remotely exotic "foreign" area as western Lake Erie. Not only was it exciting from a sailing point of view, but we also combined it with a pre-season swing through the training camps of several midwestern football powers, since I was covering football as a sportswriter.

We went to Notre Dame practice and met Terry Brennan and Paul Hornung, which was exciting enough, but the climax was a visit to Michigan State the year after they had won the Rose Bowl. We watched practice, had a steak dinner at the training table with all the Bowl heroes on the team, and then went back with coach Duffy Daugherty for an interview in his office. He was very friendly and talkative, great "copy" for a sportswriter, and while he and I were talking, he told Robby to take a look around the halls at some of the

Lake Erie was lumpy for the Comet nationals

mementos and pictures of famous MSU alumni like Robin Roberts, who
was one of Rob's heroes, and while Rob was out of the room, I asked
Duffy about his start in coaching.

He said he had been on terminal leave from the Navy in New York
in 1945 and took on, on a temporary last-minute basis, the head coach
job at Trinity School.

"Then I saw your team," I said. "My brother-in-law was playing on
the Pingry School team in Elizabeth, and I remember seeing them play
Trinity. Robby goes to Pingry now, by the way."

"I'll be damned," Duffy said. "What a small world. Yeah, I remember
that game." He shook his head in wonderment, and just then Robby
came back in.

"How do you like it here, Robby?" Duffy asked.

"Fine, sir."

"Almost as nice as Pingry, isn't it?"

The expression on Robby's face was marvelous as his eyes widened in
amazement that Duffy Daugherty knew anything about a small day
school in Elizabeth, New Jersey.

We didn't end up as spectacular heroes ourselves in the nationals,
though we did get a seventh in one race and were just below the middle
in a fleet of thirty-six in the final standings. It blew fresh from the
northwest across the open waters of the lake for the first two races, and
with Rob at 105 pounds and me and my quivery midriff, we were
having trouble keeping the boat flat. Other boats, with well-muscled
crews hiked out in a discouragingly hard-bellied display of teamwork

would plane by, as Robby kept up his litany of "Hike, Dad. HIKE!"

I was in the midst of explaining that the other crews were all college-age football types full of youthful vigor when Marcy Lippincott of the Riverton, New Jersey, family of boatbuilders and racing experts planed by in a fantastic show of flat-out hiking. Marcy was perhaps in his early twenties and in great shape, but he happened to have parted prematurely with a good bit of his hair.

"Well, look at Marcy," Rob said in disgust. "Look how he can hike, Dad, and he's BALD."

Local Knowledge

Because we had done moderately well at the nationals, we were invited to a special regatta called the Dixie Cup on the Delaware River, run by the Red Dragon Canoe Club, a hotbed of top Comet sailors. The competition was as good as at the nationals and the partying was better, but local conditions made the sailing pretty tricky. The race course was on the narrow, swiftly running river, and the current was a major factor in all race strategy.

I had been telling Robby that this was a chance for him to study how the local hotshots operated in special conditions.

"Whenever you sail at some strange place for the first time," I pontificated, "always watch what the local guys do. There are special tricks to sailing in a place like this."

We did everything wrong in the first race and ended up at the rear of the fleet with the only leg left a close reach upriver against the strong current to the finish line. Directly ahead of us was Jim Merrill, one of the veteran campaigners of the class, a former national champion, perennially the man to beat, and the guy who had done more to earn Red Dragon C.C. its reputation as a racing hotbed than any of its experts.

Most of the fleet remained near the east bank of the river after rounding the last mark, which was near that bank, and Rob started to follow them, but Merrill crossed over and began to sail up the western bank.

Deserting my designated role as non-interfering crew, I turned parental and said, "Follow Merrill, Rob."

"I don't want to," he said. "This looks like the better side."

"Remember what I told you about watching the local experts? Well, he's it here. He knows something the rest don't, and we should do what he does."

"Well," Robby grumbled, "I don't think so, but o.k., we'll try it."

So we crossed over, following Merrill, and he ended up next to last and we were last.

Later, in the clubhouse, I bearded him.

"How come you chose the west side, Jim? I kept telling Robby to follow you because you were the local hotshot and must know something, but it sure didn't work."

"It never works," Merrill said, laughing. "I knew it wouldn't, but we were doing so badly, I thought we couldn't do any worse over there and we might hit a one-in-a-hundred fluke."

Thus ended the lesson on watching the local experts.

The Test

Robby developed other interests besides one-design racing, and in 1960, at the age of sixteen, he managed to get a berth in the Bermuda Race. I was covering the race, having joined *Yachting* in 1957, aboard the seventy-three-foot ketch *Barlovento*. That was the year of the famous storm, a disturbance of near hurricane intensity that hit the fleet the last night out of Bermuda. It had been a long, slow race in fog and calms until a low-pressure system formed rapidly in the area of Jacksonville, and, without warning in any weather broadcasts, buzz sawed along a cold front that was moving out from the continent.

It was a wild night of erratic squalls, blinding bursts of rain, and steep, vicious seas. The squalls brought such violent wind changes that the big cutter *Djinn* was caught aback without warning and flipped over onto her beam-ends on what had been the windward side seconds before. In *Barlovento*, we once tried to tack and found ourselves unable to steady up for 180 degrees as the wind came around with us.

She was about as sturdy and able a vessel as there was in the fleet, but I have to admit to being more than a little bit scared at the wild behavior of the wind, the crashing and pounding as we plunged through the seas, and an angle of heel that put her deckhouse windows into the

Rough going on the way to Bermuda

ater. Through it all, my thoughts were very much on Robby, who
ad never been offshore before and who was on one of the older boats
the fleet. Aside from pure worry over safety, I also wondered how
: would react to conditions like these.

Barlovento, with most of her crew planning to continue on the next
eek in a race to Sweden, got to Bermuda a full day before he did, as
s boat was one of the last to finish, and Jane and I were really worried
out what reaction we would get when he finally arrived. When we
w his boat coming up Hamilton Harbor at last and make her way
the anchorage area, we armed ourselves with the key to the motor-
ke we had reserved for him, a cold beer, and a twenty-dollar bill for
ending money and went down to the float to meet the club launch
hen it brought him ashore. We were normally not this indulgent as
rents, but we figured the experience he'd been through merited special

attention. Privately, I expected him to come ashore asking to trade his Comet in on a set of golf clubs.

When the launch came alongside, he was the first to hop out. He was in that peculiar mid-teen stage when arms and legs were too long for the rest of him and acne fought with the peach fuzz of an incipient beard for dominance on his face. His hair was wild and spiked and his clothes looked as if he'd been in them for a week, which was probably true, and we feared for the worst, but he came toward us eagerly kissed his mother on the top of the head, grabbed the beer from me, and said, "Hey, Pop. Do you think I can get a berth in the race to Sweden?"

Baby Needs New Shoes

He was too young for anyone to take him transatlantic, but he did go in two later races, including the famous one in which *Dyna* lost her rudder and sailed the last thousand miles of the race by balancing the sails of her yawl rig. Then, in 1964, he was part of the crew of *American Eagle* in the America's Cup trials, a summer-long campaign that was one of the most exciting in Cup history before she lost out to *Constellation*.

Early in June, before the trials started, I was invited aboard *Eagle* to get some on-deck action shots in hopes of coming up with a cover we could use on the September issue of *Yachting*, the special America's Cup issue. When I came aboard, some of the crew members began to rib me about Robby's sneakers.

"Don't you buy shoes for your kids, Bill?" they said, laughing. "He looks like a charity case."

The sneakers were about as ratty as could be imagined, with the toes bursting through rips in the cloth, and big paint stains adding to the general mess. I offered to go to an Army-Navy store and buy him some new ones, but he talked me out of it.

"Don't pay any attention, Dad," he said. "We're getting our official uniforms next week, including shoes, so it would be silly to buy a new pair for me now. These will last till the new ones come."

So I did not buy him any, and we went about our day of picture taking without more thought to my son's footwear. When the pictures were developed, there was one that was perfect for what we wanted and it was chosen to be the cover. It showed four of the crew in bright orange foul-weather gear pumping away at the coffee grinders with a nice dash of spray flying away from the bow beyond them. The color and composition were fine, but when the art director put his magnifying glass on it to check out each detail for production purposes, he started to laugh.

"There's just one thing wrong," he said. "Look at the shoe on that guy. When we blow it up, it's really going to show how beat-up that sneaker looks. I thought they had special uniforms on those 12-Meters."

Sure enough, Rob's sneaker stood out like a sore thumb, and, to use the picture, we had to have a touch-up artist work on it. The bill for one "new shoe" was fifty dollars, and it would definitely have been cheaper if I had gone to an Army-Navy store and bought a new pair for about ten dollars, or whatever.

The very special shoe is the farthest one visible on the right

How They Did It on the Eagle

When the Cup campaign was over, Rob crewed for me in the fall Off
Soundings Regatta in *Mar Claro*, still full of 12-Meter doings, and he
was pretty insufferable about the way I handled things on my little
Amphibi-Ette.

"Is that the way you do that?" he would ask scornfully as we set a
sail or made a change of some sort. "On the *Eagle*—" and he would be
off on the right way to do the operation 12-Meter style. He had
crewed for me in *Mar Claro* time and again over the years in Off
Soundings and many other races, but he hadn't been on her all year
owing to his America's Cup involvement, and no doubt it was a come-
down to operate at a twenty-four-foot scale again.

Rounding a mark, we had to make a switch from genoa to spinnaker
and Rob took over the foredeck full of beans and eager to show us
"how we did it on the *Eagle*." He did a great job, and the switch was
made as fast as it had ever been done on *Mar Claro*.

There was only one problem. In his concentration on the speed of
the switch, he had managed to let the genoa halyard go up the mast.
Naturally I couldn't resist the obvious.

"Is that the way they do it on the *Eagle*?"

With that, and before I could say another word or stop him, he
shinnied up the mast. He had already reached the spreaders before I
could even open my mouth, and by then I was too scared to say anything. Ellen Horan of *Yachting*'s staff was also in the crew, and she
simply put her head down and covered her eyes, refusing to look the
whole time he was up there.

I wasn't quite sure what six foot three and 190 pounds of Princeton
football player at the masthead would do to the stability of a twenty-
four-foot boat under spinnaker in a good breeze (he had grown a bit
since his first days in a Comet), so I concentrated on steering with the
care of an old lady crossing the ice. Eventually, he retrieved the halyard and made it safely back to the deck, as the rest of us heaved
a great collective sigh.

There were no more comparisons to *Eagle* for the rest of the weekend.

Under spinnaker in Off Soundings before the halyard incident

Hotrod Alice

While Robby was having these adventures, our girls were also getting into the act. Martha had inherited the Wood Pussy when Robby moved up to the Comet, but she couldn't have cared less about competition. She loved to be on the water, but she was more interested in waving to friends in other boats and having a good time. She had a wonderful touch on the tiller, but her focus was wider than the luff of the mainsail, and she really didn't like racing.

One day, with Jane crewing for her in a heavy breeze, they were approaching the leeward mark, where they would have to jibe, but, in the manner of most catboats, the Wood Pussy had a virulent weather helm, and Martha couldn't make the boat behave. Instead, it was riding up to windward in the wrong direction, which happened to be right in the direction of our house, and Martha announced firmly, "I can't jibe this boat, so I'm going home. I don't like this."

Jane didn't like it much either, so, with a few words about "what's your father going to think?" she agreed, and home they went. Martha retired from racing except for casual forays like her victory in the Ladies' Race, and she didn't get competitive again until she was in her late teens.

Alice, on the other hand, was very competitive. By the time she was nine, a new junior class had been added at SSYC, the Turnabout, a nine-foot cat dinghy almost as wide as it is long, and she started her career in this stubby little vessel. Once more I was signed on as crew to get a beginner through the traumas of a first season of racing. I'd been kicked out of the Comet for not hiking well enough, and the Turnabout looked like a wonderful change, since there was no way an adult could hike in one. Now the problem was that I was too fat, so, as Alice gained confidence, my career as a crew for juveniles finally ended.

To aid in transportation problems and to give the girls the chance to handle machinery properly, we acquired a Boston Whaler the second year Alice had the Turnabout, and part of the deal of buying one was a free water-skiing lesson. Rob and Martha already knew how, so Alice

Alice at speed in the Whaler

was the recipient, and she learned to ski in the single lesson. She also earned some other Whaler lore that I found out about in a surprising way.

We kept the racing boats at our house, which was more than two miles from the club, and it was a long way back in a Turnabout if the tide was wrong, so Alice was allowed to take the Whaler to tow her boat back and forth. The first day that she came back from the club with it, I met her down at the beach in front of our house to help her bring the boats up. She came in, left the Turnabout at the water's edge, and took off again in the Whaler.

"Where are you going?" I asked.

"I'll be right back," was all she said.

Right behind the beach there was a small, low bulkhead, sort of a retaining wall, with a gap in it from the beach to the grass of the lawn. We used the gap to pull boats through, and they sat on the lawn when not in use.

Alice circled away in the Whaler out to the middle of the river, then turned and headed straight for the section of the beach that had this gap behind it. As I stood there immobilized and not knowing what she was intending to do, she revved the motor up and came charging at the gap in the bulkhead like a stunt driver at Cypress Gardens. The boat hit the beach at full speed and bounced up it in wild leaps. As it went through the gap in the bulkhead, the motor dropped back from a tilt-up position, still churning madly, and the propeller hit the sand. My

mouth was open in surprise, and also in a vain attempt to shout a
Alice, and the clouds of sand churned up by the motor flew into it i
considerable volume.

The boat came to rest on the grass, and Alice reached back an
stopped the motor. When I had spit enough sand out so that I coul
begin to talk, I sputtered, "Hey. Alice. What on earth are you doing?"

"I'm just putting the boat away, Daddy," she said calmly. "The ma
who sold it to us and gave me the water-ski lesson said that the bes
way to land it was to run it fast right up the beach."

It was a terrible disappointment to her when I had to lay down th
law that this wasn't really the recommended way to beach the boa
at the house.

Hard-Nosed Competition

Alice progressed from the Turnabout to a Blue Jay after a few year
and she continued to be very competitive in every way. In fact, sh
became the first girl ever to win the North Jersey YRA junior cham
pionship, a step on the route to the national championship for Junior
known as the Sears Cup, a sister trophy to the Adams Cup for womer

The regatta Alice won was sailed in borrowed boats at anothe
club, and the committee there ran off eight races in one day becaus
they wanted to take advantage of a good breeze. When I came hom
from work, Alice, victorious but knocked out, was lying down in he
room. I went up to congratulate her, and asked her, since she seeme
so beat, whether she had a headache.

"Yes, I do," she said. "It starts at the top of my head and ends a
my toes."

Another big regatta in our area is the National Sweepstakes Sailin
Regatta on the Navesink River, twin to the Shrewbury, in Red Banl
Alice had had a year-long battle in Blue Jay racing with a girl who w
a couple of years older and who was also a hard-nosed competito
There was nothing in the world Alice wanted more than to beat th
girl, and, in the three-race series at the Sweepstakes, she went into th
last race with a twelve-point advantage on her rival. This meant tha
Alice could finish as far down as twelfth in the fleet of about thirty boa

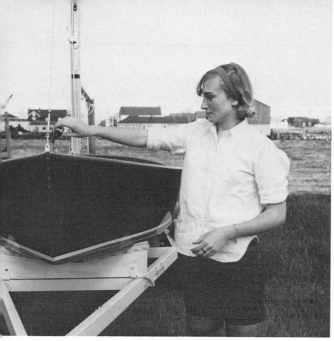

Alice christening her Blue Jay

Racing the Blue Jay

and still win the series even if the other girl won the race, but Alice was not going to sail it conservatively. She went all out to win the last race too, and she was so eager that she set the spinnaker when she didn't have to while leading the race in a blustery, puffy northwester. The other girl was several boats back, and Alice had clear sailing to the title, but overconfidence raised its ugly head, a puff caught the spinnaker aback in a violent wind shift, and Alice capsized. The boat was wallowing down in the water and if it filled any more could not be righted, when the other girl came sailing by. Alice and her crew had resigned themselves to being out of the competition, when her rival, who had a harsh, raspy voice that carried strongly for great distances over the water, called out, "Tough luck, Alice!" in the most sarcastic of tones.

This was all it took to galvanize Alice and crew to action. Bailing frantically, they kept the boat from sinking further, got her upright half full of water, and started sailing while still bailing, screaming curses all the while. Not only did they finish high enough in the fleet to clinch the series, they actually passed the hated rival just before the finish, and Alice delivered the final blow by not saying a word as they sailed by.

What's the Course?

With Robby college age and the girls in their mid-teens, he went his own way most of the time, and I ended up with an all-girl crew, Jane, Martha, and Alice, for much of the racing we did in *Mar Claro*. They were good, and we did pretty well as a rule.

One of our big adventures was to trail to the Inter-Lake YRA regatta at Put-in-Bay, Ohio, an island in the middle of Lake Erie's western end off Port Clinton. This was billed as the world's largest freshwater regatta, and I went there to do a feature for the magazine while racing *Mar Claro* in Cruising Class C for the smallest-size auxiliaries.

The only problem with racing there was that they started the race at 0730 under the theory that morning winds were better on the lake

Racing at Put-in-Bay called for dawn harbor starts

a reversal of what we were used to on the seacoast, and it was a daily struggle to get my crew organized in time to make the start.

We would leave the harbor with hair curlers, bobby pins, cold cereal, and filmy underthings scattered all over the cabin and cockpit while I tried to organize for the race and talk the girls into getting dressed. One day we were so late getting out there that the starting signal for our class had already gone and the course information had been replaced by the sign for the next class. We knew the first leg was directly to windward, so we could head in the right direction, but when we arrived at the mark, there was going to be a 180-degree choice of which way to go.

There was a rather slow ketch in our class that was not too far ahead, and we figured we could ask her crew. We soon caught her and called over, "What's the course?"

All we got was a shrug in answer, so we kept on going, feeling that, since we were so late, the other boats in our class would get there first anyway, and we could follow them. As we neared the mark, though, we got a tremendous lift that the rest of our class missed, and it looked as though we were going to be first to the mark. I had visions of having to sit there in stays until one of the other boats came along, a ridiculous prospect, but we were saved this embarrassment at the last minute when one boat picked up a good slant and beat us there by a couple of hundred feet.

Once around the mark in the right direction, the rest of the course was automatic, so we didn't have to wait for anyone and went on to win the race and the series. Everyone made a great fuss over my all-girl crew, but no one else had to get them up in the morning.

Ungraceful Exit

The last time I raced with the girls as crew was in the Prince of Wales competition. This is the North American match race championship, sailed like a tournament elimination between clubs. We had got by one round, and the second step was to race a boat from the Navesink. They provided Lightnings and brought them over to the Shrewsbury, and my opponent was June Methot, Jane's old nemesis from the Adams Cup elimination, who had sailed Lightnings in top-flight competition for years.

I had only raced a Lightning once or twice about fifteen years previously, and Martha and Alice had hardly ever been in one, but we gave it our all and managed to be in the lead at the first windward mark by a few lengths. It was a breezy day, and the girls were hiking out well and holding the boat flat.

The second leg was a spinnaker reach, and Marth and Alice hopped to it smartly to get the chute up. It went up quickly all right, only it was upside down. In the confusion, June passed us, and we were one down in a two-out-of-three series.

We had got the first start, an all-important factor in match racing, but June had me by a length or so after the second one, and we had a close battle all the way up the first leg. The girls promised they would have the spinnaker right this time, and they got it up beautifully as soon as we rounded onto the reaching leg. We picked up on a plane and were really closing fast at the jibing mark, and I figured that we could get June's wind by jibing inside as we rounded and then should be able to take her on the run.

She jibed rather wide, and the opening was there if we could take advantage of it. I pulled the tiller over to cut inside her close to the mark, and Martha and Alice jibed the spinnaker without a flaw. It was my job to jibe the mainsail, and I pulled the mainsheet across as we swung in. The boom came in toward me and was right over my head as the stern crossed the wind, and there it stayed. For some reason, and I'll never know why, though the owner of the boat later admitted that the mainsheet block sometimes jammed on the traveler, the sail never ran out on the other side. With it stuck amidships, as soon as the wind caught the other side of it, we whapped over in one of the fastest, noisiest capsizes I've ever seen or been in.

We were still carrying plenty of momentum from the plane as we turned, and the force of it threw all three of us far out onto the sail in flat-out racing dives. I later asked June if she saw what had happened, and, laughing, she said, "No. I only heard it, and it sounded like an explosion."

As we surfaced from our dives and began wallowing around in the usual embarrassed frustration, Alice, squirting out a mouthful of water, asked ruefully, "Was that my fault?"

I had to admit it was the skipper's.

The Joys of Scandalizing

One of the best things we've ever done was to acquire *Polly,* an eighteen-foot Sanderling class catboat. She is a fiberglass replica of the classic Crosby Cape Cod cat, with aluminum spars and a 265-square-foot Dacron sail, and it is amazing what these modern materials have done to improve the sailing qualities of these broad, shallow center-boarders. The mast can be big enough to carry the load without shrouds and still light enough so that the bow doesn't root, with that overwhelming urge to broach up to weather on a broad reach or run, and the bow sections, hollowed and fined down by the man whose brainchild the Sanderling was, Breck Marshall, make her adequately close-winded and lively on the wind.

She is the perfect boat for us to have at our house, since she draws eighteen inches and the water is two feet deep at our pier at low tide. When we look out the window and see that conditions are right, we can be sailing in five minutes. We can take two couples with us for pleasant party sailing, and we can race her at Shrewsbury Sailing and Yacht Club in the closest kind of competition. All the boats are exactly alike, with the same sailmaker, and all fittings have to be fleet-approved, so the boats are virtually interchangeable as long as their bottoms are clean and their sails are not out of shape.

She takes me right back to the Baby Rainbows at Nantucket, in a real exercise in nostalgia. We have a buff deck, just as my two chartered Rainbows did, the only color for a catboat deck if you ask me, and I really enjoy sailing a gaff-rigged boat. It adds such a wonderful extra dimension to sail handling, and there are so many variations to a gaff sail that are completely out of the question in a triangular one.

We have a condition at our pier that seems to guarantee that we will be making a landing with the wind and tide opposed, and the gaff sail is a wonderful aid in this situation. The doctrine is to come in downwind against the tide, gradually lowering the sail, but with the peak still raised, so that there is a controllable triangle of sail gradually descending down the mast. If the timing is right, the gaff comes down onto the boom just as we nestle alongside the pier end

The Sanderling fleet in action

at zero speed and quickly grab the dock lines. If the timing is wrong, we end up with what we call a "bulrushes landing," with our bow on the bank and everything in a snarl. Fortunately, we have almost no neighbors to see this happen, and we eventually straighten things out, so a bulrushes landing is no great tragedy.

One time we were invited to a party at the house of friends who live on the river beyond a fixed bridge that is too low for a catboat with peak halyard two-blocked to pass under. Several catboats live up there and either come through under power or with the gaff well lowered, and we figured we could make it if we dropped the gaff far enough. This is known in catboat parlance as "scandalizing the peak." I don't know where the phrase comes from, but it's a delightful one, and I've always been kidding Jane about how great it is to do it.

"Here's our chance," I said. "We'll go to the party with a scandalized peak."

We approached the bridge with caution and scandalized the peak slowly, dropping it until it seemed low enough to clear the bridge, then started through, reaching in a light breeze. Everything went beautifully except for one hitch. There was a red warning light extending down from the bottom of the bridge. We had lowered the peak enough to clear the bridge proper, but this light caught the peak halyard, and suddenly there we were hung up under the bridge. I had visions of hanging there for hours, or of having to somehow get up on the bridge, but I didn't know what we could do. I tried lowering the peak more, but it didn't free the line from the light. A small outboard came by, its occupants gazing at us in some wonder, and I thought they might pull us sideways, but I was afraid that would prove too complicated.

While I was sitting there feeling foolish and pondering the problem, the boat slowly spun around until she was headed out again, and then, with a slight tweak of the halyard, we were free. On the second try, I lowered the peak more and kept an eye on the light and we made it through. I was just raising the peak on the other side of the bridge, with a great sigh of relief, when we ran into a new hazard. Some kids were flying a kite on the shore, and the first thing I knew, its line was around our gaff and tangled with the mast.

There was great screaming and yelling on shore, and I jibed away trying to free it quickly. Just when I thought it might be working, the kite string parted, the kite skittered off to leeward over the water, and we had a tangle of string on our sail and mad kids on shore.

Another time we were in a race in the club championship series on a day of humid, threatening weather and a hint of thunder to come, reaching along the northwest shore of the river in a fitful

Polly's gung-ho crew

westerly. We were in the lead, concentrating hard on making the
best of every puff, when I heard that dreaded sound behind me, the
gurgle of the fast-approaching bow wave of an overtaking boat.
Looking back, I saw that the second boat had a new breeze, and it
was just about to reach us. It was a dark line on the water coming
off the nearby shore, and my first reaction was to hope that it would
reach me before the second boat did. The jibing mark was just a couple
of hundred yards away, and I wanted to hold our lead and a controlling
position till we got there. Then the puff hit us, and my next reaction
was strictly one of handling my own boat. It was a strong gust, and
we leaped ahead.

In just a few lengths, we were really flying, with the bow beginning to bury and the boom bellying up in the new blast of air. There was a strong weather tug on the tiller and we were heeled well over.

"Are you going to jibe the mark?" Jane asked with a touch of anxiety in her voice.

"Sure," I said. "We can handle it."

As I spoke, the wind doubled in strength and a line of white froth skittered madly across the water. We heeled rail down, and the weather helm became more than I could counteract. This was no trifling little shift of breeze. It was a heavy line squall that had been hidden by the closeness of the shore. It was no longer a question of jibing the mark, but of staying upright and intact. And then the phrase came to me that we kidded about so often.

"Scandalize the peak!" I cried, and Jane knew just what to do. She let the peak halyard off the cleat at the forward edge of the cockpit, and the gaff suddenly dropped behind the sail, flogging crazily, but cutting the area of the sail in half in a few seconds. With the pressure off the sail, we were able to round up safely, wrestle the rest of the wildly flapping sail down to the boom in a quick, rough furl, and then get the anchor over. With everything secure, we ducked into the little sitting-headroom cabin and crouched there in comparative comfort while the quick blast of the front blew itself out. Most of the boats had done something similar and no one was in real trouble.

We hated to lose a first place, but it was good to learn how easy and effective it was to scandalize the peak when you had to.

~~~~~~~~~~~~~~~

PART VII

With the Big Boats

Much of my racing was with the family, and we also cruised a great deal, but in the course of my career as a boating writer, first as a newspaperman and later as an editor of *Yachting*, assignments took me aboard a variety of boats in most of the big races. Some of it was routine, and sometimes funny things happened.

What a Little Hiccup'll Do

My first distance race was perhaps my most unusual. It was in the summer of 1941, and the event was the Cornfield Lightship Race on Long Island Sound. At that time there was a lightship on Cornfield Reef off the mouth of the Connecticut River, and one of the fixtures on the calendar was a race from City Island around it and back. It was a kind of race that was popular in those days and has since all but died out except for the Jeffrey's Ledge Race in Massachusetts Bay. The participants were given a certain gas allowance and the trick was to figure out when to use it to best advantage. I think it was probably good for about 10 percent of the course distance.

I took one of my first Corinthian crew calls, preceding the Block Island Race in the slender Scandinavian boat, in the Cornfield Race. The boat was a handsome Geiger-designed cutter named *Deep Water*, whose picture and plans I had seen in *Yachting*, and it was very exciting to sign aboard her as crew. The owner-skipper was a radio actor whose best-known role was Buck Rogers, and who also had been in a serial soap opera named "Pepper Young's Family" for years. As crew we had his wife, an actor who had played his twelve-year-old son in "Pepper Young's Family" for at least twelve years and was about twenty-six years old, a sound man from the program, and another bright-eyed Corinthian, like me completely new at it and eager to please.

The first leg down to the lightship was an easy reach in a moderate southerly, and I began to feel that this ocean racing business (even though we were inside Long Island Sound, I considered it an ocean race) was not too bad. Just as we rounded the lightship sometime in the hours around midnight, however, a cold front came slashing through with a fresh northwester behind it, and things were a bit different when we started back into it. In the face of a growing breeze and steepening seas that sent cold spray dashing across our deck, we were not doing as well as we had been on the outward leg. We were carrying too much sail and sagging far off to leeward in the widest part of Long Island Sound. With only my summer on *Bona* as back-

245

ground, I could still see that this wasn't doing us much good, but, as a new hand aboard, I had no intention of speaking up.

I was amazed, therefore, when the skipper came to me and asked, "What do you think we should do?" Evidently he thought all Corinthians were a font of nautical knowledge, not realizing that I was a bushy-tailed new member.

When I swallowed my surprise at being asked, I stammered out something about reefing the main and using our gas allowance to head up under the Connecticut shore, where the seas would be smaller and would have less effect on our speed. Here we were pounding up and down and punching into them.

"Would you reef her then, please," the skipper said to me.

"Me?" I gasped. "Reef this boat? Don't you know how?"

"No, I don't. I thought you knew how," he said, as though I had just told him a big lie, or something.

"I can try if no one else can," I said. "Have you got lanyards for the gooseneck and outhaul?"

"Lanyards?" was the weak reply.

Eventually he came up with a couple of short rope ends, but, between my ignorance, the lack of experience of the rest of the crew, and the general difficulties of bouncing around in the spray-blown dark on a strange boat with inadequate lines, we could not effect a reef. Instead, we took the main down and eventually were able to rig a storm trysail. It was not the most effective sail to windward, but, with a staysail, the storm trysail (the only one I have ever been under sail under), and our gas allowance, we managed to slug our way slowly westward through the howling night.

After a while, the engine began to have difficulties, and the sound man, who had been helpless with sailing gear, said he knew what to do about engines and went below to blow out the fuel line. His only problem was that he inhaled when he should have exhaled as he tried to blow out the line, hiccuped in a mouthful of gas, and was lost for the night. From then on, his upheavals made better sound effects than anything he had ever devised for the Buck Rogers show.

Also among the missing were the skipper's wife and the twenty-six-year-old twelve-year-old, as the other Corinthian, the skipper, and I kept her going through the long, cold night. Came the clear, frigid dawn, with the northwester giving that hard, steely look to the water as it kicked up steep chop and whitecaps, the juvenile finally popped his head out of the hatch with a beer in one hand and a piece of chocolate cake in the other. "My breakfast," he said, beaming. "Oh, what an exciting morning!"

He took a bite of the cake and washed it down with a big swig of beer, and my Corinthian friend promptly joined the sound man in the sound effects department. If I'd had anything to get sick with, I would have been right along with them, but all I could manage was a weak retch or two.

By midmorning, the skipper's wife, freshly made up and with her hair carefully coiffed, appeared for the first time since supper the night before, took one look at the waves, said "My, it's rough, isn't it?," and disappeared for the rest of the race.

It was a long day of slugging our way the length of the Sound, and would you believe that, in a fleet of about twenty, we were third, just twenty-eight seconds out of second? If the sound effects man hadn't hiccuped, I'm sure we would have made up that twenty-eight seconds.

Dick Bertram and Ladies' Day

After the war, in my first summer as a boating writer for the *Newark News*, I was invited to crew in the Bay Head Yacht Club Ocean Race Series aboard *Searader*, Jack Harkrader's thirty-nine-foot Geiger-designed centerboard sloop. This was a hotly contested series of half a dozen races in the ocean outside Manasquan Inlet for about eight or ten boats from BHYC. The owners were all close friends, neighbors, and drinking buddies at the club, and emotions ran extremely high in the series, extending beyond the race course into the whole fabric of Bay Head social life.

When a skipper protested another, repercussions were violent, but not on the nautical merits of the case. One wife once persuaded her husband to drop a protest "because I have to play bridge with that man's wife every Wednesday, and I don't want to hear about it for the rest of the summer."

I unwittingly created a very embarrassing situation by my reporting to the paper. One of the leading boats was owned by a man named Ed, who was aboard during the races, but she was actually sailed by a local expert named George. I didn't know this, and every time our crew discussed a move by the other boat, someone would say, "George is about" or "George has his spinnaker up." For the first few races, my accounts in the paper, which were unfortunately read with great avidity by the Bay Head community, listed the owner of the boat as "George" with his correct last name.

Understandably, the owner took this personally and was becoming increasingly upset until someone finally took me aside and explained the situation.

One of our crew was Paul Johnson, who ran the Morton Johnson boatyard, one of three confusingly named Johnson yards in the area, and while Paul ran an excellent yard, he was not noted for buttering up his customers. One owner noted for his pomposity came up to him after lucking out in a win and said, "Paul, you haven't congratulated me on winning today."

"Well, I will if you really want me to," Paul said dourly, fixing his eye on the other man, "but I'll also say if you'd kept *your* hand off the wheel, you'd have won by a couple of miles more."

To get to the ocean, we had to go through Manasquan Inlet, and the highway drawbridge just inside it had been damaged, so only one leaf was open. This was a narrow fit for the racing boats, and one of them directly in front of us didn't make it one day. She tangled her spreader in the draw, and the rig collapsed in a sickening jumble.

Before the mess had even landed on deck, Paul cocked one eye at the situation and dryly announced, "That'll be about a three-thousand-dollar job, I reckon."

In my first race, the first leg was down the coast to a mark off Chadwick, just below Mantoloking. It was supposed to be a special buoy put out by the club's committee. When we got there, with the fleet closely bunched, there was no buoy to be found, and there was a scene of milling confusion as the boats hung there deciding what to do. This was in the days when pound nets lined the Jersey coast. These were elaborate fish traps set on heavy stakes just off the beach.

In the confusion of wondering what to do about the missing mark, one of the boats got into irons and couldn't break free. Out of control and pounding up and down in the considerable chop, she drifted back into one of the pound nets and became entangled. As her bowsprit rose and feel, it tore the nets, and the boat also smashed a few of the stakes as she heaved up and down. By the time she worked clear, she had caused heavy damage to the pound and had also ripped some of her own sails and done some hull and rigging damage. As a result of this episode, the owner was sued by the fishermen for the actual damage plus the value of the potential catch lost because of the damage before the nets could be repaired. He never raced again.

There was a great deal of socializing in connection with the racing, and a highlight was the special race around Barnegat Lightship to Little Egg Harbor, an all-day affair. The fleet was rafted at the bulkhead of Little Egg Harbor Yacht Club in Beach Haven after this race, with sterns to the bulkhead and the bow anchor of the boat at one end of the raft holding everybody, when a line squall came

Dick Bertram with another "ladies' day" crew (an SORC party)

howling through at the height of the cocktail hour. Most of the crews were in the clubhouse, but one crew member on the windward boat, the one with the anchor out, had done his considerable drinking right on board. His solution to the situation when the squall hit was to take the strain off his anchor by cutting the boats to leeward loose. He staggered through the driving rain to the bow, and was poised there, knife in hand, when the owner of the next boat to leeward came dashing down from the club to see how things were going.

When he saw the man with the knife in hand, he grabbed a winch handle and jumped across to the other boat. Just as the knife began to touch rope, he grabbed the knife-wielder by the shoulder, spun him around, and raised the handle over his head. With the rain streaming over them, they stood there in tableau, winch handle poised and knife at the ready, until finally the knife wavered and slowly dropped to the man's side.

P.S. The anchor held.

Amid all of the social bantering, a plan was hatched for what was billed as a Ladies' Day. On *Searader* we were given the word that all the boats in the special race to Shrewsbury Rocks Buoy and back would have females aboard, and we all lined up our wives and lady friends for the big day. Arriving at the start, we were met by loud jeers and catcalls from the all-male crews of the other boats, yelling, "Party boat!," "Powder-puff boat!," and other such examples of sparkling wit. It had all been a plot to load us with extra weight and the distraction of feminine company.

But we also had another added attraction. Dick Bertram, who later became one of the world's best-known yachting figures, was an ex–Jersey Coast boy who happened to be back on a visit that day and had been asked aboard at the last minute. The race was a light-air spinnaker run up the coast and a beat back into a growing afternoon southwester, and Dick, by request, took over as sailing master. On the run, he played the spinnaker for every inch and ounce of benefit, keeping Jane chain-smoking in the hatch to give him smoke to watch, and we left the other boats far in our wake as we ghosted along in a masterly display of zephyr hunting.

Even with our extra weight, we were able to hold on to the lead during the beat back, and the gun was a wonderful sound. We waited around the finish as the other boats came by, calling over, "Hey! We've been waiting to ask you to a party on the party boat."

Coming Left Non-Stop

My own first experience as sailing master was during a New York Yacht Club Cruise in the 1950s. My friend, big Jim Davis, who later navigated us so well in the Lipton Cup Race in *Jaan*, had been handling that chore on a fifty-foot ketch for most of the cruise, but he couldn't stay with it for the last day off Marblehead, Massachusetts, and he asked me to fill in for him.

I had never been aboard the boat, and I didn't know any of the people, so it presented quite a challenge. Jim told me that the owner always wanted to be at the wheel, but he had to be told every move to make. He loved to steer as long as he was under direction.

"Just don't leave him on his own, and he'll be all right," were Jim's parting words as he took the launch ashore.

The race was a run south from Marblehead to a buoy off Boston and a beat back, and we managed the start pretty well. The crew was a young, eager group of the owner's college-age kids and friends and they did a perfectly good job of getting the spinnaker up.

Things went well, and we were the first boat in our class to reach the turning mark, with the rest of the fleet hot on our stern. We would be jibing around it after dousing the spinnaker, then setting the genoa for the beat back to the finish, and I gave the order to the owner to "Come left around the buoy."

Then I concentrated on the problem of getting the spinnaker in properly and making sure the genny went up and was trimmed correctly as it filled, and I didn't think about the helm again.

It was something of a shock, therefore, to find the boat continuing to "come left" until we had rounded up completely, head to wind, and were bobbing there in irons as the rest of the fleet whooshed by our stern, gennies filling nicely, and took off on the windward leg. By the time we had recovered and had way on again, we were well back in the ruck, and we stayed there.

By gosh, I reflected as I watched the transoms of the other boats, Jim *really* meant it when he said you couldn't leave the guy on his own.

Happy Ship

My first Miami-Nassau Race was in 1961 aboard *Hilaria*, Hugh Schaddelee's fifty-five-foot Sparkman & Stephens yawl from the Great Lakes, and it was an exciting one as we fought the famous *Ticonderoga* for the first two legs, both to windward, to Great Isaac, and then Stirrup Cay, finishing with a fast reach from Stirrup down to Nassau. We had saved our time on "Big *Ti*" and we thought we had the race won until a new fiberglass yawl, one of the first of that construction to show up in top competition, *Paper Tiger*, designed by a young sailmaker named Charley Morgan, breezed in way ahead of her class and saved her time on us.

That was later, but when we arrived at Yacht Haven, we knew we had *Ti* beat, and we also knew we had the boat behind us tucked away because she gave us time, and she was hull down on the horizon when we finished. She was one of the best-known and most widely campaigned boats in ocean racing, and it was a thrill to sail her under. I was also eager to get a first-time closeup of her when she followed

Headed for Nassau in *Hilaria*. As usual, I'm getting wet on the windward rail (dark hair, hatless)

us into Yacht Haven by over an hour. Here was one of the legendary boats of ocean racing, and I had heard a great deal about her.

As she rounded the little island in front of Yacht Haven, she managed to find the one coral head that sits off the end of it and perched there for a few minutes before working off. Then, as she came into the marina entrance across the usual swiftly running cross tide, her skipper misjudged the current, and she was swept sideways into the boomkin of a cruising ketch in one of the slips. There was a great amount of grinding and wrenching, and a lot of yelling and pushing, before she worked free from that one.

And then, as she finally made it into the basin and approached us to raft alongside, there was one of her crew perched right at the rail in street clothes, seabag in hand. He didn't even wait until there was a line aboard us before he leaped the gap between the boats, and, standing on our deck, turned to the skipper he was leaving, and in loudly enunciated tones cried, "That's the last time I'll ever sail with you, you son of a bitch."

Poor Man's Lightning Rod

One of our favorite regattas when we were campaigning *Mar Claro* during the 1960s was the Off Soundings Regatta at the eastern end of Long Island Sound. It was a chance for us to mingle with some of the more famous ocean racers while engaging in some great competition, and we made it a point to enter if we possibly could.

As we went out one morning for a start in Gardiner's Bay after partying in Deering Harbor, Shelter Island, the night before, one of those unsettling rarities, an early-morning thunderstorm, descended on the fleet as we milled around in the murk. The visibility was just about zero, and out of this miasma came some of the most terrifying cracks of lightning I have ever been near.

They were so close that the thunder was simultaneous in a loud, explosive blast, not the usual distant rumble, and each flash unleashed a cold, slashing cloudburst of rain. It was as terrifying as being under air attack, and there is no more naked feeling than standing in the cockpit of a sailboat as lightning zaps all around you. I hung a piece of wire from the backstay down into the water, but had no faith in its efficacy.

There's always safety in numbers in the Off Soundings fleet

There was certainly no place to hide, but I decided that there was one way to minimize our chances of taking a direct hit. We were only twenty-four feet, with a mast height of about thirty feet, one of the smallest boats racing, and, in a desperate stab at logic, but with no scientific knowledge, I figured that taller boats would be more likely to be hit than we were if we were close to them, so I picked out the tallest spars I could see through the near-zero curtain of wet visibility and cuddled close to them.

Scientific or not, it worked. Within the space of a couple of minutes, a thirty-six-foot ketch on one side of us and a forty-eight-foot yawl on the other were both hit. The noise and the spectacle were both terrifying, as the electric blue of the flashes connected with the mast trucks, and we could feel the whole atmosphere crackle with the charge of it. (We later found out that the ketch had all her rigging fittings fused and her electronics blown out, while the big yawl only had a small hole in her wooden mast near the end of the burgee stick.)

Moral of the story: Don't own the biggest boat in the fleet.

Greek Lesson

It's difficult enough to step aboard a strange ocean racer and figure out all the strings so that you can be of some help aboard, but how about stepping aboard a strange Greek ocean racer? Talk about confusion!

I was thrown into this situation when I was invited to sail in and cover the Aegean Rally in Greece in 1966 aboard the venerable but well-found cutter *Toxotis*, British-built before the war and well known there as *McNab* before she was bought by John Sikiarides of Athens.

The only other time I had felt quite as lost trying to figure out what the crew around me was saying was aboard the 12-Meter *Vim* with an Aussie crew in Sydney Harbor in 1962. The peculiar twangy Australian "strine," their shorthand slang, was all Greek to me, and so was the chatter of the crew of *Toxotis*. They were expert sailors, as two of them had been crew for the then Crown Prince Constantine when he won the Olympic Gold Medal in Dragons in 1960, and they still sailed with him whenever he had a chance to get in his boat—a not so frequent occurrence once he took on the uneasy duties of wearing the crown.

Now, however, they were on loan to John Sikiarides for the Rally. He came along for the ride but turned over the racing completely to sailing master Odysseas Eskitzouglou, and it was a hard-working, efficient crew, ever alert to sail trim, sail changes, and the fickle summer winds of the Aegean.

It was also the noisiest, most argumentative crew I have ever seen. Every maneuver was carried out in a torrent of rapid-fire comment and controversy, all, of course, completely incomprehensible to me, but a simple tack or jibe sounded like mobilization day for the Battle of Thermopylae as far as I could tell. There was always one loser in the hassle, and this I could tell, because the Greek gesture of ceding in an argument is to spread both hands, palms outward, at the waist in a semi-shrug, while giving out with a nasal snort that sounds something like "enhh!" This is all very well, except for the fact that it is done no matter what the loser is doing at the time—working a halyard, steering, or trimming a sheet. The spread-hands becomes a vivid drop-everything move, and it was a wonder that there were no disasters in the process.

Toxotis at Tourkalimano, Piraeus, with the Royal Yacht Club of Greece in the background, before the Aegean Rally

Our skipper, Odysseas, during "happy hour"

After an argument, they would turn to me all smiles and say, "No mind us. This the way we do always. It just the Greek way." And everything would be fine until the next chance for a difference of opinion.

Gradually, I could pick out some words they were using that were general nautical terms, with no counterpart in Greek, such as "walkie-talkie," "genoa," "chart table," "handicap," and "boom vang." Every time we made a move, the torrent of orders would usually end up punctuated by "boom vang" as the last item to be attended to, and I soon made it my job to hop to the boom vang every time this happened. This struck the crew as hilariously funny, and thereafter the order would be given as "Bill—boom vang," only "Bill" in Greek comes out as "Mbeel," and the order sounded like "Mbeel—mboombang."

There is a Mediterranean lingua franca of sailing terms used in most countries along its shores, and I began to pick up a few of these words too, such as *flocca* (jib), *panni* (mainsail), and *baloni* (spinnaker—what else?), and *lasca* for "let out" and *ferma* for "trim in," but the "mboom-bang" was still my No. 1 job.

Despite their intense desire to win and their basically serious ap-proach to the racing, the crew never missed a "happy hour" in late

Two of the crew perhaps just before or after one of their famous arguments. Themis of the six toes is at the wheel

Celebrating in Ios after winning the first leg of the Rally

afternoon, with ouzo, and bouzouki music on the record player, amid all kinds of horseplay and even dancing in the cockpit.

The first day, as we were having happy hour, Odysseas happened to see that I have only four fingers on my right hand, a congenital lack that very few people notice and that I almost never think of, since, having been born with it, I don't miss anything. He started to laugh uproariously and then explained that this would be too bad for a Greek, since the most violent, obscene, and supposedly effective whammy you can put on someone is to hold both hands open, palms turned upward and out at the shoulders, and then give a short, jerking push outward in the direction of the whammee with all ten fingers.

The others were all amazed and amused, but then Themis, usually quieter with me than the others because he had only a word or two of English, really started to break up and, amid gales of laughter, took off his shoes and showed us that he had six toes on his right foot. So, aided by ouzo, we worked out a special Greek-American whammy to flash back at the rest of the fleet. I gave them the old "push" with my nine fingers, and Themis, sitting on the deck with his feet over the rail, really gave it to them with eleven toes.

P.S. It must have worked. We won the Rally, and what a celebration when Greeks are victorious! They all said I did it on the mboombang.

The Power of Suggestion

Before my adventures with Jack Sutphen and Mort Engel in *J & B*, and the wreck of the *Mary E*, I had sailed with them several times in SORC races, and there always seemed to be something happening. The first time was in *Bones*, a Halsey Herreshoff–designed forty-foot sloop that earned her name because Mort had skinned her out to her bare bones for racing.

We had a mild Miami-Nassau Race for a change, but the day of the final race on the SORC calendar, the thirty-mile Nassau Cup Race in Northeast Providence Channel, saw a blustery east wind of perhaps 22 knots kicking up big blue rollers in the open water off Paradise (formerly Hog, until they put hotels on it) Island.

As usual I was huddled on the windward rail trying to keep the spray

Jack Sutphen working up to "fighting pitch" before a start

from getting inside my foul-weather gear while we slugged into it on the first windward leg, and I noticed that the boat was setting up a peculiar vibration as she pounded into the seas. There would be a shudder and a quiver in a rhythmic pattern, and it didn't feel quite healthy. In fact, it set a thought in motion, and I found myself realizing that I had never been dismasted in an ocean racer.

The thought had barely crossed my mind, and I was trying to will it away, like some bad omen, when there was a loud, explosive *crack* overhead. I felt the boat lurch heavily to windward and looked up to see a great midair tangle of rigging and collapsing sail off to leeward. My instant reaction was one of surprise that things could get into a mess so quickly, and then there was a splashing and thrashing as the collection of junk hit the water alongside, followed by a sudden comparative silence, almost eerie, in the aftermath of released tensions. A spreader had failed, followed by the failure of everything else.

It was a long, tedious job getting the sails and salvageable spar parts aboard, and the rigging untangled and lashed, before we were finally ready to head for port, and then we found that a piece of rigging was wrapped around the wheel, so we had to have a tow.

All through it, I was obsessed with a feeling of guilt for having had that thought about never having been dismasted at just the wrong time. Had I done it?

Catch Her, Bill

Bones never recovered from this ignominious event, and she was replaced for the next campaign by *J & B*, a stock thirty-nine-foot sloop that was a whiz in light air and smooth water but notoriously skittish downwind in heavy air. She was one of the new breed with short keel and separate rudder and very little else under her to give her stability. (She was later succeeded by the second *J & B*, the Carter 39 involved in the *Mary E* episode.)

We had a fast passage through the first two legs of the Miami-Nassau Race in a fresh northeaster of perhaps 25 knots, with more in the gusts, and the change of course at Stirrup Cay meant that we would be on a run for Nassau for the last leg, time to put up the spinnaker. I happened to be on the wheel at the moment. It was my first race in the boat, and I felt that I had her under control on the beat and close reach we'd had so far, but it was my initiation into the special delights of handling one of these babies on a run. There was a good sea running, with the usual short, steep, and eccentric wave pattern.

With what I thought was a considerable measure of over-optimism, we put up one of the biggest chutes on the boat, a high-shouldered thing that stood far up above and in front of the masthead when it snapped full and began to draw.

I have always thought that I could "feel" a boat well and had the knack of timing to anticipate an incipient broach with counter-helm, bringing the boat back again before this helm action took her too far. I had sailed a separated-rudder, short-keel boat in the 'Round Grenada Race on a wild sleigh ride down the windward side of that island in marginal conditions without a single broach just the year before, so I started with at least a fair bit of confidence.

The first *J & B* at least temporarily under control under spinnaker

This lasted less than ten minutes. As an extra puff hit, along with a larger than usual kick in the ass from a wave that was out of the usual pattern, I felt the need to catch the boat when her bow started to root and round up, and I zinged the helm over fast and hard.

"Catch her, Bill!" Jack yelled.

"I got her!" I cried confidently, "I got—" gargling and giving up, "God—dammit!"

J & B, with her helm all the way over the other way, continued to root and broach in the opposite direction until she was flat on her beam ends, spinnaker flogging in the seas to leeward, and everyone scrambling to hold on for dear life while yelling insults at me.

We got her back on her feet fairly soon, as I muttered a weak "Sorry, boys," and off we went again. This time I lasted for maybe six minutes before the whole performance was repeated, and I abdicated the wheel in a huff.

"Here, Jack, you take her. I'm too old for this sort of thing. I can't make her behave," I said, retiring to the after end of the cockpit to sulk.

Jack, one of the best helmsmen I have ever sailed with, stepped in with great confidence, and, much as I hated to have to go through the wild gyrations of another broach, there was a measure of personal satisfaction, mean as it was, in seeing her take off on him in a very few minutes with a carbon copy of my act.

"We've got the wrong chute," Jack said. "Let's get the bulletproof. This one's too far up there."

So the chute was changed, and it did help a bit. After that, she only broached twelve more times, by my own personal, small-minded petty-jealousied count.

Next year, she had a bigger rudder, and she only broached about half as much under similar conditions.

Immortal Fighting Words

Jack Sutphen, as I've already mentioned, is about as competitive a sailor as I've ever known. Ashore he is mild-mannered, soft-spoken, and a model of politeness. On his boat, especially when at the wheel, there is a visible change in him, almost as dramatic as the Jekyll-to-Hyde transformation, as his competitive drive takes over.

He is one of those sailors who have to take out their tensions verbally. The first time we sailed with him in *Scorpion,* his forty-foot sloop, I couldn't believe the stream-of-consciousness catalogue of worries that poured out of his mouth. Thinking he really meant them, I figured he had given up and was not trying to win, and I kept urging him to hang in there, which he was actually doing with every ounce of concentration he possessed, and we went on to win. Gradually, I became accustomed to his pace, a driving, work-off-everything-verbally will-to-win that really pays off.

Sometimes it has to be curbed a bit, as when we were approaching the finish of a race around Block Island during the Storm Trysail Club's Block Island Week in absolutely zero fog. I was navigating, and we were beating down the northwest shore of Block Island along the sandbar that stretches out from its north point. Working by the clock and the depth finder, I had us tacking on and off the bar with feet to spare, since it was a good reference point. We were right at the end of an inshore tack, with seconds to go before we were on the bar, when I yelled up "Come about!" to Jack at the wheel.

"We've got a lift," he called back, holding on.

"It'll lift you right onto the sand if you don't tack," I said with some urgency, as the gap between little red blips on the depth finder dial was rapidly disappearing. "Come about NOW!"

We did, and we again went on to win.

It was this concentration on the elements of the race, and of trying to get the most out of the boat and the wind every second of the time, combined with the verbal release of tensions, that gave us our favorite racing quote of all time, one that Jane (who has learned a few things since her bridal days and O'Hegan's arm) savors as the ultimate in competitive zeal, and one that fits so aptly in so many contexts when things happen to go wrong.

It was during the same Block Island Week in which we had been doing so well (and eventually won), in one of the final races, and we were rounding the south end of the island in a good fresh, puffy southwester on a spinnaker run. As we turned the southeast corner, it was time to jibe, and, at the moment, we were gunwale-to-gunwale with a couple of our closest competitors, surging along almost out of control. It was going to be a hairy, exciting one, and every inch counted if we were to keep the boats near us from gaining an edge during the jibe. Rick, an agile foredeck type, went forward to handle the pole, and we went into the jibing routine.

Suddenly, as he started to move it, the inboard end of the pole jumped out of the bell on the mast, and the pole zinged across the foredeck with tremendous force and caught Rick on the shoulder and side of the head. Jane, Jack's wife, Jean, and I gasped in horror as Rick

Getting ready for the near-fatal jibe, with Rick just heading for the foredeck (*Stanley Rosenfeld photo*)

was poleaxed to the deck in a heap. We were sure that he had a broken shoulder or fractured skull, and we forgot the race situation and were thinking only in terms of a medical emergency. It looked bad, and I jumped up to go to his aid.

But Jack, at the wheel and seeing the pole and sail go awry as Rick hit the deck, screamed out in anger.

By the time I reached Rick, thinking I had a stretcher case to contend with, he was struggling to his feet and making a stab at wrestling the pole under control.

He said later that, as stars spun around him and his ears were ringing from the blow of the pole, the first thing he reacted to was Jack's agonized scream. Despite the pain and confusion, he knew he had to do something to prove Jack wrong. The immortal line that spurred him on, screamed by Jack, was, "There goes the whole fucking race!"

Hitting the Deck, Swedish Style

When we bought our Morgan Out Island 36 cruising sloop *Tanagra* in 1973, Jane made me promise that the boat would not be used for racing, which was not a great sacrifice, since a full-cruising auxiliary was never meant for competition. We would do all our racing in *Polly*, our eighteen-foot Sanderling catboat, and *Tanagra* would live a life of ease.

In the summer of 1974, *Tanagra* was based in Newport, Rhode Island, for the America's Cup campaign. She was used for taking *Yachting* guests and staff out to watch the trials, and as a barracks boat for anyone from the magazine staying over in Newport, saving a tremendous sum in restaurant and hotel bills. In charge of her was Tom Bixler, who had just graduated from St. Lawrence University and took the job as *Tanagra*'s captain for the summer before entering his family's insurance agency in the fall. Cheerful and eager, with a round, youthful face and pleasant manner, he was an excellent skipper in every way, handling the boat well in the sometimes hairy conditions in the spectator fleet that pounded around Rhode Island Sound in pursuit of the Twelves, and acting the host role well for the dozens of guests who came aboard.

During the midsummer break between the Cup trials, there was the annual New York Yacht Club Cruise, a traditional event going back to the club's founding in 1844, with its daily port-to-port races and the usual in-port festivities each evening. We happened to have a young lady from Sweden staying with us at the time as part of a sailing exchange program with Scandinavian clubs, and I thought it would be a great experience for her to take part in the cruise, so I went back on my promise to Jane and entered *Tanagra* in the Cruising Canvas Class. This meant no spinnakers or other light sails, so the racing would not be too tough, but Jane has never liked the business of getting a sheet on a winch quickly and clockwise (it's a long-standing joke that she then says "Which way is clockwise?"), and she still took a dim view of the idea. I convinced her it would not be a high-pressure affair, which mollified her some, and she was thoroughly enchanted with Mikaela, the eighteen-year-old Swedish girl, so, with Tom as the fourth, we made up *Tanagra*'s racing crew.

Mikaela

I had visualized reaching and running through Nantucket Sound and Buzzards Bay in the usual fresh southwesters of summer, and all we had was light air on the nose for most of the cruise, so the racing was not a howling success, but we were never dead last, though we did have to power in several times.

Socially, though, we were the hit of the fleet, at least with the college-age set. There were many more young men than young ladies in the crews, and no others had an attractive young Swedish girl with a centerfold-type figure, so each port saw a steady procession of young men descending on us by dinghy from all over the harbor. Mikaela handled it all very well, but there were a few nights when she didn't get back till very late, and most of the harbor starts were quite early in the morning.

Tom, who was engaged to be married that fall, had been doing his best to act like a Dutch Uncle to Mikaela, helping her pick her dates from the swarm of besiegers and more or less keeping an eye out for her at shore functions. Several times, he was kidded about his luck at having her as a shipmate, and he would shake his head and smile ruefully, saying, "But I'm engaged." But he never deserted the helpful uncle role.

There was one morning when Mikaela had been out until three o'clock or so that we had an especially early start. Tom, who slept in the forward cabin, was always up first and would start breakfast. Mikaela had the bunk that converted from the dinette table in the main cabin, and Jane and I were in the after cabin. On this morning, Tom had the coffee perking and was well into scrambling the eggs, and Mikaela was still sleeping blissfully a couple of feet from where he was vigorously stirring away.

"Come on, Mikaela," Tom called. "Time to get up."

Mikaela slumbered peacefully on, so Tom raised his voice.

"Hey! Mikaela! Come on, it's late. You gotta get up. Hit the deck," he said, stirring away, and turning toward her for emphasis.

Mikaela went from deep slumber to complete wakefulness in an instant, threw the covers off, and stood up calmly, without a stitch on, stretched, and moved past Tom to go to the head, while he dropped the scrambled eggs all over the galley.

America's Only Race

The most glamorous yacht I have ever raced in is *America*, the 103-foot replica of the schooner that brought the cup that bears her name home from England in 1851. The replica was contracted for in 1967 by Rudi Schaefer as the centerpiece of a TV documentary about her sponsored by his beer company. Her launching at the Goudy and Stevens yard in East Boothbay, Maine, on May 3, 1967, the hundred and sixteenth anniversary of the launching of the original *America*, was a colorful ceremony as her black hull glistened in the slanting light of late afternoon, flags fluttered, and bands played.

Schaefer, a Bermuda Race–winning yachtsman himself, had her copied in every detail abovedecks, and her lines were taken off the old plans and adapted for modern boatbuilding by Olin Stephens. Below-decks she is a modern yacht.

When Schaefer retired, *America* was sold to Pres Blake of Somers, Connecticut, for use as a private yacht. He cruised her in New England and the Caribbean for several years and then decided to take her to

Europe for OpSail 74, which was to go from Copenhagen to Gdynia, Poland, and then back to France and England, ending up in the Solent, scene of the original *America*'s triumph.

I joined *America* in Copenhagen as she lay alongside a quay in the inner harbor of that colorful seaport city, surrounded by tall ships and by hundreds of small craft there for an antique boat show and parade as part of OpSail. There were Viking ships, *botter* boats, trawlers, converted fishing smacks, rowing shells, an old 12-Meter (the British *Evaine*), and many sail training vessels of every size and description from all over Europe, but we were the only American representative.

America attracted tremendous crowds of the curious, and it was like living in a boat show exhibit or a museum to have hordes of strangers ogling you from a few feet away and asking all sorts of questions. Anyone who had an American connection let you know that he had a cousin in Brooklyn or Minnesota or whatever, and a surprising number of American tourists came to pay homage to the Stars and Stripes.

Blake, who made the money necessary to support *America* as a private yacht from the Friendly Ice Cream Company, which he started in 1937 with a loan of $530, was well aware of her symbolic role, and he played "American Ambassador" to the visitors with genial patience, answering all sorts of questions. He also enjoyed going ashore and testing the product of the street vendors selling ice cream to compare it with "The Product."

"Not enough butter fat," was his usual verdict as he licked a cone or bit into a popsicle.

The day of the start of the race to Gdynia, which was to be preceded by a marine parade out of Copenhagen's harbor, was overcast and blustery, but there was no way that any more vessels could be crammed onto the water or more people along the banks. The focus of the parade was the Danish royal yacht, an immense, white, clipper-bowed vessel that loomed over the spectator fleet like a mother hen over chicks. Somehow, she reminded me of *Corsair*, years before, dominating the boats around her at the Yale-Harvard crew race.

The Queen of Denmark stood on the top deck and took the salutes of the vessels as the cadets on the tall ships manned the yards, whistles blew, horns tooted, flags fluttered, ensigns dipped, and the crowd on shore cheered, and it was a lively, dramatic spectacle under swiftly blowing clouds and an occasional pale patch of sunlight.

The start was outside the harbor in the Oresund with a reaching leg of fifteen miles to a lighthouse, which had to be rounded to port as the start of a long leg to the eastward out into the Baltic. The tall ships, six of them, were to start from anchor an hour before our division, which contained the smaller sail training vessels. These included *Evaine*, a Swan 48, sister ship of the boat that had won the 1972 Bermuda Race, and several big schooners about the same size as *America* from Sweden, France, England, and Holland. It seemed interesting that *America* was to race a Twelve in the only formal race she's ever been in.

The Russian *Tovarishch*, the German *Gorch Fock*, and the Polish *Dar Pormorza*, graceful white full-rigged ships, blasted away from the anchored start and were soon dark towers on the horizon, but the big Russian barque, *Kruzenshtern*, was slower in getting her hook up, as were two smaller ships, the Danish *Georg Stage* and the East German *Wilhelm Pieck*. The wind had piped up to about 25 knots, freighted with rain, as the square-riggers started.

When our time came, it was still blowing as hard, with a few stronger gusts, and we charged out beyond the windward end of the start intending to run back outside the line, then dip it and harden up on course. The sailing master was having trouble locating the other end of the line, and he was also preoccupied with the crew's work on the sails, since we had three young Danish naval cadets aboard just for the race in order to qualify as a sail training vessel. Pres was having a real wrestle with the wheel, and we kept riding up to windward instead of bearing off for the line. The sailing master was not really aware of this, and, at the last minute, he picked out a boat that was not the other end of the line, thought that it was, and that we were behind the line, and gave the word to Pres to harden up as the gun went off. As a newcomer aboard, I was only spectating, but I was sure that we had never dipped the line. I hoped that the Sail Training Association, which runs OpSail races, would not be too strict with us, but I had no way of knowing.

When we squared away on the reach, with the breeze still a good 30 knots and spitting rain, *America*, under main, foresail, and working jib, took off like a Le Mans racer. I know I have never been faster in a sailboat, even a planing catamaran, as she smoked along at perhaps 13–14 knots, and the most amazing part of it was that she didn't seem to be straining or laboring. She made so little fuss going through the water, and her wake was so flat, that you had to look straight down over the side at the water rushing by to realize just how fast she was going.

Two powerful Swedish schooners that were close astern dropped back quickly, and the skipper of one later told me that no vessel had ever sailed away from his ship like that before.

We caught *Kruzenshtern*, *Georg Stage*, and *Wilhelm Pieck* soon after jibing the lighthouse (jibing *America* is a man-sized job, but the crew did it well), and their rigs made a striking pattern against the western horizon in the lingering July twilight of that latitude.

It was glorious sailing through the night and into the next day as we followed a zigzag course eastward in the Baltic. The breeze mod-

Screaming along on a reach after the start

Georg Stage, one of the Danish tall ships in the race

erated and the sun came out, and, on a direct run, wing-and-wing, we
were not moving the way we had on the reach. Modern boats like the
Swan 48 caught up under spinnaker.

We rounded a mark off the south end of Sweden's Oland Island for
the last leg of about a hundred miles southward across the Baltic to the
finish in the Bay of Gdansk. We had been under a vast cloud of 10,000
square feet of sail, everything *America* can carry in the way of topsails,
gollywobbler, light genoa, and staysails, an impressive amount of
Dacron. Now, with the wind still west and piping on again as the day
waned, we had visions of a roaring reach to the finish and an arrival
in early morning. We began to pick up the boats that had passed us
under spinnaker, as no one can reach like *America.*

The Baltic is a fickle sailing ground, however, and its breezes seldom
hold a pattern for long, and our dream ended shortly after midnight
with fifty miles to go. The westerly quit, and in its place came a soft
southerly off the Polish coast, a fitful breeze blowing through haze,

America's graceful bow slicing through the Baltic

and we took until the next evening to finish, tacking back and forth at about 110-degree angles as the modern Marconi-rigged boats made their close-winded way past us again. Through the haze, we could see *Gorch Fock* and *Dar Pormorza* making lazy progress tacking through about 160 degrees, with glints of sun occasionally highlighting their sails as they dropped behind us.

We charged across the finish shortly after 2000 in a freshening lift off the Russian shore of the bay, not too sure of how we'd done, but thoroughly impressed with *America*'s sailing qualities. Considering her schooner rig, long keel, and oversized three-bladed propeller, her progress to windward had been pretty satisfactory, and there is nothing like her when it's blowing fresh on a reach.

When I checked in with the Sail Training Committee ashore the next day, Colonel Richard Schofield, the very proper Englishman who conducts the races, pulled at his moustache a bit and made a few noises in his throat.

"Ah, yes. *America*. Hmmm," he finally said, then paused for a while. "Are you aware that you never started the race?"

I didn't like the sound of this, as right as I knew he was.

"Well, yes," I said cautiously. "Some of us thought there might have been some confusion over the off-line mark."

"Exactly. Exactly." He made a few more "Hmmmms," then spoke again. "We have had to assess you a penalty of 2.7 hours for not making a proper start, but I'm happy to say that this does not affect your standing as the winner of Class B." He then flashed me a small smile. "Congratulations."

And so we had saved our time, and the penalty time, on *Evaine*, the Swan 48, and all the other modern boats in our class. Not bad for a 124-year-old design on the only occasion the replica was raced. And no matter what happened, the first miles of reaching after the start would have been worth the whole thing and more.

Welcome to Poland

After the visit with Colonel Schofield, I thought it would be politic as a visiting writer, to make myself known to the press officer for OpSail. Headquarters was in the Polish Naval Academy in Gdynia, and

America berthed in front of the Polish Naval Academy

I found his office and was ushered in with great cordiality. He had been with the Free Polish forces during World War II, so he spoke English well.

As I came in, he hopped up and shut the door behind me, and, without so much as a "How was the race?," "What can I do for you?," or any such normal openings, he said, "We have great news in Poland. We now have Coca-Cola and Pepsi-Cola. In Warsaw is Coca-Cola's district. Here in Gdynia, is for Pepsi-Cola."

Taken aback a bit, I nodded politely, not really knowing what to say, as he went quickly to a small refrigerator against the wall and brought out a bottle of Pepsi-Cola and a bottle of Polish vodka—which is excellent, by the way. With great ceremony, he filled two cups with vodka and Pepsi-Cola, then handed one to me and raised his in a toasting gesture.

"I now give you new Polish toast. Welcome to Poland from Pepsi-Cola."

I raised my cup to him, and at about 0845 we sat down to our vodka and Pepsi. He then became all business, saying, "Well, how was the race? Is there anything I can do for you?"

PART VIII

~~~~~~~~~~~~

Cruising Excursions

Cruising is a tamer pursuit than racing, naturally, and it is less likely that odd things might happen. In fact, the essence of good cruising is to have nothing untoward happen at all, but any combination of people, boats, and weather has inherent possibilities for incidents to develop, and develop they have at various times in the later years of the more than half a hundred cruises I've been on.

Fig Newtons and Booze

About the most "liquid" cruise I've ever taken was a ferry trip from the Chesapeake, helping a friend bring his forty-foot Owens cutter to New Jersey one spring in the early 1950s. He had just bought her, and he was very proud of her except for the fact that considerable dry rot had been discovered after he took possession and was having her worked over at a yard.

He used to stand at the stemhead and look back at her as she sailed along, shake his head, and say, "Forty feet of dry rot—and she's all mine."

I don't know whether it was this, or just normal routine, but I have never seen so much steady drinking on or off a boat over such a long number of hours. In my time, I have hoisted glasses with some pretty good ones and been in on some fairly strenuous parties without feeling that I was not holding my own, but I drank more on this cruise than I ever have in my life, and I was light-years behind the others. It was steady from before breakfast till long after midnight for three days, and I was beginning to fear for my health, or at least my liver, despite my poor performance in the group.

There were four of us aboard, and all were experienced sailors, so we had practically no nautical misadventures. In fact, the other three seemed to be able to carry on perfectly normally in sailing routines without ever being without a glass in hand.

The oldest member was a yacht broker who was a perfect figure of a Harvard man. He had a trim moustache, spoke in a clipped accent with a trace of New England broad "a," did the cooking expertly, and was a font of stories. (One of his favorite gags about himself was to say "I'm called Dusty because my faahts are so dry.") In later years, he was to run into financial difficulties with his business, and he was down to his last nickel and in desperate straits while in Florida when he came across what seemed to be a perfect solution to his problems. He met a woman who had been recently widowed and who was living aboard a large power yacht her husband had left her. After a whirl-wind courtship, in which the broker acted the part of sophisticated man of the world to the hilt, broadening his Harvard accent and dropping all the names of the wealthy people he knew in the yachting world, he married the lady and they started north on a honeymoon cruise in her yacht.

Our friend figured that he finally had it made, and he was relaxing happily in the lap of luxury when they came to their first fuel stop on the Waterway.

"Will you pay the man, please, dear," the bride said sweetly.

"Pay the man?" was the surprised response. "Ah—ah, I don't have any cash with me, my pet. Don't you have an account for the yacht?"

"No. I don't."

It turned out that the lady had the yacht and nothing else in cash or credit and had thought she had found the savior of *her* situation.

Thus ended the honeymoon, and in fact the marriage.

When he was with us, before he got into that mess, his only problem was the location of his next drink, and he was the champion of the whole group. Because of this, his advanced age compared to ours, and his labors in the hot galley, he did have a tendency to doze off after dinner when the party was just really getting going, but he always did it with the utmost dignity.

After three days, weather delays had held us up so that we were only in Forked River, New Jersey, on Barnegat Bay, forty miles from home, instead of Atlantic Highlands, where we were supposed to have been and which is four miles from home, and I had to be back in the office the next day, so I was forced to call Jane and tell her to come get me. This went over like a lead balloon, as she had to arrange a sitter and then drive through rainy darkness over strange roads to find me, but she agreed to come.

Meanwhile, we were having cocktails (and cocktails and cocktails) and dinner, and near the end of it, as we were having dessert, the yacht broker advanced to his usual state of doze. He happened to have helped himself to a couple of Fig Newtons just before this, and he had them clutched in his hand when he nodded off. After a while something jarred him awake, and he opened his eyes and looked down at his fist which had just unclenched at the moment.

With sheer horror in his voice, he looked down at what the Fig Newtons had turned into and said, "What the HELL is this?"

We calmed him, gently removed the gooey mess, and watched him drop off again. He remained that way until Jane arrived. As she started down into the cabin, her wet feet slipped on the ladder, and she came kerplunk down the rest of it to land with a solid *splat* on her fanny on the cabin sole. The discomfort and the ignominy did nothing to improve her already touchy humor any more than the cold-sober sight of a bunch of drunks did, and at that moment the broker woke up again, saw her sitting on the sole, and said, in his most lordly accent, " I never did approve of women drinking on boats."

Salty Talk

Favorite cruising companions over the years have been Mason and Julia Gross, neighbors in Rumson who have similar ideas on how to relax afloat, especially important to Mason when there were very few other ways he could escape the pressures of being the president of Rutgers University during the years of its great expansion from small college to the State University of New Jersey.

Mar Claro with her "thing closed"

Julia always looked on the romantic side of life afloat, keeping a notebook of impressions, working in a sketchbook, and reading up in guides about the waters where we were cruising. One of her favorite pursuits was to collect nautical phrases that she had never heard before so that, she said, she could sound knowledgeable in talking to sailors at parties or boating gatherings.

"It's great to be able to start a conversation by asking someone, 'Can you lay a grommet?'" she would say.

One year we took *Mar Claro* to Maine by trailer and launched her at the South Freeport yard where she had been finished off while being built. It was run by an old Navy friend, Harry Parker, and Harry, his wife, Woofie, two of their kids, and another couple were going to cruise in company with us for a few days in an Amphibi-Con, a twenty-six-foot sloop of the Controversy type, which *Mar Claro* also was.

The night before taking off, we were discussing plans at the Parkers' house and generally going over operations. Both boats had outboard motors for auxiliary power. They were located in an enclosed space aft of the cockpit with a well down into the water, a very handy rig, but there was a problem with getting enough air to the motor. If the hatch over the well were kept closed, there wasn't enough ventilation. If it were kept open with the motor running, the ventilation was fine, but the noise was much louder, so there was a constant concern over which way to operate. We were talking about this, and Harry asked me, "Bill, do you run with your thing open?"

I said that I did, while noticing out of the corner of my eye that Julia had her notebook out and was jotting something down.

"Learn something?" I asked her.

"That's the best nautical phrase I've picked up yet," she said. "That's marvelous: 'Do you run with your thing open?'"

Cruising in Company

The first night of our cruise in company with the Parkers was spent at anchor in the little harbor of Ash Point Cove on Harpswell Neck, not far to the eastward of South Freeport. It was small and snug, and we rafted together for congeniality as well as to save space.

Mar Claro and dinghy were added to this tow of Harry's

While making plans for the next day, we found ourselves in a small disagreement. Harry started making noises about an 0600 start. With six aboard, including two children, he would be up early, which was his wont anyway, and he wanted to get a good start. We were just un-winding from city life and long auto trips, and the Grosses and Robin-sons said they thought 0900 would be a much more civilized hour.

This was unresolved when we turned in, but it was thoroughly well resolved in the morning without our having anything to say. I did wake up at first light and could hear some stirrings on the Amphibi-Con, but I settled back to sleep comfortably. The next time I woke up it was to the gurgle of water past the chine and a sense that the boat was moving.

"Hey!" I said, and sat up. We definitely were moving.

I jumped up to the cockpit, and there we were at the end of a towline from the Amphibi-Con. Behind us was a small sloop the Parkers were using for a tender, and aft of that was a little pram that was our dink.

I called something rude over to Harry, who was standing at the tiller, and he smiled and waved back cheerily.

"I told you we like early starts," he called.

Just then I spied an anchored Concordia that belonged to a good friend of mine, one of my companions from the "Monster" Officers' Club at Milne Bay, Shorty Greenwood. I knew he was cruising Maine, had told him our plans for cruising with the Parkers, and wanted to hail him, so I called over to Harry to circle near the Concordia.

Shorty was just coming out of the hatch for his first look at the new day when his eyes fell on the strange sight of a four-vessel tow circling him like Indians around a covered wagon. He rubbed his eyes, blinked, and looked again, and then broke into a broad grin as he saw who it was.

"Is that what you mean by cruising in company, Bill?" he called over.

Very Funny

Our cruise to the eastward in Maine was to end at Mount Desert Island, where *Mar Claro* had been born. Her hull had been built at Farnham Butler's yard on Soames Sound, home of the Controversy-type boats, before being sent down to Harry Parker's at South Free-port for finishing, and it seemed appropriate to hold our cruise between these two historic, to *Mar Claro*, ports.

After a few days in company with the Parkers, Harry sailed off into the sunrise early one morning while we were still asleep (by prearrange-ment), and we were on our own for the last few days into Mount Desert. There was fog offshore, and most of our passages had to be under power in the bays and rivers that formed a network of water-ways in from the coast. We were "running with our thing open" to give the hard-worked outboard as much help as we could, but it had another problem. When all four of us sat in the cockpit, the motor was too low in the water and the exhaust didn't exhaust properly, backing up into the motor and stalling it.

The only solution was to send Mason, as the heaviest person aboard up on the bow to change the trim, and then the motor ran beautifully He had a fairly lonely cruise, but we occasionally sent him beers or martinis or peanuts to keep him happy.

When we got to Mount Desert, I flew back to South Freeport in a charter plane and drove the trailer to Mount Desert, and Farnham loaned me one of his yard men for the day to help me unrig *Mar Claro* and get her on the trailer. The only hoist capable of handling her was at Northeast Harbor, several miles from Farnham's yard.

I had rigged and unrigged *Mar Claro* for trailing countless times, and the drill wasn't difficult, but somehow this wasn't the day. First we had to wait for the tide to get her alongside the hoist, and then, in lowering the mast, which was stepped on deck, we ran into more trouble. The step consisted of a pair of "ears" on the bottom of the mast that went over a "knife-edge" fitting on top of the cabin trunk. The ears had holes in them, and a bolt went through these and through a hole in the knife-edge fitting to hold the mast in place.

In lowering the mast, I had always left the shrouds loosely attached and had never had trouble, but this time there was too much tension on the lowers, and, when the mast was about half down, with the workman easing on the halyards and me under the mast to support it from below and gradually bring it down, the ears both cracked at the base. It was an unnerving thing to have happen, but, with the builder's yard so close, it couldn't have happened in a better place, since a spare was at hand. Still, I wasn't happy.

The day of "a million laughs"

Then, when we finally got the boat on the trailer in the position she'd always ridden in, which balanced her with enough weight on the tongue so that she rode well, and so that you could walk on her without upsetting the balance, the workman and I went aft to check the rig, and she began to tilt backwards, with the trailer tongue rising in air. Both of us scrambled up the deck like rats deserting a hulk, and we just caught her before she upended on her stern.

I was a nervous wreck by then, and Farnham Butler happened to stop by just at that moment to see how we were doing.

"How's it going?" he asked his workman casually.

"Oh," the man said, chuckling delightedly, and in his broadest Down East accent. "We've had a million laughs, Farnham—a million laughs."

Happy Birthday, Alice

Ever since our brief adventure in Bimini and Cat Cay the first time we had taken *Mar Claro* south, I had wanted to get her back to the Bahamas, and I was able to arrange it in the fall of 1962. At that time, the Bahamas government had a contract with a ship running a weekly service from New York to provide special mail and freight service and to receive reciprocal promotional benefits from the government, and one of the arrangements they had with the ship, S.S. *Italia*, was for Olympic class sailboats to be carried as deck cargo at very low rates in order to promote special world class regattas in the Bahamas, bringing foreign boats in to compete.

Mar Claro was of the approximate dimensions of the 5.5-Meter sloop, the largest Olympic class at that time, and arrangements had been made with yachting people in Nassau for her to be shipped on her trailer as a 5.5. I had a call one day from the shipping office about making the final arrangements, and the man said, "Mr. Robinson, are you the one who's shipping a 5.5 slop to the Bahamas?"

I said yes, I was shipping a 5.5-type boat.

"And it's a slop?" he asked.

Not wishing to go against him in any way, I agreed that "it is a slop," and off she went on the deck of *Italia*.

She was ideal for cruising the Bahamas, as her two-foot-four draft let her go anywhere, and she was underrigged enough to handle the

The pier at the Current Club, *Mar Claro* at the outer end

strong breezes easily, and we had a great winter of commuting to her whenever possible. Over Christmas, we had the whole family for a few days of messing around Nassau, day sailing and snorkeling along the shores of Rose Island, until Robby went back north to go skiing, and Jane and the girls and I then took off for Eleuthera.

It happened to be December 27, Alice's birthday, which was always a problem. When she was little, we used to give her a midsummer party on July 27, or something, but we were inclined to slight the occasion now that she was older, and the whole trip was a family treat. We were planning to leave Yacht Haven at 0830 when, at breakfast, I remembered that she was fourteen that day, and I dashed down the street to the East Bay market to find some sort of cake. There was no bakery, but I finally found a Sara Lee applesauce cake in the grocery store and smuggled it aboard.

At lunchtime, as we were reaching along the cays east of Rose Island in a pleasant southeaster on a day of bright sun and sky, we plunked a big fat candle from a coffee warmer onto the cake and broke it out for her with the usual fuss, and she was suitably impressed, in fact quite touched.

We were aiming for the Current Club at the northern tip of Eleuthera, and we made it just at sunset, with the whole population of

The Cockney Lotharios of the Current Club

the club out on the pier to greet us. This was one of the typical little out-island resorts, with a few bedroom units around a central bar-restaurant-entertainment center, and informality the key. Visiting yachts are usually welcome for dinner, and there is always great camaraderie and easy talk around the bar and dinner tables.

The club was managed by an English couple who had two teen-age sons. One did handy work around the club boats and docks, and the other, at the advanced age of eighteen, was the chef for the club, and a very good one—that is, if his mother could find him at mealtimes. After dinner, there was a movie, shown against a sheet hung up in the bar, and the two sons of the establishment did a quick flanking movement on our daughters and had them quickly surrounded, to everyone's mutual delight.

After the show, we wandered back to *Mar Claro* at the end of the pier, and Jane and I had a nightcap while the boys and girls sat on the pier and chatted. Our girls had never dated anyone with a Cockney accent before and they were fascinated. In fact, Alice had never really dated anyone. We soon hit the sack in the forward cabin, leaving them chatting away, and the next thing I knew, I was awake, it was a bit after two o'clock, and, just to make sure, I looked into the main cabin. The bunks were empty.

This was a shocker, and I really didn't know what to do. There was no doctrine for fathers whose daughters are missing on Eleuthera at 2 A.M. I wandered quietly up to the club, but it was completely dark and closed, and no one was around the beach or the other parts of the pier. I was really worried, and I went back to talk it over with Jane. We had just decided that I would have to go up and wake up the manager when we heard feet coming down the pier, a rustle of hushed giggling, and then a soft "Good night, good night, good night" all around as they came to the boat.

The girls came quietly aboard, but they were beside themselves with suppressed giggles and postmortems about an auto ride they'd been taken on.

"Wow," Alice said. "What are you supposed to do about things like that?"

Martha was really laughing. "Boy, you had a rough one, didn't you?"

"I'll say. How are you supposed to handle them?" Alice kept repeating.

"It's tough," was all Martha would say, laughing all the while.

They subsided a bit as they got into their bunks, and finally there was a deep sigh from Alice. "Well. It certainly was an interesting fourteenth birthday."

Years later, inscribing one of my books as a present for Alice, I wrote, without thinking, "To Alice, who has interesting birthdays."

She looked up from reading it, and her eyes lit up. "Daddy!" she cried. "You were listening!"

The End of a Perfect Day

At Easter time, Jane and I went back by ourselves and had nine days of cruising the Exumas that were about as perfect a cruise as anyone could ever hope for. The weather was ideal, we had reaching breezes everywhere we went, mostly at hull speed, and everything fell into place beautifully.

We alternated anchorages between spots with some life, like a revisit to the Current Club on our way back, or Staniel Cay, with a lively

The dark blue of the channel at Warderick Wells winds among white flats to a secluded anchoring hole

touch of activity at its yacht club, with splendid isolation in the hundreds of coves and cuts that abound throughout the Exumas.

By day we would fly across the pale pastels of the Great Bahama Bank, whose great shining expanse spreads westward from the Exumas through water so clear that we seemed to be in air rather than liquid, marveling at the subtle changes in color as the bottom changed, here a powdery blue, here a pale, pale green, here almost pure white, and then a ribbon of brilliant blue winding in from the deeps of Exuma Sound off to the east.

It was glorious sailing of the most romantic kind, and after one of the best days of all, we beat our way up to the northern end of Warderick Wells and turned to starboard to reach along a deep blue channel between banks of blinding white to a protected pool well inside, surrounded by small cays. We had it to ourselves, one of the most perfect settings imaginable for a cruising anchorage, and I was filled with the beauty of it as we had a cool anchor cup of Mount Gay Rum on the rocks, and sat in the cockpit watching the sun go down changing the colors around us as each new hue blazed into the sky.

The colors faded, it grew dark, and the sky filled from horizon to horizon with the brilliance of the stars. Not a human light could be seen as it came time for supper.

Jane's system for cruising meals when we are away from sources of fresh food is to put the makings of one meal of cans in a plastic bag so that one grab in the locker, instead of a lot of fumbling and label reading, brings it all out at once.

And what, on this most romantic of nights in this most perfect of settings, at the end of this glorious day, was the ambrosia suitable to the occasion that was in the bag she pulled out? Just the two things I really don't like to eat if I have any choice, all wrapped together—spaghetti and beets.

Special Treatment

In 1966 we cruised the Virgin Islands in a Columbia 29 operated by Harry Parker's charter service, when the idea of bareboat chartering was just beginning to catch on. There were eleven boats available that year (compared with the more than 120 based there ten years later), and my account of the cruise was some of the earliest publicity that bareboating was to receive.

As a result, we were wined and dined and entertained at every stop, with considerable fuss made over us by local yachtsmen and officials and people in the marine trades. There was a reception for us at the St. Thomas Yacht Club, where we met a great many members, and the hospitality was overwhelming at all points.

Our companions on this cruise were Ray and Dennice Carey, good friends and racing competitors from home, but they had never cruised with us before, and they were also new to Virgin Islands cruising. Ray is a Holy Cross and Harvard Business School graduate who had a meteoric business career, became president of his company in his early thirties, and has since moved on to the presidency of bigger companies as a much sought after executive.

In most circumstances, he and Denny would be getting the VIP treatment while Jane and I tagged along, but here it became a local joke for the four of us that no one could quite catch their names, and they were always being introduced as sort of an afterthought as "Oh, yes—and these are Bill Robinson's friends." I was embarrassed, but they took it all as good for a laugh and played it that way as it kept happening over and again.

We had a wonderful cruise, with excellent sailing and weather and a lot of fun and laughs. After we got back, I happened to see a mutual friend of ours and the Careys at a party.

"Ray tells me you had a great cruise," he said.

"We sure did."

"Sounds like you really got the treatment."

"What do you mean?" I asked.

"Well—I asked Ray what it was like to go cruising with Bill Robinson from *Yachting*, and he said, 'It's what I imagine it would be like to visit East Boston with the Pope.'"

The Problem in Denmark

The Fyn Archipelago in the center of Denmark, between the Jutland Peninsula to the west and the big island of Zealand in the east, is an interesting cruising ground. There are hundreds of islands, large and small, and the waters between them are well protected. Quaint little towns, ancient seaports, and a good-sized city or two provide a wide choice of harbors. The land is low and gently rolling, with forested areas setting off farmlands, and hundreds and hundreds of small auxiliaries cruise there in midsummer.

Jane and I were eager to cruise there, and we arranged a week in a bareboat charter, a Danish-built fiberglass sloop with small Bukh diesel engine, beautifully appointed and equipped, known as a Bianca 27.

We were warned, though, about three things: the weather, the language, and the possibility that Americans wouldn't be too popular. The Danes make jokes about the weather and their language, such as, "We had a lovely summer last year; it was on a Friday," and "Danish is not a language; it is a disease of the throat." As for the popularity of Americans in the late Vietnam era (1971), we would just have to see.

We were prepared for anything, but the weather solved itself. In early August, we had eight beautiful days of warm sunshine and good sailing breezes, with almost no rain. The forests and fields basked pleasantly in the sun, the water danced and sparkled, and the villages and farms nestled picturesquely in the trees. Scratch Worry No. 1!

As for the language, in three visits I have been constitutionally unable to say any Danish word or place name and not get a blank stare back from any Dane. On the third try at a simple name such as

Under way in the Fyn Archipelago

Mullerup, the harbor we started from, said distinctly in English phonetics, there might finally be a delighted awakening and an "Ah, yes—Moolairoop," with guttural undertones impossible to duplicate on paper. As for the yachting center of Skovshoved, I never had any success whatsoever in getting a Dane to admit to what I was trying to say, even though I did my best to duplicate the Danish sound, which seemed to come out somehting like "Scot's Hole."

We were told that English would be spoken everywhere, which wasn't quite the case in the outlying islands, and with the older people who had gone to school before World War II. There is no anchoring

Our Bianca 27 (center) at the marina and boatel in Mullerup

out in the archipelago. All overnight moorings are in incredibly crowded little harbors behind artificial breakwaters, as there are no natural anchorages, and, since we only had a Danish ensign and a permanent metal burgee from a local club, harbor masters' instructions were always shouted in Danish.

I would call back "English only" until someone could be found to translate the directions. Someone was always found.

Via phonetics, we learned three key words for eating ashore, which we did every night in a spirit of adventure, and to give Jane a vacation from galley work—she had become very adept at concocting her version of open Danish sandwiches for our lunches. The words, sufficient to take care of our needs in a restaurant, even in the most remote little ports, were, in the order to be served, *schnapps* (akvavit, as a cocktail), *url* (rhymes with "girl" with a subtle little pursed-lips difference—which is beer, and is, of course, related to ale), and *fisk* (fish). We did very well with these basics and only had one surprise when we departed from the formula, thought we had ordered smorgasbord, and ended up with beef stew.

There was only one serious language impasse. After the first night aboard, I realized there was no flashlight, and I went to the general store in the little fishing village of Lohals, where we were, to try to buy one. I looked around the jumbled stock of the store and couldn't find any, so I went to the counter. A young girl waited on me, and I drew a complete blank when I started out in English. (There went the theory that all youngsters had English in school. If she did, she hadn't reached "flashlight" in the vocabulary lesson yet.) Gradually, I drew a crowd of customers and the other clerks, as everyone in the store tried to solve my problem, and, in desperation, I began a pantomime act, imitating pushing a button on a cylinder, and it somehow came out as a suspiciously indecent gesture.

I kept saying "flash," "light," "beam," and any other illumination words that came to mind, feeling sillier by the minute as the entire assemblage hung frowning on my every word, and finally I came out with "battery." That got a response, and the girl sped to a far corner of the store and held up a flashlight battery. I followed her, and there, next to the batteries, was a flashlight.

I picked it up happily and pointed to it, and everyone in the store gave a great simultaneous sigh, chorusing, "Ahhhh—HAND LAMP." (See, they do speak English.)

Many Danish terms had a relationship to English, and I could figure out most of the sailing directions in the guides this way simply by saying them phonetically. For example, a yacht harbor is a *lystbadhavn*. If you equate lust with pleasure and fudge on the pronunciation of "bad" to "bod," it isn't hard to figure that one out.

As for anti-American feeling, we did notice a certain coolness when we would enter a shop or restaurant and it was obvious that we were not Danish. Before long, though, we realized that this was because we were assumed to be Germans. (Jane is very blond.) Hundreds of German boats cruise the area, as Kiel is only ninety miles away, and they are received with formal but cool courtesy. World War II and its occupation have not been forgotten.

As soon as it was realized that we were Americans, however, there would be broad smiles, an attempt to talk English, an inevitable cousin in Milwaukee or Bridgeport, Connecticut, and the greatest effort to please. There was no variation in this, and the warm friendliness and desire to please were extremely welcome after all the warnings.

There was just one difficulty that we had not been warned about, and it was a simple one, but tough—ice. The profusion of ice machines taken for granted in American yacht harbors didn't exist, and it was extremely difficult to track the stuff down. We had been told that akvavit *had* to be served ice-cold, and beer the same, as we took off on the start of the cruise, so we assumed ice would be a part of the scene. No such luck.

For the first few times, we would ask for ice and be politely directed to a place that would turn out to be a Danish version of a soft-ice-cream stand. *Eis* can evidently mean the cold hard stuff or ice cream. We started when our original supply began to disappear, and by the time it was gone we were getting a bit desperate. In the sizable town of Svendborg, we were directed to a hotel about a mile inland, so, carrying a plastic bag, we set out for it. The girl at the desk was most helpful, nodded a "Yes, we can sell you ice," gave our plastic bag to a bellboy, and sent him off into the nether regions of the hotel. We waited in the lobby, smug about how smart we were to work this one out, and finally the boy came back. In the very bottom of the bag, about half a tray's worth of slender, sick-looking cubes barely made a bulge. Rather than argue, we paid the small fee and dashed the mile back to the boat before the cubes melted completely. We had some martini makings aboard but had not been using them, since gin is such an expensive luxury in Europe, but we decided to have martinis while the precious cubes were still alive. We managed a couple before they were all gone.

Finally, we found the solution. The only place to get ice in Danish ports is at the fish-packing plant. Once we discovered this, we wallowed in the stuff, and our akvavit and *url* were as deliciously cold as the most demanding Dane could require for the rest of the cruise.

Meltemi

After racing in the Aegean Rally in *Toxotis* in 1966, we were invited to cruise back toward Piraeus with John Sikiarides, the owner, another American friend of his, and Markos, the paid hand and one of the best seamen I have ever been shipmates with. John was the perfect host, making sure that everything was just right for us at all times and taking us ashore to see the sights from the point of view of the local people in such interesting islands as Symi, Cos, and Patmos.

We visited the almost deserted monastery at Symi, a long, low, red-roofed building with a clock tower, where an abbot and two monks tried to keep the order going by renting out their empty cubicles to Greek families as vacation rooms, and the monastery was a peculiar mixture of laughing children, accordion music, flapping laundry, and the peace and serenity of their order. We were received by the abbot

Jane at the wheel of *Toxotis*

At the pier in Patmos, next to *Aries*

The monastery of St. Christodoulos atop the highest peak of Patmos

in his "state" living room, where the Bishop of Rhodes was entertained on his official visits, and ceremoniously served wine and candy. The abbot was particularly proud of a small marine museum maintained there, and especially wanted me to see it when he learned I was a boating writer.

In Cos, there was the Asklepieion, the magnificent ruin of the world's first real hospital, where Hippocrates taught and practiced. Jane has been fascinated by archeology since majoring in Greek in college, and this was the most successful kind of cruise for her, combining sailing in the Aegean setting of brilliant blue seas against the stark brown of the islands and their white chapels and villages with visits to antiquities she had longed to see for most of her life. John was, as ever, a most knowledgeable guide, adding a great deal to the information tourists would normally gather.

Patmos was the most fascinating of all. Its azure circle of a harbor was lined with the whitewashed buildings of a modern Greek village, but far above it, on the highest ridge of the sere, brown island, an ancient village, Chora, crowned the rise with a fringe of buildings spread across it like snowdrifts. Towering out of these low-lying huts were the great walls of the monastery of St. Christodoulos, pinkish gray in the slanting light of late afternoon, and we taxied up there to stand on its battlements at sunset and look out at the vast Aegean panorama below us. A monk who knew John's father was standing at the wall with binoculars, looking at the shipping in the harbor, his hair drawn back in a small pigtail, and a stubby cigar poking from the gray of his beard. He invited us to visit the chapel and museum, dimly lit and glowing in candlelight that added extra richness to the ornate artifacts, many of them gifts of the Russian imperial family.

From this most romantic kind of reminder of departed eras, we were back in the present the next morning, after a night of listening to bouzouki music at a waterfront taverna, where Greek men did the traditional whirling, introspective dances. *Toxotis* headed out of the harbor in a flat calm, and we powered westward toward Mykonos in the lee of Ikaria, one of the highest islands in the Aegean. Its great bulk loomed over us as, up ahead, at the point off its western end, we could see a thin tail of whitish mist streaming off to the south.

The water around us was completely calm as we chugged along, but I noticed that Markos was reefing the mainsail and getting our smallest staysail rigged. I raised my eyebrows to John, and he read my thoughts.

Aries plugging into the meltemi off Mykonos

"It's calm now," he said, "but Markos thinks that we may have some wind when we get past the next point."

Markos was so right. We cleared the last point of Ikaria in brilliant sunshine under a cloudless sky, with an unruffled, cerulean sea beneath us, and it was as though we had opened the door to a giant wind tunnel. In less than a minute, we went from a flat calm to rail down in a howling norther, whitecaps close together on steep, breaking seas, spray breaking over the bow. *Toxotis* leaped ahead like a hopped-up horse on a jumping course, but we had the right sail combination, and she was taking it well. The little tail of mist off the point had tipped Markos off.

And so we met the meltemi.

This was the fabled summer wind of the central Aegean. The Greeks blame it on the Russians, saying that it builds up on the steppes of Russia, gathers strength crossing the Black Sea, and vents itself when it

Toxotis buried her rail and really charged through it

The sea wall at Mykonos protected us from the meltemi

reaches the warmer climate of the Aegean. It definitely is one of nature's more monumental thermals, and it dominates sailing conditions in the Aegean in July and August. We had been just ahead of it in the Rally, but now we had the original, one-hundred-percent genuine, full-bore thing, and it was some sail.

Toxotis was a sturdy vessel, and she took it well, but there was still a steady hosing of needle-like Aegean spray, surprisingly cold in the mid-seventies air temperature, dashing over us with each plunge of the bow. When we got to Mykonos, it was not high enough to give us a lee. Instead, the meltemi accelerated down its leeward slopes and blasted out at us in darkly ruffled wind streaks patterned by long lines of white foam. It had been a good 45 in the open Aegean, and now it was well over 50, but she labored sturdily along.

The last couple of miles into Mykonos had to be dead to windward under power in the narrow channel between Mykonos and Delos, and we made it at about a knot and a half in one of the hardest slugs I've ever been through.

Nowhere else in the world is there "fair-weather sailing" like the central Aegean when the meltemi howls down out of the beautifully clear Grecian skies of summer.

"Crash" Landing

Tanagra, our Out Island 36 sloop, has pretty well followed the dictum that not much is supposed to happen in cruising boats, but there have been a few oddments in her career, like the first time we ventured into the Gulf of Mexico with her from her base during her first winter, Clearwater, Florida, heading for St. Pete.

Clearwater Pass (a "pass" is an inlet in Gulf of Mexico terminology) has a drawbridge at its land end and then runs northwest between extensive shoals for about a mile, with a width of a couple of hundred yards between the shoals, before reaching the open Gulf.

Right after we cleared the draw under power, with the mainsail up as a "safety valve," heading directly into a fresh northwester of about 18–20 knots, the Perkins diesel coughed a couple of times and died. On a lee shore, with shoals on both sides of us, there was no time to mess with the engine (it turned out later to have dirt in the fuel), and it was a question of sailing her out of there or anchoring. I didn't want to sail back through the draw, and it was no place to anchor, as the onshore breeze was kicking up a good chop, so it was up to *Tanagra* to prove herself by clawing out of there under sail.

"Let's see if she can do it," I muttered to Jane as I put the wheel over to fill the main. And she did, making progress to windward under main alone for a couple of tacks. Then, when I had my bearings, we broke out the roller-furling jib (a lazy old man's delight) with a simple tweak of the sheet, trimmed it, and really began to move. *Tanagra*, whose hull mold was originally for an ocean racer in the days of the Cruising Club Rule, tacks quickly (which some Out Island models do not), and she makes little leeway, so it turned into a routine sail to tack our way out the channel to open water.

With a favoring wind, we flew south on a fast reach and negotiated Pass-a-Grille Channel and a drawbridge or two on our way into Tampa Bay and the Sheraton Bel-Air Marina, where we were to meet friends. It was all reaching and running until the last mile, which was directly to windward to the marina entrance, and we beat slowly toward it in the last gasps of the northwester that was fading with the afternoon.

We almost made it, but not quite. In the narrow entrance to the

Tanagra

marina, the wind quit completely, and we barely drifted up to a stake marking the other side of the channel, about a hundred feet short of the first pier, so near and yet so far. As we hung on there with our hopes for a spectacular entrance under sail dashed, the marina attendant came out on the pier and called over, "Why don't you use your engine?"

I would have thought any idiot could tell I wouldn't be in this position if I had one, but, trying to keep my voice mild and free of sarcasm, I said, "If I had one I would. It doesn't work."

"Oh," he said, thoughtfully scratching his head for a moment. "I see— Well, I'll come tow you over in the Whaler."

After our brave start, it didn't seem right to end with just a "whimper" this way, but that's how we finally arrived, in tow of a Whaler.

No Time to Relax

Another "adventure" involved the Perkins when we were heading south in the Intracoastal Waterway in the fall of 1975. We had been having lube oil troubles, but I had had the engine checked by a mechanic the night before, and we started out the channel from Oriental, North Carolina, into the Neuse River on our way to Morehead City.

As we cleared the last buoy, I turned the wheel over to Jane so that I could go below to the head, and I had hardly assumed position on it when the engine set up a tremendous clanking and rattling, gave two loud thumps and a horrendous, clashing *clank*, and froze up dead.

When I had collected myself, we made sail quickly and managed to squeeze back up the narrow channel to the marina, hard on the wind, with inches to spare, as I feathered her up like a racing machine (there was no room to tack) and shot the gap across the turning basin for a landing at the fuel pier. Eventually, we got the news that we had thrown a rod through the block, meaning the complete demise of the engine. The pin holding the rod had failed.

Ever since then, Jane is terrified every time I leave her at the wheel to go to the head with the engine running, and I must say it has taken any sense of relaxation out of the procedure for me.

Mystery Port

Cruising in the Bahamas with Martha, her husband, Hank, and their daughter Julie, then four months old, as crew, we were on our way from Nassau back to Florida via the Berry Islands, Grand Bahama, and Palm Beach, and were making the long hop across Northwest Providence Channel from Stirrup Cay to Grand Bahama. This time, that so often unfriendly body of water was calm and serene on a lovely May day, and we were approaching Grand Bahama in late afternoon, thinking to make Lucaya for the night.

Against the lowering sun, landmarks in the west were hard to identify, but we could see the occasional high-rises that dot the Lucaya-Freeport area as black silhouettes up ahead. We came to an unmarked sea buoy off two big concrete jetties, with a high-rise building inshore of them, and I asked Hank and Martha, who had been to Lucaya several years before, if this was it. I'd never been to it myself, but it didn't look right. Also I thought we had come on it too soon, but they thought it probably was, and there was no other place on the chart or in the *Yachtsman's Guide to the Bahamas* that had a sea buoy and jetties, so we turned to starboard and powered in.

Once inside, we realized it couldn't be Lucaya. There were big dredged lagoon fingers extending off into empty brush on each side of the main channel as we came in, but none of the facilities or buildings of Lucaya so clearly indicated in the *Guide*. There was just one lonely high-rise, evidently occupied, but with no sign of life at the moment, well up the channel.

There was definitely no such place in any navigational reference we had on board, but it looked snug, darkness was descending, and we decided to stay right there. We anchored in the first lagoon inside the entrance for a quiet, completely undisturbed night in what we could only log as "Port X," thoroughly mystified.

In the morning, we found that Lucaya was a few miles to the westward, and we still had no clue as to where we had anchored. It was a complete mystery, but I thought I could check Harry Kline, editor of the *Yachtsman's Guide*, when we got back to Florida, to solve the riddle of Port X. I called him, but he was just as mystified as we were and had never heard of the place. He said he would check into it, and he eventually discovered that it was a real estate development that had been started after the last charts were printed and that had failed before it was given any publicity.

Now it is official. It is called Grand Lucayan Waterway, described in the *Guide*, and it is no longer possible to "discover" it the way we did. How often can you find an undiscovered harbor in the middle of a busy cruising ground in this day and age?

PART IX

~~~~~~~~~~~~~~~

Names and People

In moving around the world in pursuit of yachting stories, the opportunity to meet famous "names," both from the sailing world and in other contexts, is always there, and the encounters can be very interesting, since people are usually their most relaxed and informal selves in boats. Here, then, are a few names that can be "dropped."

Introducing the Aga Khan (right) to a colleague

Seeing Corsica with the Aga Khan

In 1971, we were invited by the publicity firm handling the Aga Khan's Costa Smeralda resort on the Italian island of Sardinia to come have a look at the facilities there to see if they were suitable for holding major sailing events. This is a thirty-mile stretch of mountainous coastline on the northeast side of that big Mediterranean island, which has been very carefully developed as a premium resort for the jet set.

To discuss the trip, we were to have a meeting with the Aga Khan and his publicity man in New York, who asked me to suggest a good location.

"His Highness is here incognito, and the meeting must be in complete privacy, with no publicity or attention whatsover," he said.

I told him that a Tuesday 3 P.M. meeting at the New York Yacht Club would be as private as anything that could be arranged, and I would reserve a meeting room upstairs to make sure that privacy was complete. He agreed that this seemed like a fine plan.

The day of the meeting, I arrived at the Yacht Club a little before three to find the street filled with police cars with their rooftop lights flashing, while crowds of the curious milled about the sidewalk. Inside, the grand staircase of the clubhouse was lined with professional-looking types in trench coats with turned-up collars and fedoras with turned-down brims, all carrying walkie-talkies. Pacing the lobby in a panic was the Aga Khan's publicity man, beside himself with agitation.

"What the hell's going on, Bill?" he moaned. "Do they know His Highness is coming?"

"I haven't told anybody," I said. "I just reserved a room upstairs in my name."

"Well, he'll never come in here with all this going on. He'll drive right by, and I'll be fired; that's what will happen."

I inquired at the desk about all the fuss and was told that Prime Minister Heath of England was a guest at a small luncheon given by Olin Stephens, the yacht designer who had designed Heath's newest ocean racer. He was in New York to visit the UN, and the security precautions were extremely heavy because there had been some terrorist incidents in Quebec in the past few days, and a British diplomat had been kidnapped. At the moment, the luncheon party was being shown through the Model Room, with its unique collection of half models and a series of cases showing the entire history of the America's Cup. They were expected to leave soon, but it was almost three o'clock, and the Aga Khan's man was only slightly mollified.

"Well, I'm glad they don't know about his visit, but he still won't come in," he said.

We stood tensely by the door, wishing Heath to make an exit and wishing the Aga Khan to stay away for a few more minutes, and finally Heath descended the staircase in a grand procession. Flanked by the trench-coat brigade, with the Yacht Club chambermaids also lined up and waving little British flags, he took each step slowly, giving the Prime Minister version of the Queen Elizabeth wave, shook hands with the luncheon party with much ceremony (with the publicity man practically ready to take him by the scruff of the neck and throw him out), and was finally ushered into his limousine. Amid a great wail of sirens and flashing of lights, the entourage blasted off down Forty-fourth Street, and the club lobby quickly returned to normal. Not two minutes later, a black limousine pulled up in the now deserted street, and the Aga Khan, a pleasant, unassuming young man, very polite and quiet, and two aides, came into the club. No one knew he was there, and the meeting went off smoothly, except for the slow subsidence of the publicity man's ulcer. (Two years later, I met Heath sailing on the Hamble in England, and he was amused to hear of the near-miss, and the concern he had caused the publicity man.)

As a result of the meeting, it was arranged for us to visit Costa Smeralda that July, and we spent a lush few days as guests of the management in their fanciest hotel, the Calle di Volpe, being wined and dined in jet-set style, while incidentally contemplating the waterfront facilities (which were fine). There were confusions like ending up at a party for the Sail Training Association, to which we were not invited, thinking it was the right one, when we were supposed to be at a reception for a Yugoslavian mezzo-soprano, whose concert we later had to suffer through. She was large and loud, with a frontal construction that went with her trade, but she made the day anyway for an epicene German society photographer who was part of our party. Overcome with glee, he said, "Do you know what that awful woman asked me in her terrible German? She wanted to know if I had been well eaten."

We were included in parties with the Aga Khan and his friends, and it was fascinating to hear the trilingual conversation that bounced back and forth in English, French, and Italian, with everyone speaking whatever suited him best.

The Aga Khan's express cruiser

On our way to Corsica

Bonifacio was well worth the visit

The main purpose of the visit was to inspect the offshore waters to see if they would be suitable for major, world-class regattas, and this was to be done in the Aga Khan's own express cruiser, a needle-nosed fifty-footer with twin 18-cylinder, 1,300-hp diesels. They were housed under a "flight deck" aft, with a small but lushly appointed cockpit-bridge forward of that, and a cozy two-bunk cabin and head in the forepeak. We reported aboard at 1100, at the yacht harbor of Porto Cervo, helped over the stern gangplank by a uniformed crew of two, and were greeted by the Aga Khan with the question, "Would you like to see Corsica?"

"Well, that sounds very interesting," I said. "How far is it?"

"It's forty-five miles, across the Strait of Bonifacio. These are the waters I want you to see."

"If it fits in with your schedule, we would certainly enjoy it," I said.

"Well. We must be back by one o'clock, since we are having lunch on my big yacht with some rather sticky people." He laughed apologetically. Pretty sure I had read the signals correctly, I shrugged in acquiescence, and he burst into a big smile.

"We shall see Corsica!" he cried.

He pressed buttons, bells clanged, and sirens screamed, as the various engine alarms registered, and the twenty-six hundred horses rumbled to full-throated, urgent life. In minutes we were arrowing away from the narrow harbor entrance of Porto Cervo over a fortunately glass-smooth gray-blue sea, and the passage past many little islands was more like a flight than a boat ride. In less than an hour, the high, corrugated cliffs of Bonifacio at the southern tip of Corsica loomed over the bow and were soon towering over us. Our wake, which had stretched for miles behind us in a great white-winged vee, subsided as we came off the plane and entered the winding harbor entrance, a narrow cut in vertical stone cliffs that opened out slightly to a harbor lined with the umbrellas of cafés, yachts moored stern to, and tier on tier of ancient houses, oddly proportioned cubes that hung from the cliffs like birdhouses. They were seemingly ready to topple to the water in the lightest puff of wind, but had been there for centuries.

Our exhaust thundered and cannonaded around the shoreline, echoing off the cliffs, as we took a complete turn of the harbor at idle on one engine (probably 8 knots) and then made a quick exit to the open water outside, where the throttles were pushed forward, the boat rose back on her plane, the wake again veed out into infinity, and the blue mountains of Sardinia grew rapidly closer.

It was actually 1310 when we came alongside the gangway of his big motor yacht and were welcomed aboard for lunch by the Begum.

The King Is a Sailor

That was a year for royalty. After Sardinia and our cruise in Denmark, the last stop on our trip was Norway, where we had been invited for the weekend to visit Finn Ferner, one of Norway's leading sailors and sailing officials. His son, Christian, had stayed with us on the Scandinavian sailing exchange the first year we had done it, and Finn and

The Ferners' house on the Oslofjord

The royal Norwegian yacht *Norge,* formerly T. O. M. Sopwith's *Philante*

his American wife, "Monk," had asked us to be sure to come stay with them if we ever got to Norway.

Their house is a handsome multi-level one of California redwood rising in stages to the top of a bluff overlooking the Oslofjord, a dramatic setting with a gorgeous view, and their weekend entertainment for us consisted of sightseeing such fascinating items as the restored Viking ship, and Amundsen's *Fram* and the *Kon-Tiki,* side by side in dual museums, sailing on the Oslofjord, and a dinner party for King Olav, a dedicated sailor, and, incidentally, a *Yachting* subscriber.

It was a revealing glimpse of the informality of Scandinavian royalty, combined with the real reverence and affection with which the royal family is regarded. The Ferners are practically "family," since Finn's brother is married to the Princess, and Finn crewed for the King for years in International One Designs and Six-Meters.

A lone driver deposited the King, a widower close to seventy, at the door, and he made his way up the stairs to the cliff-top living room with the dog barking at him, as he shushed it and played with it. Heavyset, with the outdoor look of a sailor and skier, he was wearing a yachting blazer and gray slacks.

He proved a knowledgeable reader of *Yachting,* discussed several articles in the latest issue, and asked after American friends like our publisher, Bob Bavier, and Harry Morgan. After a short cocktail hour, sit-down dinner for a dozen was served buffet style, with everyone helping himself, as there were no servants in the house at all.

"No one in Norway has them," Monk explained.

Supper over, we all, including the King, helped clear the table, taking our plates to the kitchen, and we then settled down to watch the televising of an astronaut re-entry after the second moon landing. Everyone congratulated us, much to our embarrassment, on its success, as though we were personally responsible.

After the King was picked up by his driver, the rest of us chatted on, and stories were told about his great love for sailing. He has a large vessel as his royal yacht, but his real love is racing, and he is an insatiably keen competitor. Finn told of returning to port after a long, hard race in an IOD a few years previously on a cold, rainy day. The crew offered to take the helm, but the King said he wanted to keep sailing, so the others huddled below in the cuddy to keep out of the rain.

Suddenly they noticed that Olav was concentrating harder, adjusting the sheets a bit, and obviously tending the helm with care.

"What's the old boy up to now?" Finn murmured to the other crew, and, as Olav continued to give every evidence of being in a race again, they peeked out to see what was up. Ahead of them was a motor launch chugging sedately along, and the King was making every effort to pass her.

"He's so competitive, he has to pass everything that floats," Finn said, laughing.

The King's Dragon

When I sailed with King Constantine's Olympic crew in *Toxotis* in the Aegean Rally in 1966, we found that after the rally we were all going to Denmark for the festivities in connection with the centennial of KDY, the Royal Yacht Club of Denmark. A Transatlantic Race was ending, which I would be covering, the One Ton championships were being held, and a great many one-design classes were conducting regattas. One of them was the Dragon Gold Cup, the world championship of that class, which was then an Olympic class, and Odysseas and his sidekick, Yorgo, were going right from the Rally to trail Constantine's Dragon to Copenhagen.

When we had a reunion there, I found out that Constantine had not yet arrived, and Odysseas and Yorgo asked me to crew with them in the tune-up race for the Gold Cup. Top sailors from all over the world were in the regatta, and it would be a great experience. Fortunately, this was not the race in which printed instructions, which were handed out in either Danish or English, contained a lulu of a mixup. The Danish instructions had the fleet rounding the first mark to port, and the English ones called for a starboard rounding, and the resulting confusion

Dragons in the yacht harbor at Skovshoved

King Constantine (left) arrived by powerboat

was one of the classic shouting matches of all time (the race, of course, had to be canceled).

We had a very exciting race in a fresh, puffy land breeze, and rounded the last leeward mark in first place. Right behind us were two of the top class hotshots, the Americans Bobby Mosbacher and Buddy Friederichs, and we had to make the unavoidable decision on which one to cover. We chose Mosbacher and held him, but Friederichs naturally split tacks, and he took us both.

It had been a hard race, and we were glad to break out a beer and relax a bit as we jogged back to the KDY small-boat club at Skovshoved. I knew the beer was going to tax my bladder after a long afternoon, but I figured we would soon be in, and it tasted great. Halfway back to port, we saw a powerboat heading for us at top speed with a man standing on the bow wigwagging madly, and suddenly Odysseas and Yorgo braced up and looked sharp (what they said to each other in Greek I have no idea), because it was Constantine, tall, dark, youthful, and very excited. He wanted to come aboard.

Jumping over eagerly from the powerboat, he greeted his crew with joyous cries as they handed him his sailing jacket. "Ah! My boat. My lovely boat!" he said, laughing happily. "I am so glad to see her again. It is so long since I have sailed her."

We had met briefly when he came to wish *Toxotis* luck at the Rally (and his first sentence was "How is Bus Mosbacher?"), and he shook hands warmly now and asked about the race. As he shrugged into his sailing jacket and grabbed the tiller, he turned to me and asked, very politely, "Do you have any plans, Mr. Robinson? I would love to sail my boat for a while if you are not in a hurry to go ashore, but we can take you in if this is inconvenient."

So how do you answer a request like that? Tell him your bladder is about to burst?

Instead, I mumbled what I hoped was a polite and diplomatic version of "Go ahead, King. Sail your boat," and settled onto the cockpit sole with my legs crossed, wondering about the protocol of taking a leak over the side of a royal yacht.

I knew he was far from stuffy and had a sense of humor, judging from a story Bus Mosbacher told of a time when he was crewing for Constantine in the Dragon at Piraeus. Bus was tending the spinnaker sheet, and there came a time when he wanted to trim it and found that Constantine was sitting on it. With the diplomatic tact that kept America's Cup crews at top form for him and earned him the job of Chief of Protocol in the State Department, Bus asked, "What does one say to a King who is sitting on the spinnaker sheet?" and Constantine's answer was "Tell him to get his royal ass off it!"

Still, I didn't have the guts to stand up and use the lee rail, so I suffered in silence while we ranged through the fleet, and Constantine renewed acquaintances with his friends and competitors in the class. Finally we came to Prince Juan Carlos, at the time the designate to the throne of Spain in Franco's plans, and now the King of Spain, who is Constantine's brother-in-law. English is their mutual language, and they greeted each other with glad cries. Juan Carlos is slender, blond, and so handsome as to be almost pretty.

"Hello, brother-in-law," Constantine called. "How's my sister? How's the folks?"

"Everybody's fine," Juan Carlos said.

"How did you do in the race?"

"Don't ask."

"What's the matter?"

"Last night!" Juan Carlos cried, holding his head. "The Spanish Ambassador came aboard the yacht for one drink at nine o'clock, and would you believe FOUR O'CLOCK—" He held his head again and rolled his eyes.

After some more banter we sailed on, and Constantine chuckled over Juan Carlos' plight.

"What yacht is he staying on?" I asked.

"My father-in-law's. The royal yacht of Denmark."

"Why does he live there instead of ashore?"

Constantine laughed and gave an expressive shrug. "If he lives ashore, we can never find him," he said.

In my condition, laughing was difficult, but I kept up a brave show, and finally we made it ashore. I departed with what I hoped was not too unseemly haste, not knowing the protocol for going ashore from royal vessels, and safely managed a stiff-legged walk to the place I had been dreaming of for the last hour.

Uppercutting the Prince

Jane was waiting for us at the club after the race, and we all gathered in a group to have the usual postmortems, now that I could think of something else besides going to the head. After a while, Juan Carlos came up and was introduced all around. When Jane and I met him, we both gave regular, informal, American-style handshakes, which seemed the right thing, with everyone in sailing clothes.

While we were talking, our son Robby, who had been in the Transatlantic Race, came up and was also introduced. After a while, people began to drift away, and it was time to say goodbye. Juan Carlos, who had given Jane that straight American handshake when we met, evidently realized that she was a more senior matron than he had first thought, judging by the size of her six-foot-three, 190-pound progeny, and decided to give her the more respectful European-style kiss on the hand in parting.

The only trouble was that, as he leaned over suavely to kiss her hand, Jane, who had never had anyone perform that gesture in all seriousness before, and remembering how she had been greeted when they first met, pumped her hand up in a good, hearty handshake.

The timing was perfect. As Juan Carlos leaned over, Jane caught him square on the jaw with her firm gesture. He reared back with a startled, hurt look in his eyes, gasped out something like "Adieu, Madame," and quickly faded away from her solid right uppercut.

Jane, who blushes easily, blushed about as purple as I have ever seen her in the more than fifty years I've known her, and sighed, "Wouldn't you know? The first time a Prince ever kissed my hand, and I have to go and punch him in the jaw."

A Greek Challenge

While Constantine was still on the throne in Greece, his heart's desire was to become involved in America's Cup competition, and he made serious noises about a Greek challenge. He visited Newport, Rhode Island, at the height of the 1967 activity, when Bus Mosbacher in *Intrepid* was defeating Australia's Jock Sturrock in *Dame Pattie*, and designated a well-known, experienced Greek yachtsman, John Theodoracopoulos, as his official representative.

We had met John during the Aegean Rally in 1966, when he was sailing his big ketch *Aries*, which had formerly belonged to R. J. Reynolds. All Greeks overwhelm you with hospitality, but John seemed to have an extra knack for it. We had been entertained royally on *Aries* several times, and later, on a return visit in 1967, he had given a big dinner party for us at the Athens Hilton. Martha and Alice were both

John Theodoracopoulos on *Aries*

with us, and during dinner one of them, making conversation, asked, "When are they going to start breaking plates?"

"You want to break plates?" John asked.

"Oh, I was just asking. I didn't mean—"

"We shall break plates," he announced firmly. "Not here. It is no longer legal in Athens. After *Never on Sunday* so many tourists wanted to do it that we were running out of plates. No one does it at the Hilton, of course, but there is a special place out in the country. We shall go there."

No protests over too much bother, etc., etc., could deter him, and the entire party of more than twenty people was transferred in limousines to a country inn about an hour out of the city. Evidently he had phoned ahead, because they were all ready for us. We were the only people in the place, but a good-sized bouzouki orchestra was on the bandstand and burst into frenetic music as we entered. We were seated at one big table and ordered drinks, and then great stacks of plates were passed around to each place. Everyone stared at them timidly, afraid to make the first move.

"Go ahead," John said, smiling at Alice. "Break one."

Alice stared at him, looked at a plate, giggled, then gingerly picked one up and dropped it. It broke with a timid tinkle of china.

"Good!" John cried, "but you can do better than that. Martha, you do one, and really break it."

After a moment's hesitation, Martha picked one up and dashed it down with some authority, so that the pieces scattered across the floor. One by one the other guests got into the act, and soon plates were crashing and cascading all over the floor. When enough debris had gathered, a waiter would come out with a broom and sweep everything into a trapdoor under the bandstand.

There were interesting sidelights. The wife of a couple that was known to be having difficulties broke one over her husband's head, drawing blood, and he sat there with a martyred look from then on, ignoring the activity as the smashing continued. The dignified wife of an admiral, regal in furs and long gloves, had been loftily aloof when the fun started, but I watched her as the spirit of the occasion began to catch up with her, and finally I saw her gloved hand reach out sneakily and flick one plate to the floor. The sound of its crashing brought a beaming smile to her face, and soon she was hurling them down with the greatest abandon.

The supply of plates would come in waves, and in between there was general dancing. No one's glass was ever allowed to remain empty, as John presided over everything with that wonderful imperious gesture of a raised arm and snapping fingers to keep the waiters hopping. Short and stocky, with big dark eyes perpetually twinkling in humor and a devilishly gleeful expression on his face, he was very much the master of the revels, and some revel it was.

We also have John to thank for the name *Tanagra* in our family. After the 1966 Rally and cruise in *Toxotis* (the Greek name for Orion, the Hunter), I was asked to give a slide show on the Greek islands at the New York Yacht Club, and, knowing that John was in New York at the time, we invited him to be our guest for dinner and the show. While making introductory remarks before starting the slides, I acknowledged John's presence and asked him to stand and take a bow as a Greek yachtsman who had been most hospitable to us. The audience of about two hundred and fifty, packed in the Model Room, gave him a warm hand, and he beamed in obvious pleasure.

Afterwards, he kept repeating what an honor it was to be introduced and applauded at such a gathering, and the next day a messenger arrived at my office carrying a box that he would only deliver to me personally, not trusting it to be left at the reception desk.

"In gratitude from Mr. Theodoracopoulos," he said. "Very old. Very fragile. Very valuable. You must be very careful with it."

It was a Tanagra figurine, about ten inches high, of terra cotta, dating from about 450 B.C., of a graceful woman dressed in flowing robes. Tanagra is a town in Boeotia, north of Athens, where hundreds of these artifacts have been found. They represent a lady dressed to go traveling, and they were placed in the tombs of noble ladies after the funeral to be pleasant companions for them on their onward journey. The word Tanagra has come to be a synonym for grace and delicacy, and our Tanagra lady is our prized possession. When it came time to name our boat, we liked the sound of the word as a name, and we explain it as a "lady dressed to go traveling," which *Tanagra* definitely is.

When it came time for the New York Yacht Club to accept challenges for 1970 at the end of the 1967 activities, John entered one from the Royal Yacht Club of Greece, and Australia, France, and England also placed challenges. I asked John how they expected to turn out a 12-Meter in Greece, since the boat had to be designed and built in the country of challenge, and nothing approaching a Twelve had been turned out there (although he had bought *Nefertiti*).

"Are you going to import Olin Stephens and make him Olino Stephanos?" I kidded.

"We have smart boys," John said. "Very smart boys working with the U.S. Navy in Washington as designers."

"What are they working on?" I asked.

"Propellers for aircraft carriers."

With Constantine's political problems and eventual loss of the throne, the Greek challenge naturally died before anyone had to find out whether these smart propeller designers could turn out a Twelve, but while it was still on the books, I wrote an editorial in *Yachting* suggesting that the method of selecting a challenger be changed to provide more competitive experience for the boat that had to meet an American defender fresh from the most intense kind of summer-long battling in our selection trials. Previously, one club's challenge was it, and anyone else wanting to get into the act had to wait a turn in another challenge year. If all the challengers were allowed to sail off in an elimination series, I suggested, it would be a fairer, more interesting, and more competitive way of arriving at the ultimate challenger.

The idea was well received by interested groups in England, France, and Australia (and has since become the system in effect), but John, who was in New York at the time, wrote me a letter saying that Greece did not like the idea.

I telephoned him at his hotel and said, "John. You're out of your mind. The New York Yacht Club would never pick Greece ahead of the other three countries. If they picked the most inexperienced one, they would make a laughingstock of themselves. The only way Greece can become involved is through a sail-off."

"King has no time for sail-off," he said.

"Look. You know as well as I do that he has to spend a lot of time in a boat all summer. He can't hop aboard one cold on September 15 against somebody like Bus Mosbacher. A sail-off would help him," I said.

There was a pause on the other end of the line, and then a sigh from John. "I tell you the truth," he said. "We don't trust the French."

A Scoop in Sydney

The sailing world was really startled when Australia entered the America's Cup picture with a challenge for 1962. It was a good enough story for me to head for Australia to take a look at their preparations, and I worked an arrangement with Pan American known as a "letter of agreement" in which they paid me a sum roughly equivalent to the air fare to perform a public-relations assignment for them. This consisted of making sure the airline was identified in anything I wrote about the trip.

The head of the Australian challenge was Sir Frank Packer, a brash, autocratic Sydney publisher and yachtsman, and arrangements were made through the New York office of his syndicate for me to stay at the Royal Sydney Yacht Squadron as well as to write some articles for his papers and be interviewed on his TV stations. I was told that I would be met on arrival for a TV interview.

Since I was coming in from Europe, my last leg from Bangkok to Sydney had to be on Qantas, as Pan Am didn't fly that route, and I was thoroughly travel weary and jet-lagged when the plane finally touched down at Kingsford Smith Airport. I looked out the window and saw several TV cameras and photographers with still cameras and thought that it seemed like quite a contingent for one boating writer, but I had expected to be interviewed when I arrived. Then I realized that any photos would show me coming out of a Qantas plane, while I had this special arrangement with Pan Am, and I didn't know what to do about that.

I really didn't have to worry, though. When I stepped out the tourist-

Sir Frank Packer watching *Vim* and *Gretel* practicing

Alan Payne

class doorway onto the landing steps, braced for cameras, there was no one there, and I could see that the collection of cameramen and press were all at the first-class steps. It seems that Miss Australia had just won the Miss World beauty contest and was returning home in triumph on the same plane.

Eventually, a man from Sir Frank's TV station did find me as I waited at customs, and I was taken into a small reception room for the interview. In it, I came out looking like a fugitive from a Georgia chain gang, as twenty-two hours of flying doesn't set one up so well to look fresh and sparkling on black-and-white TV. Miss Australia looked fine, though.

The Yacht Squadron is an active club with the atmosphere of an old-line English one, and I enjoyed my stay there. A few old members lived there permanently in retirement, and the first morning I came down to breakfast, one of them was the sole occupant of the dining room. The waitress had been warned about the special guest from America, and she cooed and clucked over me like a mother hen, making sure that I felt at home. She introduced me to an old codger, a retired admiral who mumbled a welcome, and, since he was all alone at a large table, I thought the expected thing to do would be to sit next to him.

"May I join you?" I asked almost rhetorically, starting to pull out a chair, and the old gentleman turned red as a beet and started sputtering.

"Oh, no, love!" the waitress cried, taking me by the arm. "Mustn't sit there. That's the Colonel's place. Here we are," and she led me to the next table and plunked me down back to back with the Admiral. It seems that the permanent residents had their special seats, and the Colonel would have died of apoplexy if he had found a strange American in his, if the Admiral hadn't done so already at the enormity of the thought. He was well on his way to it when the waitress intervened. So we sat, the only two people in the room, and carried on a rather stiff conversation over our shoulders.

Alan Payne, the designer who had created Gretel, the Australian challenger, in a monumental achievement of imagination and hard work, also knew I was expected, and he called me almost as soon as I entered the club to see if we could have dinner that night. He was very anxious to have the information on Gretel reported on in Yachting, and there was method in his grabbing me that early. Through dinner, he filled me in on his thinking, his problems, and his activity, and made arrangements for me to go aboard Gretel the next morning to take pictures of her special gear and fittings. Most of the items had been custom designed by Payne and built one-off in machine shops, since there was no stock stuff like it available.

"Sir Frank doesn't know you're here yet," Payne said (presumably

Packer didn't watch his own TV station all the time), "and I know what he's going to say when he finds out, so I think it's best if we get you aboard *Gretel* as quickly as possible."

It was only after I'd had my tour and taken a ream of pictures that Payne called Packer and told him I'd arrived.

"Oh, he's here, eh. Well, help him all you can, but he's not to get on the boat," Packer said.

"Yes, sir," Payne said, winking at me, since he knew I had my story, and, telling the truth literally, promised, "He will not be getting on the boat."

When the Aussie contingent arrived in the States in the spring, Packer held his first press conference in his New York hotel room. Although we'd met several times in Australia, he didn't acknowledge it when I walked in, but as soon as the questioning started, he indicated me rather sourly and said, "Why don't you ask your Mr. Robinson about those things? He knows more about the boat than I do."

A taboo closeup of *Gretel*'s special gear

Gretel off Sydney Heads

A Special Wife

A year before the Olympics were to be held in Mexico, a pre-Olympic Regatta was held in Acapulco in the same week in October 1967 that the regular Olympics were scheduled for in 1968. There had been considerable discussion about the ability of the Mexicans to handle a major regatta like this, plus concern over the light air expected, and the heat, so a look at the pre-Olympics seemed like a good story as an advance on what to expect in the real thing.

The pre-Olympic Regatta was run completely on Olympic lines, with the organization administration and race committee work set up exactly the way it would be, plus a full social schedule. The only difference was that anybody who wanted to could come. It attracted a worldwide entry of top sailors, and the regatta went off beautifully.

As part of the setup, all official visitors, including the press, were assigned hosts to make sure that everything went smoothly for them. We would be driven to and from parties, introduced to the right people, and generally shepherded around in great style under this system, and our host was a very pleasant American named Lew Riley.

He took excellent care of us, and, since he was a sailor, we naturally talked about our boats. It seems he lived in Mexico City but kept a little Cal 24 sloop at the Club de Yates de Acapulco for weekending.

"I come down here to relax on her," he said. "I just get a bottle of wine and go anchor in a cove after a nice sail and have a quiet evening. We don't even keep an apartment here. The boat's enough except when my wife comes. Then I have to get a hotel room so she can have space to keep her clothes and do her makeup and things."

Poor fellow, I thought, as he talked, conjuring up the image of a spoiled, anti-boat wife and an uncooperative poor sport, but I understood the situation a bit better when I found out just who his wife was. He was married to Dolores Del Rio.

PART X

~~~~~~~~~~~~~

Operation Sail

One of the unique nautical events of all time was Operation Sail 1976, the visit of "tall ships" from all over the world to the United States in honor of the bicentennial, with the grand climax the parade up New York Harbor on July 4. No other bicentennial event stirred the hearts and minds of Americans the way this one did, and it was a day that will never be repeated. I was fortunate enough to be quite deeply involved with OpSail, and during the course of this involvement a great many things happened. This, then, is a look at OpSail from the point of view of my own experiences.

The OpSail Caper

It started quietly enough. When I had been in Poland for OpSail 74 aboard *America*, I had met some TV cameramen there who later compiled an excellent film for national television in Poland and Russia. They came to the United States the following winter and wanted to show their film around, so they looked me up for introductions to people who would be interested.

A showing was arranged at the OpSail 76 headquarters in the World Trade Center, and I went down there to see it. Afterwards, chatting with Frank Braynard, the ship buff who fathered the whole OpSail idea back in 1964, when the first American one was held, and built it to the mammoth undertaking it became for 1976, he asked me where I lived.

"Rumson, New Jersey," I said.

"I thought you were from New Jersey," he said. "Al Lyon here is from the New Jersey Bicentennial Commission, and they are looking for someone to head up OpSail activities over there. You'd be just the man!" Frank always talks in enthusiastic superlatives.

Lyon had been a guest at the film, and I was introduced to him.

"I thought you had a chairman," I said. "Some guy has been calling me up every once in a while to talk it over."

"Well, we've had some problems," was the answer, "and he's no longer involved. Would you be able to do it?"

I went into a "this is so sudden" act, not knowing what it really entailed, but a couple of days later, after a few follow-ups, I agreed to take on the job.

"What does it involve?" I asked.

"That's up to you," was the answer. "We have no program for New Jersey yet. The tall ships are scheduled to anchor in Sandy Hook Bay on the morning of July 3, and they will stay there overnight before forming up for the July 4 parade under the Verrazano Bridge."

"Have any plans or ideas been started?"

"That's the trouble. The previous chairman was working on radio communications, but nothing else was set up. It's wide open."

"How about a budget? Is there one?"

"Ha!"

So much for a budget.

So I was a committee of one to entertain up to sixteen tall ships for a day, on no budget, and with no precedents or directives, but I wasn't long in my isolation. From Trenton came lists of names of people who had written in that they would like to work on OpSail for the bicentennial, and I was given the name of a Mrs. Rosario Federici who was sort of the Perle Mesta of New Jersey, an unpaid party-giver for the administration of Governor Byrne. She had staged vast charity balls, receptions, and galas, and could turn out brass bands, armies of bishops, monsignors, and assorted padres with their flocks, and organize grand-scale feedings for any size of gathering, so we got together for lunch and talked over her ideas.

About the smallest one she had in mind was to take over Monmouth Park Race Track for the day, and other ones involved great tents at Atlantic Highlands or Sandy Hook, but she had no experience in the problems of moving people by water on and off a big collection of ships.

Despite the fact that we started on different wave lengths, she was a lady of intelligence and adaptability, and she certainly knew her way around the halls of power (social, at least) in Trenton. Before it was all over, she proved to be one of the few people who stayed with it all the way and came through with what she said she would do, from all the great lists of people who "wanted to help."

"You'll have all sorts of volunteers," Frank Braynard said confidently, since his system was never to say no to anyone who said he wanted to help.

"Fine," I answered. "I have nothing for them to volunteer for yet, but it's nice to know."

My first concern was with the Coast Guard, since they would be in control of all activities afloat over the OpSail weekend, and I wanted to see what their plans were before making any of my own. I went out to the Ship Movement Office on Governor's Island, and a young officer showed me the mooring plan for Sandy Hook Bay.

There was room for up to twenty tall ships to anchor in the area between the tip of the Hook and the outer end of the two-mile-long Navy Ammunition Pier that juts northward into the bay from Leonardo, and the anchorages were all neatly plotted with circles around them. Depths ranged from eighteen to thirty-five feet, and only one or two of the ships drew over twenty-five.

Would the area be patrolled?

Yes, it would, and the anchorage area would be restricted during the time the ships were anchored there. This was definite.

With this knowledge, I formulated a plan that would provide a gesture of welcome from the State of New Jersey and take care of the budget problem all at the same time. We would sell a specially designed flag to boatowners who wanted to take part in a parade of welcome through the restricted area, and any surplus over the small amount of administrative funds needed would be a donation to OpSail. We would ask Governor Byrne to be the chief reviewing officer of the parade, and other state and municipal officials would be included. The Coast Guard assured me that this parade would be permitted.

Next, how did we entertain personnel from the ships? There was no way we could have a big catch-all party for all crews. It would involve thousands of people, and the logistics would be staggering. Paying for it would be even more of a headache, and moving people around would be impossible. Already, local police officers of the communities along the Bayshore area of Raritan Bay were in a public panic over the traffic problems they would have that weekend.

The best way, it seemed to me, would be to involve the yacht clubs in the area. They all had facilities for entertaining large groups, they had boats for moving cadets from ship to shore and back, their members would have mutual nautical interests with the young sailors from the ships, and the sailors would have a chance to see a typical aspect of American life, nautically oriented.

With this in mind, I asked each club in the area to designate a delegate to the New Jersey OpSail committee, and I called a meeting at my house in the spring of 1975 to get the ball rolling.

Everyone bought my plans in principle, so we had a program to work on and a year to go. Somehow the meetings seemed to attract all sorts of extras, visitors from Brooklyn who were to have a few ships in Gravesend Bay, bicentennial officials from local towns, and an assortment of ladies who wanted to do something social.

Meanwhile, my phone rang daily with all sorts of requests. Could a school library have OpSail pictures? Were there movies available? How could you get to see the ships if you didn't have a boat? Would I be interested in paintings of the ships by a ninety-year-old retired Lithuanian boatswain's mate? Where would the individual ships be anchored?

Despite these distractions, we had a working plan, and we went ahead. The list of ships participating was far from final yet, so we could not assign them to the individual clubs, but we got a burgee designed and ordered and things were looking good.

Then OpSail officials, who had told me I had carte blanche to make plans, said they didn't want a separate New Jersey OpSail flag, because they were selling an official OpSail flag, and they refused to lend us the money to place the order. I said we couldn't function without our own flag and that I would borrow the money personally, and there was finally an about-face on both counts, thanks to the chairman, Bus Mosbacher, listening to my story.

Next, the Coast Guard said that all the ships were going to be shifted to Gravesend Bay because the water was too shallow in Sandy Hook Bay. This order was short-lived, and we were guaranteed at least twelve ships. We were given the names of those that were definite, and the latecomers were to be sent to Gravesend Bay, so we held a name-drawing meeting at my house. There was a mixture of elation and disappointment as the names were drawn, as some of the ships seemed more desirable than others, and there was one complication in that our one all-Jewish club would only entertain a ship from a country that had not voted to censure Israel in the United Nations. Everything was eventually smoothed out to almost everyone's satisfaction, and each club then had the problem of making its own arrangements with the representatives of the ships in their consulates and embassies. Some became intimate friends with the ship representatives over the next few months, holding frequent meetings, while others had a hard time locating anyone to deal with. All found it a fascinating exercise in international relations. All clubs did an excellent job, and the festivities were uniformly successful.

Another part of the plan was to have four cadets from the U.S. Coast Guard *Eagle*, the host ship for OpSail, come to each club to mix with the foreign cadets and to represent the United States at the various parties, but try as I could through every channel imaginable, I never got an answer, much less a commitment, from *Eagle* for this, and the Coast Guard missed a good chance to make friends.

The Coast Guard was also being difficult over our parade of welcome. No longer would the anchorage area be restricted for the visit of the ships. As soon as they were all anchored, it would be wide open, so the only time we could hold our parade would be while they were anchoring. As yet, though, no one knew the hours for this. All this was arrived at after repeated changes in information and directives, and once we were told we couldn't have the parade at all, and I began to think the Coast Guard was somewhat over its head in what it was trying to do.

It was a bit difficult to plan ahead on a time for the parade and on signing up large yachts as reviewing vessels with this sort of vague information, but I made a trip to Trenton with OpSail officials early in January for a ceremony in which the Governor officially recognized OpSail and New Jersey's participation in it, and accepted my personal invitation to act as chief reviewing officer of our parade. I don't know whether it was a significant omen or not that the statehouse had to be evacuated during the ceremony because of an electrical fire on one of the upper floors, but from then on my problems compounded. I had never before had to deal with politicians, or, more specifically, their aides. Byrne, a fellow Princeton alumnus, was very pleasant, and surprised me by saying that he had written me a letter when I was on the *Newark News* (over twenty-five years ago). It was in dealing with the people who make his appointments, lasting over the next few months, and right up until 5 P.M. on July 3, that I made a solemn vow never again to become involved with politicians or the need for their presence at a function.

I'm a mild-mannered sort, and the only time I admit to a real stack-blowing was in the case of Robby's withdrawn protest, but I found myself in screaming matches on the phone with people who acted as though I thought I was a man on horseback about to stage a coup. We had agreed to a perfectly simple program in which Byrne would board a reviewing vessel at 0930 Saturday morning, watch the parade, spend midday at whatever pursuit he chose—we would get him a tennis game if he wanted it—and then come for dinner to the Rumson Country Club, where the crew of the Norwegian ship *Christian Radich* was to be entertained, and which was to be my base for the evening.

This program was established months ahead, and I won't attempt to go through the variations on it that were played back and forth, day by day, until the whole thing was over. At one point, I was yelling "Are you calling me a liar?" to the most disorganized of his aides, when he insisted that I had never mentioned 0930 as a starting time. That had been it since the moment we began our plans.

At one point, he said, "The Governor doesn't spend two hours a week with his cabinet, and you are asking him to sit on a boat for four hours." This was months after we had originally agreed to the schedule. Did he think I was playing games?

Along with the problem of the Governor's schedule, we had to find a suitable yacht to be the parade leader. Most of the bigger vessels in the area were tied up in charters or with private plans of their owners, but a solution appeared in March when we were tied up next to a ninety-five-foot yacht from New Jersey at a marina in the Bahamas. The owner asked me what was the best way to become involved with OpSail when he brought his boat north next summer, and I asked him if he would like to take part in our parade as the lead reviewing vessel, carrying the Governor.

"I'll put the son of a bitch in the dinghy and tow him," was his first response, as they had had some personal differences over my friend's company and industry not too long before. Then he smiled and said, "That's silly, really. OpSail shouldn't be political, and I'd be happy to do it."

We announced the availability of the special flags for the New Jersey parade of welcome at twenty-five dollars a throw from my office, in a release to New Jersey papers, and the response was overwhelming. We had ordered five hundred flags as the absolute maximum that might be requested, a bit in awe of what a five-hundred-boat parade would look like, and they sold out completely, with quite a few requests turned away, making an eight-thousand-dollar profit for OpSail.

So everything seemed fairly well organized and on an even keel. The spring was advancing, interest in OpSail was burgeoning in a great ground swell, and all our plans were fairly well set.

Then it hit the fan.

First of all, the Governor had another fight, evidently a four-letter-word shouting match on the phone, with my industrialist friend who was supposed to take him in the parade, and I had word from both sides that there was no way that the Governor would be found dead aboard, or would be allowed aboard, my carefully selected reviewing vessel. This is where Rosario Federici came to the rescue, locating a hundred-foot yacht owned by a North Jersey trucking executive who would be delighted to have the Governor review the parade from his vessel. She also came up with such a long list of VIPs, prelates, distant relatives of the Governor, and just plain hangers-on who should be invited out to review the parade, that we figured we needed two vessels anyway, and I kept the first boat signed up with the proviso that he didn't have to take "that son of a bitch."

The next splash against the fan was a syndicated column by Jack Anderson, which appeared in local papers. It stated, without proof or confirmation, that the Chilean tall ship *Esmeralda* had been used as a torture ship during the coup that overthrew the Communist government of Premier Allende. There wasn't a substantiated fact in the column, but it painted a lurid picture and made reference to the irony of the fact that this Fascist instrument was taking part in the celebration of American freedoms.

There was an immediate outcry of bleeding-heart motherhood, and a great fuss was made in the press over this "outrage," with the eager journalists failing to realize that, whether the allegations were true or not, they were buying the Communist party line in toto by playing it up this way. No one mentioned the fact that there was hardly a vessel in OpSail whose political background was pure. There were ships from Russia, Rumania, Argentina, Portugal, Poland, Colombia, Spain, and many others whose recent political history didn't quite jibe with the principles of the Declaration of Independence, and our own *Eagle* had once been the Nazi training ship *Horst Wessel*. But there was no logic in the situation stirred up by this innuendo-filled column.

The Keyport Yacht Club was the unfortunate victim of it. When I read the Anderson column, I groaned to myself, and thought, "Those poor guys at Keyport. They're really in for it." They had drawn *Esmeralda* strictly by lot out of the hat passed around my living room, just as all the other ships had been assigned, and they had already progressed far in their plans for the July 3 party.

While the local politicians they had invited to the dinner (and who had accepted eagerly) all backed out with pious pronouncements, and do-gooder groups who had no idea of the real situation began to circulate petitions to ban the torture ship, Keyport's members stuck to their guns in an admirable display of cool fortitude. They announced that they had made a commitment to entertain the Chilean cadets with no regard to political considerations, and they felt they were duty bound to stick by their word.

As chairman of the New Jersey Committee, I began to receive calls from the local papers asking for my stand on the situation, and I said that I thought the Keyport Yacht Club members were acting like real gentlemen in fulfilling an obligation they had agreed to take on. I pointed out as forcefully as I could that OpSail was an apolitical event, and that it wouldn't exist if we began to make formal objections to the politics of the participants. The people who were "buying" the unproved Anderson column were meddling in affairs they knew nothing about and that were none of their business, and I thought it was a disgrace. We were playing host to young seamen from around the world, and they should not be subjected to political demonstrations. Obviously the cadets on *Esmeralda* were too young to have taken part in the alleged torturing in any event.

As an old newspaperman, I hate to see newspapers do a sloppy job, but it was almost completely predictable that the Asbury Park *Press* would come out with a two-column head on its front page reading, "Visit of Torture Ship Defended." They quoted me moderately accurately, but the headline, without quote marks around the words "torture ship," was enough to counteract any logic in what I was quoted on. I later had words with them about this bit of journalistic irresponsibility, and they did, in fact, show me a later edition where the quotes had been added. The first one was the edition delivered in Rumson, however.

And so, while the phone rang incessantly with people wanting flags for the parade, with friends asking at the last minute what they should do about seeing OpSail, with cranks calling about the "torture ship," and with nervous chairmen from most of the clubs going over last-minute details, we got word from the papers that there was to be a picketing demonstration at our house on Friday afternoon, July 2. A teacher from the local high school who had long been identified with Communist causes, and who bled predictably for lettuce pickers, grape gatherers, or whatever the latest cause was, had notified the papers that the affair was being staged to "demonstrate to Mr. Robinson the evil of his blind acceptance of Fascist torture." By now, I had talked to people at the paper often enough so that they were beginning to come awake to what their eagerness for a hot story had turned into, and they were a bit ashamed. The *Daily Register* decided not to send a reporter to the house at all. The *Press* did, but did not use a picture and kept the story on a back page. They had begun to realize that publicity was all the demonstrators were after, and lack of it would be the most effective handling.

On the day of the demonstration, we had a jammed household, and two of the members happened to be under psychiatric care for temporary nervous disorders (surprisingly, I wasn't one of them). In addition, Martha and Hank were driving in from Texas in two cars, one with baby, one with dog, a woman working on an OpSail committee that was to provide spectator boats for people who made good donations was there to try to arrange for a boat, since the one she had signed up had just evaporated; and the doctor was expected momentarily to talk one of the patients into going to the hospital for treatment.

In other words, it wasn't a completely normal Friday afternoon when a group of people in long black robes and death masks arrived at the entrance to our driveway, carrying placards, and began to march back and forth. Our house is at the dead end of a side road out on a point in the river, with the other houses well separated, about as un-public a spot to stage a demonstration as anyone could pick, and the charade had a sparse audience. There was the girl from the *Press*, with a photographer, one Rumson policeman, and my next-door neighbor's father-in-law, visiting from Colorado, who stood in the bushes to watch the show. ("They hang people like that where I come from," he told the cop.) The policeman had once been in Jane's Cub Scout den, and he came up to the house as the demonstration started and the pickets began making speeches to each other.

"Just give me the word and I'll run 'em in, Mr. Robinson," he said eagerly. "Just give me the word."

"Thanks," I said, "but I just want to cool it. Don't pay any attention to them unless they do some damage. They want a fuss made, so just ignore them."

"O.k. I'll watch 'em, but you just let me know if you want me to handle it." We had a little discussion about a member of his family who

The OpSail fleet leaving Bermuda

had been injured in an auto accident, and he went back to his car in the street saying, "Just give me the word."

After a while, one of the demonstrators ran up to the front door and tossed some placards on the steps. Martha, who had just driven in, picked them up and ripped them across, the doctor arrived, the lady looking for the boat left with a promise she could take her guests on *Tanagra* with Martha and Hank the next day, two people drove in wanting parade flags, Martha's dog began to run in circles and bark on her release from the car trip, and the phone rang every few minutes. The next time we looked up, the demonstrators had gone.

One of the calls was from the professional captain of the yacht we were counting on as a review vessel, the one the Governor was not welcome on, saying that he didn't think he could get up the Shrewsbury to pick up the guests at the Rumson Club the next morning as per plan, and I used fairly strong language to tell him that unless he showed up, I was moving permanently to the Rocky Mountains. When he hung up,

Close quarters before *Libertad* (left) and *Juan Sebastian de Elcano* collided

I had no idea what he would do the next day, but I knew I had made myself clear.

Another call changed the Governor's plans for the twenty-third time, five of them in the last day, but I was beyond caring what he did at the moment.

At last, July 3 arrived, bright and sunny, with very little wind. We went to the Rumson Club not knowing whether one review yacht was showing up or not, though we did expect the trucking executive in his. The parking lot was filled with Rosario's entourage, and there, silhouetted against the low morning sun in the mid-river channel, was the reviewing yacht, on time at the appointed place, but there was no sign of the trucker's vessel. If I was to make it out to the bay in time to start the

parade, we couldn't wait any longer, so we took all Republican politicians and those of Rosario's list that she designated and headed out to
Sandy Hook Bay. As we steamed down the channel, the other yacht
arrived, covered with placards and signs welcoming the Governor,
bunting, pennants, and streamers flying from every vantage point, and
a jazz band tootling away on the top deck.

The latest plan for the Governor had him boarding that vessel in
the bay after a helicopter ride in from a carrier offshore to Sandy
Hook, where he was to be picked up by a cabin cruiser I had been able
to arrange for at the last minute.

The bay was an incredible sight. From offshore, the tracery of their
rigging outlined against the eastern horizon, the tall ships were making

The July 3 parade of welcome in Sandy Hook Bay, New
Jersey

We wound our way in among the ships

their way up Sandy Hook Channel to the anchorage, and the bay contained the biggest collection of small craft I have ever seen anywhere, even in the most crowded America's Cup spectator fleet. As we approached the rendezvous point for the start of our parade, there were our five hundred flag customers, neatly lined up and waiting for the signal to start, and it was a truly impressive spectacle. We were to be led by two Coast Guard picket boats, followed by *Tanagra*, operated by Hank and Marth with the charity donors aboard (and their check later bounced), then the yacht I was on, followed by the faithful five hundred. *Tanagra* sported a big banner saying "N.J. WELCOMES OPSAIL" in the same colors as the special parade flag, the yellow and blue of New Jersey.

Most of the tall ships were at anchor by now, and we set a course to steam by them. The myth that the anchorage area was to be restricted until they were all at anchor had disappeared in the incredible press of spectator boats, but our parade managed to keep some semblance of form as we snaked through the bay paying homage to ship after ship with waves, salutes, whistles, and loud cheering. It was a gay, infectious

affair, noisy and full of excitement, and our parade held together until
the picket boats decided for some reason to double back through the
fleet, and, like a snake eating its own tail, the columns began to dis-
integrate. This became complete when the big Spanish ship *Juan
Sebastian de Elcano* charged right through the rear end of the parade
on her way to her anchorage, scattering everyone out of her way,
but the primary objective had been achieved, and no one there will
forget the scene.

The Governor managed to arrive just as the Coast Guard boats
deserted us and went back to the Hook for lunch, but he presumably
got a view of the ships, and plenty of people saw the banners on the
trucker's yacht.

We got home to find that the Governor's aide had phoned at 3 P.M.
to say that the Governor would not be at the Rumson Club for dinner
(the head table had been remade several times in the last day), and there
was another message that the big powerboat that was to go pick up the
crew of the *Christian Radich* to bring them to the Rumson Club would
not be going because there had been a misunderstanding between the
captain and the owners. This was resolved by three more phone calls
smoothing the situation, while a violent thunder squall crashed and
splashed outside, and I wondered what this would do to the receptions
at the various clubs. Too late for me to worry.

When we got to the Rumson Club, a helicopter was just landing in
one of the fields next to the beach house, where the dinner was to be
held, and there was the Governor with his wife. I had visions of yet
another remake of the head table, but it turned out they had only come
for cocktails, one eventuality that had never been mentioned in all the
changes. He was thoughtfully wearing an OpSail tie I had given him
in January, and we had a pleasant chat for a while before the helicopter
zoomed off again, back to the Governor's mansion, Morven, in Princeton. After six months, not one plan we had originally made had been
followed, but he had been a part of the ceremonies.

We breathed easier when the powerboat with the Norwegians hove
into view, and the evening was one of the better parties the club has
ever held. The cadets entered in in lively fashion, dancing with the many
young girls that were there to meet them, and one couple was even discovered in a parked car before the evening was very old. I had sailed
in the *Radich* the previous summer and knew the officers, and, since
Norwegians all speak English perfectly, it was an easygoing, friendly
affair all the way through. When it was time for them to head back to
the ship, the orchestra led an informal parade of cadets and dance guests
from the floor across the driveway to the bulkhead where the powerboat

White Whale, the official New Jersey vessel in the OpSail parade

waited, playing the "Colonel Bogey March," and the crew was then mustered on the deck of the powerboat to make sure no one was missing. As the engines rumbled and the boat pulled away into the night, one young cadet leaned over the rail and cried "Goodbye, darling" to a girl on the shore, as everyone cheered and laughed.

After all this, it didn't seem possible that the "main event" was still to come. My responsibilities were officially over, but we still had the parade to go. It had been a tough question to decide what to do with ourselves on the big day. We had been invited aboard the carrier *Forrestal,* the reviewing vessel where President Ford would be, and the Coast Guard cutter moored next to her, but both invitations meant being in Brooklyn by 0700, and that seemed too much on top of the events of July 3.

We could have just gone in *Tanagra* to spectate, and that's what the kids did and had a fine time, but we eventually ended up running the official New Jersey vessel in the OpSail parade. Frank Braynard had asked me what a suitable character vessel would be to represent the state, and I suggested *White Whale* from Bay Head, a replica of an oyster sloop owned by Jim Kellogg, a commissioner of the Port of New York Authority and long active in public affairs. I invited Jim to do it, but he declined, saying he had to be on shore and would only use *White Whale* for the July 3 doings, and he suggested that we take her instead.

She is a colorful clipper-bowed gaff-rigger, complete with topsail, a gleaming black hull, and touches like a carved taffrail. We were warned she had been having engine trouble, but she seemed o.k. as we headed out from the berth we had arranged for her at the Rumson Club and powered down the Shrewsbury in a great fleet of boats. There was excitement and expectancy in the air, and it was a warm, pleasant, hazy day, not too good for photography (which didn't stop it from being the biggest day in the history of photo processing in New York), as we joined the swelling armada of boats in Sandy Hook Bay and headed for the Narrows along with the tall ships heading for their big parade.

There was so much to look at it was like being at a Christmas feast with a full stomach, and as we neared the Verrazano Bridge, the numbers increased even more. We were to join with the smaller training ships and character vessels that were to follow the tall ships, forming up in Gravesend Bay, where *Kruzenshtern,* and *Amerigo Vespucci,* too big for Sandy Hook, loomed over the small craft in their distinctive black and white paint jobs.

We had lots of time to mill around, and the collection of yachts was a fascinating mélange of contrasts. *America* was there and the monstrous four-masted *Club Méditerranée,* as big as the tall ships, which

The Naval Academy yawls lined up to salute the *Forrestal*

had just completed the Singlehanded Transatlantic Race. Old fishing schooners, replica pirate ships and Viking ships, *Bluenose* from Nova Scotia, the British *Sir Winston Churchill, Freelance* from the Antigua charter fleet, and hundreds of other fascinating craft moved slowly around, wallowing in the tremendous bobble set up by all the wakes.

When it came time for us to move into the parade after the tall ships had made their stately way through the Verrazano with cadets manning the yards and sails partially unfurled and were disappearing in the haze beyond the Statue of Liberty, the order we were supposed to follow lasted about five minutes, and then it seemed to be every man for himself. Suddenly, just astern of us, a blue yawl under full blue and gold spinnaker swooshed by, missing our counter by inches, and threaded her way through the mass of boats. She was one of the forty-four-foot yawls from the Naval Academy in Annapolis, and they put on a fantastic show, with four of them under spinnaker falling into an abreast formation while the crews manned the rails, as they zoomed by the *Forrestal.*

Our engine had been acting crankier and crankier, refusing to idle down. This made it especially hard to stay put when the parade mushed to a halt, which it did every few minutes, and once we passed the mammoth bulk of the *Forrestal*, I thought it best to leave what could only be laughingly described as a parade by now and head for home. We barely got past the shore side of the carrier when the engine quit completely. The wind had all but died too, and there was a flood tide, so sailing an underrigged gaff-rigger didn't look too profitable.

I could see *Tanagra* heading home under power about a half mile off our port bow, so I flagged down the nearest powerboat passing us to ask them to hail her and tell her to come back and tow us. As it happened, we knew the people in the powerboat. Oddly, they came in to circle us at high speed, yelling that their engine was acting up and couldn't be throttled back. While they banked around us, we tried to get the message across, and finally they waved an acknowledgment and zoomed off—toward the wrong boat. Eventually they came back and tried it all over again, but by now *Tanagra* had disappeared. After a while, an auxiliary came along with Rumson as a hailing port, and we whistled her down and asked for a tow.

And so the glorious adventure of OpSail ended for us in the long journey home at the end of a towline. When we got home, we thought we would at least catch the TV show of the fireworks at the Statue of Liberty, plus a rerun of the day's scenes. We sat down in front of the set, and in five minutes Jane and I were both fast alseep.

A distant view of the parade as we became a dropout

515
4495